THE
DEVIL'S

OSPREY
PUBLISHING

ANTHONY TUCKER-JONES

THE DEVIL'S BRIDGE

THE GERMAN VICTORY AT ARNHEM, 1944

OSPREY PUBLISHING
Bloomsbury Publishing Plc
PO Box 883, Oxford, OX1 9PL, UK
1385 Broadway, 5th Floor, New York, NY 10018, USA
E-mail: info@ospreypublishing.com
www.ospreypublishing.com

OSPREY is a trademark of Osprey Publishing Ltd

First published in Great Britain in 2020

A catalogue record for this book is available from the British Library.

ISBN: HB 978 1 4728 3986 2; eBook 978 1 4728 3987 9; ePDF 978 1 4728 3984 8; XML 978 1 4728 3985 5

20 21 22 23 24 10 9 8 7 6 5 4 3 2 1

Foreword © Professor Peter Caddick-Adams
Maps by www.bounford.com
Index by Zoe Ross

Typeset by Deanta Global Publishing Services, Chennai, India
Printed and bound in Great Britain by CPI (Group) UK Ltd, Croydon CR0 4YY

Front and back cover: Allied trucks carrying munitions and supplies to troops on the Western Front in Holland cross the bridge over the river Waal at Nijmegen under German shellfire, September 1944. (Photo by Photo12/UIG/Getty Images)

Osprey Publishing supports the Woodland Trust, the UK's leading woodland conservation charity.

To find out more about our authors and books visit www.ospreypublishing.com. Here you will find extracts, author interviews, details of forthcoming events and the option to sign up for our newsletter.

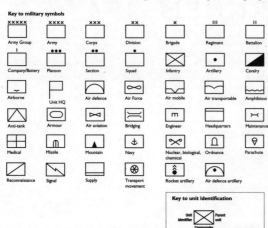

Contents

Acknowledgements

Firstly, lastly and always to my wife Amelia, without whose unfailing support I would have given up long ago.

To Matt Lowing at Bloomsbury and Lisa Thomas formerly at Osprey for giving this book a home. Lisa in particular for fully embracing *The Other Side of the Hill* approach, which had not been attempted for some considerable time. Similarly, Osprey's publisher Marcus Cowper for his unstinting enthusiasm and guidance throughout.

To fellow author and military historian Professor Peter Caddick-Adams for his astute input and for very generously writing the excellent foreword. He sets the scene with such aplomb. Likewise, to Dr Graham Goodlad, Robin Buckland and Rob Palmer for reading the manuscript so diligently. Their expert comments, observations and support were gratefully received. Also to author and writer Tim Newark for his encouragement.

Those who kindly rallied to my call for help with research include Marcus Cowper, Katie Eaton, Barbara Jones, Tara Moran, Amy Rigg and Joël Stoppels.

To Tim Isaac who first sowed the seed. Tim, thanks for letting me sit in your Horsa glider. Even firmly on the ground, it's a very sobering experience.

Lastly, and definitely not least, to my copy editor Venetia Bridges and proofreader Sharon Penlington. They are the unsung heroes in the process of pulling a book together ready for publication.

Thank you to everyone who helped.

Foreword

by Professor Peter Caddick-Adams

Watching the Allied airborne army circling, vulture-like, over the Dutch skies on the morning of Sunday, 17 September 1944, General Kurt Student – the victor of Crete – lamented that he never 'had such powerful means at my disposal! Wherever I looked I saw aircraft; troop-carriers and large aircraft towing gliders'.

It is easy to forget that Operation *Market Garden* – the Allied plan to force a 60-mile salient into German lines, outflanking the Siegfried Line (aka the Westwall) and enabling an invasion route into northern Germany – took place so soon after the collapse in Normandy. With some 50,000 Axis troops killed or captured in the Falaise Pocket when it was sealed on 21 August, and the liberation of Paris four days later, it was obvious to all that the German armies of the West were defeated. Totally and irretrievably. Including those forces destroyed in the Riviera landings from 15 August onwards, German losses in France from 6 June tallied close to the half a million mark.

This was the origin of the plan – with hindsight, absurdly optimistic – to plunge into Holland by parachute and tank. The Germans were finished, and there was nothing left with which to oppose Montgomery's headlong rush, mounted a little over three weeks after Paris was formally freed. Yet the Germans were not finished; the Eastern Front had taught them how to stitch together shattered fronts with inadequate reserves. This was where Walther Model, now Army Group B commander in the West, had earned his reputation as a 'patchwork quilt artist of the first order'.

Over the past couple of decades, dozens of books, scholarly papers, conferences and documentaries have taught us an enormous amount about the Allied airborne forces, aircrew and ground troops who invaded the Netherlands that September Sunday. Yet it is 30 years since the last study of the Germans who fought at *Market Garden*. In *The Devil's Bridge*, Anthony Tucker-Jones – using his skill as a defence analyst and a military historian – gives us the German view of the nine-day *Market Garden* campaign, using a wide variety of sources, interviews and archives. Using many sets of eyes, we are taken effortlessly from tactical combat to operational narrative and back again. We are also given the vital back story – from Normandy and Belgium into Holland, and the post-September aftermath – overlooked in previous histories.

Using a cast of over a hundred individuals, he shows us how experienced and resourceful the defenders were. Labouring under the constraints of no air cover, limited resources and manpower, this long-overdue examination demonstrates how the ragtag collection of Wehrmacht, Luftwaffe and Waffen-SS units in Holland – some summoned from far away and travelling by bicycle – overcame all obstacles, combined into *ad hoc* battle groups and crushed their opponents, usually with no intelligence preparation, and little battlefield reconnaissance. Time and time again we encounter the legendary Nazi fanaticism. When SS-Major Josef 'Sepp' Krafft advanced to fight the British at Oosterbeek, he sent his personal effects in his staff car home to Germany, observing, 'I don't expect to get out of this alive', but nevertheless pressed home his attack and survived.

We meet Erwin Kirchhof, a war correspondent, who explained the recipe for success. 'Only 24 hours before they had not known each other: the aeroplane technicians still worked on their planes; the soldiers of the Waffen-SS were refitting; the reserve units were still employed as guards; the naval coast artillery men had just returned; the boys of the Reich labour organization were still constructing field positions. Only a few of them were familiar with the principles of fighting… but they fought…'

In total contrast, Tucker-Jones describes the truce arranged on 24 September between British medical officer Colonel Graeme Warrack and SS-Major Dr Egon Skalka, his opposite number from the 9th SS Division. The humane gesture saved the lives of 450 British, German and Dutch casualties, and was followed up by SS-General Wilhelm Bittrich presenting Warrack with a bottle of brandy, 'for your general'. One of the few Allied eyewitnesses (for this is the German story) we meet is Captain Derek 'Pip' Bogaerde, who witnessed the final British evacuation from Arnhem. We all knew him better as Dirk Bogarde, master of stage and screen.

The Devil's Bridge provides a great service by examining at length what the Allies did and didn't know beforehand of the German dispositions, and logs the Wehrmacht's reactions to the battle, with the lessons they identified and should have learned. However, in the aftermath of this strange victory – the last the Germans would achieve in the West – Hitler was possessed of exactly the same overconfidence that had gripped Montgomery after Normandy. In December he sent three armies through the Ardennes in a poor imitation of *Market Garden*. *Wacht am Rhein*'s aim was to carve a 120-mile Panzer corridor from the Westwall to Antwerp.

The Führer had overlooked the fact that if Montgomery couldn't manage 60 miles in September with air cover and in good weather, the Germans certainly weren't going to achieve double that in atrocious conditions with no air support. In this way, the successful defeat of *Market Garden* helped sow the seeds of the disastrous Ardennes offensive and final military collapse of Germany in the West.

This is an important and timely operational analysis of the events of September 1944. It is a mark of my respect for Anthony Tucker-Jones' work that I wish I had researched and written *The Devil's Bridge*. Thus I am more than happy to commend his scholarship to you.

Professor Peter Caddick-Adams
Salisbury

Prologue
Model Gets Indigestion

Field Marshal Walther Model was a prompt man. He was also a very calm man. A veteran of the highs and lows of the Eastern Front, he was by and large completely unflappable. He had seen it all, including the catastrophic German collapse in Russia. Model looked at his watch; it was one o'clock on Sunday 17 September 1944. He then nodded to his chief of staff Lieutenant-General Hans Krebs, adjutant Colonel Leodegard Freyberg and operations officer Colonel Hans Georg von Tempelhoff. Model rubbed his hands together with anticipation; it was time for a nice pre-lunch aperitif, a chilled Moselle.

'Whenever he was at the headquarters, the field marshal was punctual to a fault,' recalled staff officer Lieutenant Gustav Sedelhauser. 'We always sat down to luncheon at 1300 hours.'[1] Despite the pressures of command, there had to be some pleasures and eating with his staff was one of them. Earlier that morning Model had stood outside his headquarters and watched the distant vapour trails of Allied bombers. He concluded they were off to pound his homeland and hoped the Luftwaffe gave them a warm reception.

As far as Adolf Hitler, the German Führer, was concerned, Model was a safe pair of hands. He was always in the right place at the right time. Hitler had recalled Model from Russia to take command of Army Group B in France from that traitor von Kluge. After the disintegration of the German army in Russia, Model had successfully held the Red Army outside Warsaw. Hitler now needed another miracle. Model's arrival had not been soon enough, though, to help stave off the German defeat in Normandy. Instead he soon found himself abandoning his headquarters outside Paris. Model had not wanted to be posted to the West, as he considered himself quite rightly a Russian Front expert. He had no time for the notion of withdrawing exhausted troops, declaring, 'On the Eastern Front we rest and recuperate in the frontline.'[2]

Although Model could not prevent the disaster at Falaise or flight across the Seine, by early September 1944 he had managed at least to stabilize the situation. Hitler, scrabbling around for reinforcements, had come up with General Kurt Student's 1st Parachute Army. This was hastily scraped together and deployed between the depleted German 15th Army in Belgium and the remains of 7th Army that had escaped Normandy.

Model established a new headquarters at Oosterbeek on 11 September 1944, just to the west of the Dutch city of Arnhem located on the banks of the Lower Rhine. Lieutenant Sedelhauser said Arnhem was ideal, as 'it had everything we wanted: a fine road net and excellent accommodations. But it was not until we drove west to the outlying district of Oosterbeek that we found what we were looking for.'[3] This was in the shape of two quaint hotels, the Hartenstein and Tafelberg. Sedelhauser, who had been with the scouting party, recommended the location to Lieutenant-General Krebs. Model in turn had approved and selected the Tafelberg for himself. Sedelhauser was relieved they would be settled for a while after the constant moves, plus he noted it offered 'a chance to get my laundry done.'[4]

In contrast, staff officer Major Horst Smöckel was not altogether content. He had drawn the short straw and found himself under remit to stock Model and Krebs' larder. Armed with a shopping list, Smöckel had set off to scour the local stores. Although there was a war on, he ordered much of what they wanted and asked for it to be delivered to the Tafelberg Hotel. He went to one shop and asked if they had any gin. The owner explained that it was difficult to obtain and would be expensive. Not a problem, replied

Smöckel. After the German officer had departed, the shopkeeper called Dr Leo Breebaart, a general practitioner in Arnhem, and asked to speak to his assistant Henri Knap, who was the Resistance's local intelligence chief. After a brief exchange, Knap called Pieter Kruyff, the head of the Dutch Resistance in Arnhem. Smöckel had inadvertently revealed that Model was in the Netherlands.

Krebs had joined the field marshal only on 5 September, though this was his third posting with Model as his chief of staff. The pair had previously served together in France and Russia. Model liked Krebs because he was a doer, rather than forever finding reasons for not getting things done. Krebs was lucky, as Model had a reputation for treating his staff officers badly. Krebs enjoyed working with Model because he was clearly highly competent. However, on this occasion Krebs was a little disappointed that he had not been given a corps command, which would have got him a little closer to the front and advanced his own career.

They had just sat down to eat lunch when the telephone rang in the outer office. The Field Marshal was lifting his glass of Moselle to his lips when the Tafelberg was rocked by several explosions. Model dropped his wine, and along with the other startled diners, dived under the table.[5] 'Look out! Bombers!' yelled an officer, leaping to his feet and running to the window.[6] In the meantime, Sedelhauser had answered the phone and barked, 'Sedelhauser here.' 'It's Sergeant Youppinger,' yelled a voice on the other end of the line, 'gliders are landing in our laps.'[7] This cannot be good, thought Sedelhauser. Youppinger was with a unit assigned to protect the field marshal, which was stationed to the northwest at Wolfheze.

Hanging up, Sedelhauser dashed into the operations room and reported to the deputy operations officer. The pair then ran to the dining room, where the latter blurted out, 'I've just had news that gliders are landing at Wolfheze.'[8] Krebs blinked and promptly lost his monocle. 'This will be the decisive battle of the war,' he said.[9] 'Well, now we're for it,' added Tempelhoff unhelpfully.[10]

Model was highly displeased by such negativity; besides he needed a fuller picture of what exactly was going on. 'Don't be so dramatic,' he warned his officers. 'It's obvious enough. Tempelhoff, get to work!'[11] Tempelhoff went out and got on the telephone. When he glanced out of the window, his jaw dropped at the sight of not only gliders, but also enemy paratroopers in the distance. First he called the headquarters of SS-Lieutenant-General Willi Bittrich, commander of the 2nd SS-Panzer Corps, and then Field Marshal von Rundstedt's, who was Commander-in-Chief West. Rushing back in to Model, he cried, 'What an absolute swine! There are two parachute divisions right on top of us!'[12]

Rather than panic, there was a palpable sense of excitement in the room. Everyone looked to the field marshal for leadership and to galvanize them into action. This was exactly the sort of emergency that Model revelled in. 'Right!' he responded. 'Everyone out!'[13] As they sped on their way, he communicated his immediate conclusion, 'They're after me and this headquarters!'[14] They all began grabbing their kit for a quick evacuation. Lieutenant Sedelhauser's hope of a more settled existence had gone out of the window.

As they left the room, Model and Krebs felt a flicker of embarrassment. Just after they had set up shop at Oosterbeek, they had received a courtesy call from SS-Lieutenant-General Hanns Rauter. He was responsible for ruthlessly suppressing the Dutch Resistance and rooting out Jews in the Netherlands. With remarkable foresight, Rauter had warned them the British might use paratroopers to grab the Netherlands' bridges. Model recalled dismissing such a notion, saying, 'Montgomery is a very cautious general, not inclined to plunge into mad adventures.'[15] Krebs had been in agreement. The distances were simply too great. Model had been adamant, 'Arnhem is not possible.'[16] Besides, at the beginning of the month he had concluded, 'The anticipated large-scale air-landing appears most likely in the West Wall [Siegfried Line] region.'[17]

To the west of Oosterbeek, at Driesbergen, Major Friedrich Kieswetter, deputy head of German counter-intelligence in the Netherlands, had received warning of an Allied airborne attack. This had come from a decidedly disreputable-looking Dutchman and he chose not to relay it to Model. On 15 September 1944, double agent Christiaan Antonius Lindemans, who was working for Kieswetter's boss, Lieutenant-Colonel Hermann Giskes, had been brought to Driesbergen. Lindemans said the British were going to launch a ground attack on 17 September – this was hardly news. What was of interest was when Lindemans added that the attack would be supported by an airborne operation at Eindhoven. However, according to Kieswetter's briefing for Giskes, Lindemans 'did not mention Arnhem... obviously because the objective of the planned air-ground offensive was not known to him.'[18]

Kieswetter looked at the six-foot Dutchman, who was known as 'King Kong', and asked him what the basis of his intelligence was. Lindemans explained he was a double agent, who had been sent by the Canadians to warn the local Resistance not to send any more Allied pilots into Belgium. This was because British forces were planning to break out from their Neerpelt bridgehead in the direction of Eindhoven. Giskes was away, so Kieswetter had to make a decision about what to do with this intelligence. To him it just did not make any sense. Why would the British use paratroops to take Eindhoven, when British ground forces could easily fight their way to the town? He decided not to bother Model or Student. Kieswetter prepared a report for Giskes, but the latter was not due to get it until the afternoon of 17 September.

Just four days earlier, Luftwaffe Colonel-General Otto Dessloch, while at Rundstedt's headquarters in Koblenz, was so alarmed by talk of an airborne assault that he had resolved to alert Model. Dessloch called him on 14 September, warning, 'If I were you, I would get out of the area.' Model in response had laughed and invited him to dinner. 'I have no intention,' snorted Dessloch, 'of being made a prisoner.'[19] Major-General Walther Grabmann, the Luftwaffe fighter commander at Deelen airfield, north of Arnhem, also tried to warn Krebs. He had highlighted that the heathland to the west of Arnhem was ideal for paratroopers, but it was to no avail.

Over at the Hartenstein, Major Winrich 'Teddy' Behr, first assistant staff officer to General Krebs, was relaxing after lunch on 17 September.[20] In the room next door his colleague Lieutenant von Metzsch, the artillery staff officer, was lifting a spoonful of soup to his lips. Both were suddenly startled by the loud roar of enemy fighter-bombers zooming overhead. Leaping to his feet, Winrich Behr ordered several soldiers to get on the roof to see what was happening. The sight of parachutists seemed to indicate some sort of commando raid.

Behr then dashed off to Krebs' headquarters at the Hotel Feldberg. Finding that he was lunching with Model, Behr arrived at the Tafelberg to discover everyone leaving the building. Krebs instructed Behr to find out if the enemy was landing to the north or east of Arnhem. Back at the Hartenstein he made a few calls, then packed his shaving kit and a change of clothes.

In the meantime Private Frombeck, Model's driver, was summoned and he brought the field marshal's staff car round to the front of the Tafelberg. Model in his haste had forgotten to fasten his case and when he emerged from the building it burst open. His spilt clothing and toiletries had to be hastily gathered up. Sedelhauser watched as Krebs, minus his belt, cap and pistol, jumped into his car. He was hotly followed by Freyberg and Tempelhoff. Freyberg's parting orders were, 'Don't forget my cigars!'[21]

Once seated, an annoyed Model leant forward and instructed Frombeck, 'Quick! Doetinchem, Bittrich's headquarters!' First, though, he roared off to Arnhem to see the town commandant, Major-General Friedrich Kussin. The pair met on the open road as Kussin was heading for Wolfheze to see what was going on. Model ordered him to signal Hitler's headquarters about the landings and inform him of the field marshal's escape. Model then drove on to Terborg and then Slangenburg Castle at Doetinchem.

When the dust settled, Sedelhauser found himself alone. He then proceeded to authorize the immediate evacuation of all remaining personnel from the Feldberg, Hartenstein, Schoonoord and Tafelberg hotels. When he wandered back into the operations office, he saw that Tempelhoff had left Army Group B's situation maps on the table. He rolled them up, stuck them under his arm and prepared to make his way to Doetinchem. As he did so a final report came in. British airborne forces were not much more than two miles away. It was definitely time to go. Sedelhauser not only forgot his laundry, but also Freyberg's cigars. Smöckel's delicacies were likewise abandoned to the enemy. It clearly had been a close call for Model.

When the order to leave came through to the duty officer at the Schoonoord Hotel, it caused some panic. This was home to German signals units that included German female auxiliaries. The French had dubbed them 'Grey Mice' because of their uniforms; they were more scurrilously known as 'Officers' Mattresses'.[22] The women had enjoyed their occupation duties in Paris, but now they once again found themselves fleeing the encroaching enemy. They scattered in all directions as they rushed off to their lodgings to collect their belongings. The escape from Paris had been frightening and like Sedelhauser they had hoped Oosterbeek would offer some stability.

At Waldfriede country estate, SS-Major Sepp Krafft was not a happy man. His 16th SS-Panzergrenadier Training and Reserve Battalion had originally been billeted in Oosterbeek, but was ordered out to make way for Model. He redeployed to the northwest outside the village of Wolfheze, though some of his men were in Arnhem. From his headquarters in the Wolfheze Hotel, he watched as enemy gliders landed on Renkum Heath to the southwest less than a mile away. 'The only military objective I could think of with any importance was the Arnhem bridge', said Krafft.[23]

Krafft was not altogether surprised by what was happening. Just two days earlier he had dined with Major-General Hans von Tettau, chief of staff to the armed forces commander in the Netherlands. Over dinner Krafft had briefed Tettau on the condition of his depot battalion. It was a convivial meal and afterwards they had settled down to a cigar and a glass of port. Tettau then began to muse on how the war was going.

The elderly general was uneasy. 'Today over the whole Reich and England too we had the nicest weather,' said Tettau, 'but in spite of this, not a single big bomber came.' Krafft agreed that it did seem odd, as the Allies normally made use of clear skies. 'It proves they are preparing something in great style,' concluded Tettau prophetically.[24] What had the chain of command made of his concerns, enquired Krafft. Tettau scowled. 'They treated me like an old man', grumbled the general. 'They only laughed at me.'[25] Krafft felt rattled by such complacency. When he got back to his headquarters, he instructed that a lookout be placed on top of Waldfriede house.

On the morning of 17 September, Krafft sensed that something was not right. After breakfast American bombers hit a target not far from Waldfriede. British aircraft had also hit a target in Arnhem. He wondered if the Allies were going to try to grab Deelen airfield seven miles to the north. Certainly it had been bombed several times in recent weeks. Then of course there was the bridge at Arnhem.

By midday Krafft had put his battalion on alert and confined his men to their quarters. To keep them happy he had issued a ration of gin. The Dutch owner of Waldfriede realized his unwelcome house guests were edgy when one of them said in passing, 'Mark my words, something is turning up. They always give us gin when important things have to be done.'[26] The Dutchman hurried away, alarmed by the prospect of his home becoming a battlefield. Shortly after, the landings started.

Krafft knew that by deploying between Wolfheze and Oosterbeek, his unit was the only one in the area that could block a British advance on Arnhem. In total his battalion mustered 425 men, most of whom were just teenagers.[27] Krafft appreciated it was vital that he gained time for Bittrich to gather his forces, so he instructed one of his companies to attack the British landing zone.

He was in the process of ordering his reserve company from Arnhem when Kussin arrived. The general was shocked by the size of the landings that were taking place to the southwest and northwest. Krafft explained that all he had to hold the British at bay was an understrength training battalion. Kussin gave an undertaking to get him reinforcements by 1800 hours. When the Arnhem commandant prepared to leave, Krafft warned it would not be wise to use the Utrecht–Arnhem road, as it 'may already be blocked.' Kussin, who was in a hurry to get back to his headquarters, chose unwisely to ignore this very sound advice. Also at Wolfheze, Sergeant Youppinger was fuming. All hell had broken loose, so he had phoned Army Group's headquarters. Instead of being thanked for his warning, Sedelhauser had yelled at him, 'Are you hung over from last night?' before hanging up.[28]

'They nearly got me,' exclaimed Model when he reached Bittrich. 'They were after my headquarters. Just imagine! They nearly got me.'[29] Model reasoned this had to be the case. If they were after the Arnhem bridge what would possess them to drop six miles from their objective? It just did not make sense. When Model arrived back at his headquarters in Terborg, he was informed that no one could raise General Kussin. Model cursed the Arnhem commandant's foolhardiness. Quite frankly Wolfheze was the responsibility of the Waffen-SS and Kussin did not need to go sticking his nose in their business.

This unwelcome news meant that there was no one to organize and co-ordinate the defence of Arnhem bridge. Model needed someone to get down there and sort things out. He could not spare Freyberg or Tempelhoff, and Sedelhauser was too junior. He asked Tempelhoff who they had available. It was suggested they send Major Ernst Schleifenbaum, who was one of the older members of the operations staff. The major was immediately ordered to get to Arnhem and round up all the rear echelon personnel he could lay his hands on and issue them with rifles.[30] He was also to liaise with the SS when they arrived. Arnhem bridge must be held at all costs. The battle for control of Arnhem must not be lost.

List of Maps

List of Illustrations

Field Marshal Walther Model.
Camouflaged Waffen-SS anti-tank gunners in France.
Belgian Resistance with a captured German self-propelled gun.
General Gustav-Adolf von Zangen and Field Marshal Erwin
  Rommel.
Arthur Seyss-Inquart with Adolf Hitler.
Zangen conducted a highly successful fighting withdrawal to
  Walcheren.
Anton Mussert meeting Hitler.
General Kurt Student, founder of Hitler's airborne forces.
SS-General Wilhelm Bittrich.
The Arnhem road bridge.
Model, Student, Bittrich, Knaust and Harmel.
Model being briefed by SS-Brigadier Heinz Harmel.
A German soldier being questioned by members of the Dutch
  Resistance.
The Arnhem road bridge after SS-Captain Paul Gräbner's column
  was ambushed on 18 September 1944.
German prisoners gathered on Nijmegen road bridge.
The devastation inflicted on central Nijmegen.
German troops amongst British debris left behind in Arnhem.
A German self-propelled flak gun in Arnhem.
A dug-in German flak gun on the streets of Arnhem.
SS-Grenadiers with captured British paratroopers.
British airborne forces going into captivity.

I

Race Against Time

In the German military headquarters in Brussels and The Hague, the teleprinters were clattering noisily in late August 1944. It was official: the German front had finally collapsed in Normandy and General von Choltitz had lost Paris. The surviving German armed forces were streaming east across the Seine, heading for the Somme. A new defensive line was going to have to be cobbled together, but the question was where and with what. In the meantime, the German military police were put on alert with orders to round up every straggler and deserter. They took their job very seriously; woe betide anyone caught on the road without orders or papers.

In Belgium the Germans looked to their Nazi allies for assistance. Brussels in the spring of 1944 hosted a bizarre celebratory dinner, which witnessed senior Waffen-SS officers saluting Belgian SS veterans. There was much carousing and back slapping. SS-General 'Sepp' Dietrich, the guest of honour, had raised a toast and pinned medals on those in attendance. Dietrich acted as the representative of Hitler's right-hand man Reichsführer Heinrich Himmler, commander of the Waffen-SS.

Earlier at a public ceremony in Charleroi, looking round at the gathered ranks, Dietrich had thought to himself, 'these tough Belgians made good Nazis'. They had certainly shed blood for Hitler. Dietrich could do with more men like this, and Himmler agreed with him. Truth be told, Himmler was a terrible military commander, but the highly experienced Dietrich knew a good unit when he saw one. Quite what your average Belgian citizen made of this heroic force, newly returned from the Eastern Front, was another matter. Dietrich had done all he could to look dashing and be an inspiration to the young soldiers. For the Nazi cameras recording the moment, he wore his hat at a jaunty angle, as was his custom, and looked very serious.

The Nazi occupation and administration of France proved a headache from start to finish. In contrast, the Low Countries, comprising Belgium and the Netherlands, by virtue of their size had been easier to control. The Military Governor of Belgium and Northern France was one General Alexander von Falkenhausen, the nephew of General Ludwig von Falkenhausen who had served as Belgium's military governor during World War II.

In the summer of 1944, as the Allies were poised to liberate Belgium, Dr Hendrick Elias was an anxious man. As the leader of the Flemish Vlaamsch Nationaal Verbond, he had aligned himself very firmly with the Nazi cause. Amongst his militia commanders there was a growing sense of unease, especially once Paris was liberated. In July 1944 he watched as the German-controlled Belgian security militia, known as the Vlaamse Wacht, were issued with German uniforms. This force, some four battalions strong, was going to defend Flemish territory from the Allies, but instead they had been sent to the Eastern Front to serve with a Flemish SS division.

Antwerp was not a happy city under Nazi occupation. In contrast, despite the machinations of the French Resistance, Gestapo and Vichy police, Paris had maintained its air of gaiety. Copenhagen also managed to avoid many of the deprivations of war, such as rationing. The Danes initially had been treated with great leniency by their conquerors. When there was trouble in mid-1944, the Germans had simply surrounded the Danish capital and a negotiated settlement was swiftly reached to avoid bloodshed.

In Antwerp security around the vital port area was very tight and the Germans were poised to systematically destroy all the facilities as they had done at Cherbourg. The Belgian Resistance knew the one thing the Allies desperately needed intact was the docks.

However, the resistance in Belgium expended too much effort bickering amongst themselves and was never very strong. When active they spent most of their time killing Belgian collaborators. It had been planned that the Belgian Resistance would conduct a rising, but the swift Allied advance into their country had made such an operation almost pointless.

The province of Flanders had the highest proportion of collaborators in western Europe. This meant that Antwerp, as the capital of Flanders, was a hotbed of pro-Nazi intrigue. The Germans had pandered to Elias' strong Flemish separatist party which had set up various militias and auxiliary security forces to help maintain law and order. Volunteers had also gone to fight the Russians. Hitler had been moved to praise 'the magnificent conduct of the Flemish on the Eastern Front'.[1]

On Antwerp's streets were men of the Dietsche Militia and the Vlaamse Wacht Brigade, who worked to counter the Resistance's Witte Brigade. The militia was the uniformed wing of the Vlaamsch Nationaal Verbond. The second unit had been formed as a factory guard to protect the country's infrastructure from sabotage. The German occupation also relied on the Garde Rurale raised from the country's farmers to protect crops and farms. To the casual observer, the Wacht Brigade looked like members of the SS. It had been attached to the Luftwaffe to help protect airfields, but while the fighting was still going on in Normandy had been converted into an anti-aircraft unit. The Flämisches Flak Brigade was organized with a light anti-aircraft group of six batteries and a heavy group of four batteries. Rumour was that the brigade was going to be deployed to the Netherlands to protect German rocket sites.

In the neighbouring Belgian province of Wallonia, pro-Nazi militias had also been set up. The most notorious Belgian fascist was SS-Major Léon Degrelle, who had led volunteers fighting on the Eastern Front. He became the most decorated foreign volunteer in the SS. Degrelle attended the celebratory dinner in Brussels in early April 1944, along with the survivors of his brigade. Fighting alongside the 5th SS-Panzer Division *Wiking*, they had only just escaped the Cherkassy Pocket in Russia. Degrelle's men had covered the retreat and in the process suffered 1,368 casualties from a force of several thousand.

For his conduct, Degrelle was awarded the Knight's Cross and later given permission to form a Belgian SS-Panzergrenadier division. However, Degrelle and his men were not destined to fight the British and Americans. After refitting at Wildflecken they were sent to the Baltic coast to resist the advancing Red Army. After the Allied liberation of Brussels, Degrelle knew that he could never return home. Secretly he planned to make Spain his sanctuary should Germany lose the war. A Flemish SS division also fought in Russia. 'The Flamands have indeed shown themselves on the Eastern Front,' said Hitler, 'to be more pro-German and more ruthless than the Dutch legionaries.'[2] In stark contrast, just two brigades of Belgian and Dutch troops came ashore with the Allies in the wake of D-Day.[3]

Begium now represented sanctuary for the retreating German divisions. General von Tresckow's 18th Luftwaffe Field Division spent the battle for Normandy holding Dunkirk. It was not until mid-August that Tresckow and his men were sent south to Mantes on the Seine to the west of Paris. Fighting the Americans, they suffered heavy casualties. On 27 August an American attack split them from the flanking division. Tresckow divided his command into three battle groups and headed for Beauvais. Harassed by the Americans and Allied fighter-bombers, Tresckow took up position at Ham, on the Somme Canal near St Quentin, at the beginning of September and then headed for Cambrai.

Tresckow's forces became part of a mass of fleeing German units desperately trying to reach Belgium along the Amiens–Cambrai–Mons road. The British and Americans managed to trap three entire German corps in the Mons area. Tresckow and the 6th Parachute Division attempted to break out at 0200 hours on 3 September, but American and Belgian troops blocked the crossroads at Gognies-Chaussée. The German columns were relentlessly decimated by Allied fighter-bombers and artillery.

In just three days the Americans took almost 30,000 prisoners at Mons. Many of them came from the five divisions that had been instructed to withdraw to the Siegfried Line.[4] Amongst those units completely destroyed in the pocket was the 3rd Parachute Division, which by this stage had lost well over 15,000 men. The German position in Belgium now looked particularly precarious, but there was worse to come.

Tresckow and around 300 men managed to escape the trap. Splitting them up into smaller groups, he and a handful of survivors crossed the Maas south of Dinant. On 15 September they reached the Eupen-Malmédy region of Belgium and were met by German-speaking locals. They then pressed on to reach the Belgian-German border and safety. For his actions, Tresckow was awarded the Knight's Cross.

Meanwhile, Field Marshal Model, commander of Hitler's Army Group B, had set up his headquarters at La Chaude Fontaine to the southeast of Liège and southwest of Aachen and the German frontier. The arrival of the British in Brussels on 3 September 1944 and Antwerp the following day seemed to herald the complete collapse of German resistance in northwestern Europe. The Germans and their collaborators in Brussels fled in panic.

In Antwerp, commandant Major-General Christoph Graf zu Stolberg-Stolberg was taken completely by surprise. He was captured by the Belgian Resistance and his garrison swiftly surrendered. There had been no time to destroy the docks before the British 11th Armoured Division arrived in the early afternoon. In the face of approaching enemy tanks and a rising by the Belgian Resistance, Stolberg had been ordered by Model to withdraw behind the Albert Canal. Failing all else, Model had said he and his troops should fight their way out to the southeast. Instead Stolberg and 6,000 of his men were taken prisoner. He had wrongly assumed that he would have at least a few days' grace before the British turned up. His heart had not been in the job, grumbling that 'it would have been much better to give ground rather than sacrifice troops in tasks which were too much for them'.[5]

The loss of Antwerp's docks was a disaster, and Model was flabbergasted. He had only just ordered two infantry divisions to reinforce the defences of the city. The 719th Division was still on its way from the Netherlands and the 347th Division, taking the train from France, now kept on going. Model had just been in conference with Hitler on 3 September. Their plan had been to launch a counter-attack with all available reserves from the Upper Moselle against General Patton's US 3rd Army, in an effort to delay the northern advance of the Allied armies. Instead, in just over a week the Allies had raced from the Seine to Antwerp in the north and Verdun to the south.

The German troops in northern France and Belgium were effectively trapped. 'The British Army Group is thrusting northeast towards Antwerp with the objectives of capturing the V-1 bases and bottling up our 15th Army', warned Model.[6] He was haemorrhaging men at a rate he could not sustain; losses at Antwerp, Brussels and Mons had cost him about 40,000 troops. 'They were continually overtaken and cut off,' despaired Model, 'largely because they lacked the tanks, artillery, and heavy anti-tank weapons needed for setting up a defensive position from which to counter-attack'.[7]

Surveying his situation maps, Model could see that the Allies had ripped open a 75-mile gap in his front. The road into the Netherlands was open, as was Germany's northwest frontier. The Siegfried Line ran from Switzerland only as far as Kleve on the Dutch-German border. Once the Allies were in the Netherlands they would be able to outflank it, cross the Rhine and thrust into the Ruhr, Germany's industrial heartland. If that happened, it meant no more weapons for the Wehrmacht. In desperation, Model signalled the Führer's headquarters requesting 30 new divisions. This had fallen on deaf ears, or so he thought. The German high command responded saying, 'it is important to gain as much time as possible for raising and bringing up new formations...'[8] In reality, just four new grenadier divisions would be ready by the end of September.

Model, though, was pleased to be informed that he would no longer have to act as CinC West and commander of Army Group B. It was an impossible juggling act. The long-suffering Field

Marshal von Rundstedt had been reappointed CinC West, with his headquarters at Koblenz. Rundstedt was instructed that he must 'dispute every inch of ground'. Luckily for Model and Rundstedt, Hitler for once decreed that enemy penetrations 'must not lead to the encirclement of large German formations'.[9]

Looking closer at his maps, Model soon realized the British had committed a strategic blunder to the west of Antwerp. Its loss would mean nothing if his forces controlled the 54-mile-long approaches to the port along the Scheldt Estuary. The key to this was Walcheren Island and the South Beveland Peninsula. Model's only problem was finding forces with which to hold these areas. To the south of the Scheldt were the remnants of General Gustav-Adolf von Zangen's 15th Army. This had remained in the Pas-de-Calais during the battle for Normandy because Hitler feared a second seaborne invasion after D-Day. Many of its divisions had belatedly been sent west and subsequently lost.

Model realized he faced a race against time. Zangen still had around 80,000 men available and these needed to be got across the Scheldt Estuary before the British swept to the northwest of Antwerp. Failure to do so would leave 15th Army trapped and the German flank wide open. He was pessimistic about their chances. 'The course of the breakthrough battles of 15th Army cannot as yet be gauged', Model reported up the chain of command. 'Only some sections will fight their way through.'[10]

It did not help matters that Model and Zangen disliked each other. It was widely rumoured that Model had got Zangen's predecessor, Hans von Salmuth, sacked at the end of August for being too gloomy about the future of the Western Front. When Model then accused the newly appointed Zangen of not being proactive enough, the latter confided to a staff officer that the only solution was to shoot Model or himself.[11] Annoyed that Zangen did not seem to be getting a firm grip on the situation, Model sent a staff officer to 15th Army's headquarters with instructions to 'take a look and attempt to restore some order'.[12]

Zangen immediately realized that his job was on the line and began making plans. After the officer reported back, the field marshal stopped harassing Zangen. Model instructed him to hold the ports of Boulogne, Calais and Dunkirk to shield the Pas-de-Calais and to hold the southern bank of the Scheldt. Hitler had made it clear the Channel ports were to be held no matter what. 'There was no longer any sense in staying at the coast', complained Zangen. 'We had to try to withdraw all mobile forces from the Channel area and turn them to meet the danger threatening from our rear.'[13] He knew, though, that it was a waste of time arguing.

Zangen was also to strike northeast into the advancing British on 6 September. If nothing else, the latter would buy Model time to beef up defences along the Albert Canal east of Antwerp. By this stage 15th Army consisted of six infantry divisions, with 67th Corps controlling the 70th, 226th and 245th and the 89th Corps with the 59th, 64th and 712th. These units were far from up to strength and were not front-line material. Between the Somme and Scheldt were the remnants of a number of other divisions which had escaped the fighting in Normandy.

'With the news of the fall of Antwerp', noted Zangen with alarm, 'the envelopment of 15th Army seemed to be complete.'[14] Model and Rundstedt could not understand why the British did not attack directly north of Antwerp. It seemed to indicate that Field Marshal Montgomery's advance had lost momentum after the Allies' decisive victory in Normandy at Falaise. Rundstedt was firmly of the view that the British and Canadian armies were now at the very limit of their supply lines, which indicated, for the time being at least, that the Allied pursuit had come to an end. This meant there was hope for Zangen and his men if they acted quickly. However, he knew there was little he could do to save those forces under his command trapped in the Channel ports.

Zangen appreciated that the garrison commander in Boulogne, Major-General Ferdinand Heim, was not a happy man. He had been treated abominably by Hitler, who had previously sacked him. Heim had had a series of narrow escapes on the Eastern Front, where he initially served as chief of staff to General Paulus' ill-fated 6th Army at Stalingrad. Hitler made Heim the scapegoat for the failure to stop the Red Army's breakthrough in late 1942, after he led the 48th Panzer Corps' futile rescue attempt. The unfortunate Heim was arrested, reduced to the rank of a private and thrown out of the army. However, it meant he escaped being killed or captured, as he was sent home. He spent months languishing in Moabit prison awaiting trial for dereliction of duty.

Hitler's manpower shortages were such that Heim was recalled and on 1 August 1944 was placed in charge of Boulogne's defences. The key to these were the bunkers on Mont Lambert, as they dominated the town's approaches. He had toured the fortifications and viewed the killing grounds created by the open rolling farmland. The snag was that he lacked support from the Luftwaffe to keep enemy aircraft and warships away. His gunners could not conduct effective battery or counter-battery fire if they were forced constantly to keep their heads down.

Upon arrival, Heim found that RAF Bomber Command had visited Boulogne and Le Havre in mid-June and sunk all the German naval vessels. From these raids he knew they would not be safe in their bunkers. At Le Havre the British employed massive 12,000lb bombs to penetrate the concrete shelters, built to protect their fast attack E-boats. In one attack the British neutralized the entire German fleet operating in the Channel.

In all, Heim had about 10,000 men at his disposal, but the defences were manned by disgruntled soldiers, airmen without planes and sailors without ships. Heim was once again being made a sacrificial lamb, along with all the other Channel port commanders. He had failed with 48th Panzer Corps because of a lack of resources, and he faced the same problem at Boulogne.

Heim knew that he had a stay of execution because the forlorn German garrison at Le Havre was first in the firing line. He had contacted its commander, Colonel Eberhard Wildermuth, who spoke encouragingly of the strength of his fortress. Privately, though, Wildermuth doubted he would be able to withstand the Allies' massed firepower for very long. Once they were in Antwerp, the Allies could lay siege to the isolated Channel ports at their leisure and pick them off one by one. Zangen made it clear to Heim and Wildermuth that their job was simply to delay the enemy for as long as possible. Both men understandably felt abandoned to their fate. They knew their chances of being rescued were nil. Their main dilemma was how long to resist before surrendering.

2

Zangen's Great Escape

The British wasted 36 vital hours after taking Antwerp and this presented a prime opportunity to save Zangen's army. Rundstedt immediately cancelled Model's order for Zangen to conduct an attack on the British flank. Lacking tanks and the support of the Luftwaffe, this would have been suicidal. The chances are that 15th Army would have ended up in an even worse mess. Instead, Zangen was to march directly north with all haste and get over the three-mile-wide mouth of the Scheldt and onto Walcheren Island. Once they were safely across, Zangen's divisions could head east along the northern bank of the Scheldt across South Beveland and onto the Dutch mainland to the north of Antwerp. Initially Zangen's defence south of the Scheldt Estuary could be anchored on the cities of Bruges and Ghent.

When Zangen's orders came through he noted, 'the Scheldt Estuary was to be defended vigorously by two divisions, one north of the estuary and one south'. When he read on he was dismayed to see that 'the Channel fortresses were to be similarly defended'.[1] Model also warned that the retreating troops were full of 'whispers, rumours, haste, endless disorder and vicious self-interest. This atmosphere is... infecting units still intact.'[2] Morale had to be restored to stop the rot.

The heavy German coastal guns on Walcheren and the batteries at Cadzand, west of Breskens, would prevent Allied warships from interfering with the crossing of the Scheldt. However, the evacuation across the waters between Breskens and Flushing and from Terneuzen and Hoedekenskerke could be conducted only during darkness, otherwise the retreat would be pounced on by Allied fighter-bombers. It was estimated that the withdrawal would take about two weeks. Zangen got on the phone and instructed Major-General Eugen-Felix Schwalbe to oversee operations at Breskens. Schwalbe previously commanded the 346th Infantry Division, but it had been lost on the Seine. The anti-aircraft batteries were strengthened at Breskens and Flushing, with flak guns also placed on barges out in the Scheldt.

While General Schwalbe was glad to have another role, he had no staff. 'When I was told what my new job was to be I set up my HQ in Breskens,' he recalled. 'Gathering about me as many officers as I could find, I sent them along the roads leading to Breskens, where they set up collection posts for the assembling of retreating units.'³ In order not to attract unwanted attention, these units had to lie up during the day concealed from the air; they were then allotted a time to get to Breskens. Schwalbe and his staff had to contact all the divisional commanders so that they could organize a phased withdrawal. This was not easy as most were constantly on the move and out of touch.

Once in Breskens, Schwalbe discovered that an *ad hoc* evacuation had commenced two days earlier, on 4 September, and that thousands of men had already made the crossing. He appointed a liaison officer to oversee embarkation and sent another one over to Flushing to co-ordinate disembarkation and onward transit to the clearing depots. The latter task was greatly assisted by the railway running from Flushing north to Middelburg and then eastwards across the causeway into South Beveland.

In the meantime, Zangen established his headquarters on Walcheren at Middelburg. The Luftwaffe also had a presence on Walcheren, as it was home to one of their night-fighter control stations. Half a dozen other stations had run through central Belgium, but they were now overrun. Zangen and his staff decided to make Maria ter Heide, just three miles northeast of Antwerp, an assembly area. The evacuated divisions could be rested and refitted there, before being committed to the battle. Zangen's lines of communication on Walcheren were good, but he was concerned that the Allies might opt to breach the dykes and deliberately flood the interior of the island. If that happened, it would drown low-lying German defences and greatly hamper movement. To prevent this, Zangen ordered the air defences at Flushing, Westkapelle and Veere to be greatly reinforced.

First it was necessary to secure the Breskens bridgehead, which required withdrawing the 59th and 345th infantry divisions north to the Bruges–Ghent–St Nicholas line. They were to be reinforced by the 70th Division, which had withdrawn from the Boulogne area. Their job was to hold the Canadian army at bay. Meanwhile it was decided that administrative personnel would be evacuated first.

Field Marshal Montgomery on the British side knew what was going on. It was obvious General Zangen could hardly fight his way out, so would have to escape via Flushing. Canadian intelligence showed that Hitler was strengthening the Channel ports, which would weaken an already understrength 15th Army. It was assessed, incorrectly, that Zangen would probably reach Breskens with just three infantry divisions and the remnants of three others. The Canadians captured a copy of the order authorizing the evacuation on 6 September, confirming Allied suspicions.[4] Fortunately for Zangen, the Allied high command, with its hands full elsewhere, hardly considered the fate of his few remaining divisions a priority. They had no offensive power so posed no real threat.

What Model and Zangen could not guess was Montgomery's next move. What was clear was that General Miles Dempsey's British 2nd Army was poised to strike along the Albert Canal to the east of Antwerp. To the west, thankfully, General Harry Crerar's Canadian 1st Army seemed preoccupied with liberating the Channel ports, leaving just two armoured divisions in hot pursuit of 15th Army. Then on 5 September, British armoured cars rolled into Zwijnaarde, the southern suburbs of the historic city of Ghent. This posed an immediate threat to Zangen's eastern flank.

Major-General Wilhelm Daser's 70th Infantry Division was responsible for Ghent's defence. However, the garrison was little more than 1,000 strong, supported by some 88mm guns.[5] None of these men had any intention of fighting to the death. Daser's command was known as the 'White Bread Division', because many of his soldiers had special dietary needs. In addition, like most occupied cities, there were many thousands of non-combatant administrative staff in Ghent. These included field police, military postal services, mechanics, pay clerks, radio operators and members of the Gestapo.

Daser ordered roadblocks to be set up around the city centre and patrols be maintained. Then, in a piece of comic opera, he tried to surrender to the British 7th Armoured Division. Daser soon undermined his own negotiations by refusing to deal with anyone of lesser rank. As a result he declined to surrender to a British lieutenant-colonel and then a brigadier.[6] When Daser spoke with 67th Corps headquarters, he was instructed to carry on resisting. It may be that Daser's antics were actually a delaying tactic while his men prepared to leave.

Lacking authority to hand over Ghent, Daser withdrew his forces to the northern outskirts of the city. On their initial approach the British 7th Armoured had taken about 1,000 prisoners, but apart from snipers and a few pockets of resistance most of the Germans just slipped away. Daser's withdrawal, though, was haphazard. When those administrative staff left behind in their offices could hear loud cheering, they knew it was not for their benefit. The British had reached the city centre.

One frightened German soldier surrendered from the sanctuary of the toilets at Sint Pieters railway station. He was slightly amused when a British tank crewman entered determined to use the facilities before taking his rifle. In the western suburb of St Martens Latem, 300 dispirited Germans were rounded up. Elsewhere another group of 70 men acted as if they were on holiday, wandering around a shopping centre and the local cafés. When an exasperated British officer demanded to know if they wanted to surrender, a soldier shrugged and said, 'We won't surrender until our officer gives us the order'. In response to further questioning, he added, 'They're having a conference'.[7] Eventually a German lieutenant appeared and confirmed they would be going into captivity.

Nonetheless, elements of Daser's units continued to be a nuisance in and around the city for the next three days. His gunners seemed content to spare the city from destruction. Mortar bombs were dropped onto Adeghem, but just two shells were fired into the city, which briefly cleared the streets. German troops put up a fight at Eine, northwest of Oudenarde, but were driven off with the loss of 100 killed and wounded. They counter-attacked, briefly retaking the village and needlessly murdering 60 men, women and children.[8] A company of Waffen-SS also conducted an unsuccessful counter-attack at Wetteren. Concerned at the prospect of a major German counter-attack, British engineers blew up all the bridges over the river Lys. At Deinze the Germans tried to hold the Courtrai, Ghent and Tielt road junction. Instead another 400 men were captured and the British demolished the bridge at Deinze.

On hearing that the British were in Ghent, Schwalbe acted quickly. On the night of 6 September a fleet of two requisitioned Dutch freighters, three large rafts and 16 small boats gathered at Breskens. The rafts were capable of carrying 18 vehicles each, while the boats could take around 250 men each, and the freighters possibly double that. This meant that Schwalbe could shift around 5,000 men and 54 vehicles with each crossing, which took about an hour. However, it was best to run a staggered relay service to stop the vessels from becoming sitting ducks through sailing at the same time. Breskens and to a lesser extent Terneuzen became hives of activity.

Remarkably, by midday on 7 September, some 25,000 men had been ferried over to Walcheren.[9] The following day the British finally secured Ghent, although German troops continued to resist in the surrounding factory districts. The main blow to Zangen was that the British were claiming to have captured nearly 10,000 personnel.[10] This seems a suspiciously high number, but included non-combatants who had been unable to escape. Daser's 'White

Bread Division' lived up to its name, with around 2,000 of his men being taken without much of a fight.

Zangen still held the Zeebrugge–Bruges canal, however, and this defensive line was reinforced by the 67th Corps and the 712th Division. Zangen also strengthened the Woensdrecht bridgehead that protected the Beveland isthmus, which formed 15th Army's escape route east. All the time that the British failed to take Woensdrecht, Zangen's troops could withdraw northeastwards through Bergen op Zoom and Breda and onto Tilburg on the Wilhelmina Canal. Canadian intelligence reported 'it is certain that the German scratch fleet of fishing boats and barges is plying busily to and fro in the West Scheldt evacuating as many troops as possible for another, not far distant day'.[11]

It was at this point that Hitler got it into his head to try and simplify his tortuous chain of command. He did this by ordering 'Commander Armed Forces Belgium and Northern France, and Commander Armed Forces Netherlands, are fully subordinate' to Field Marshal Rundstedt.[12] This ultimately did nothing to make Model, Zangen and Schwalbe's jobs any easier. As far as Model was concerned, it would have been better if they came under the auspices of his army group.

The German defenders of the Bruges–Ghent canal were shelled on 8 September and then they heard the clatter of tracks. The men of the 245th Infantry Division found themselves under attack by tanks of the Polish 1st Armoured Division. They held their ground, but on the night of the 9th the Poles tried again, only to be repulsed once more. Units of the 245th and 711th divisions were also attacked by the Canadian 4th Armoured Division at Moerbrugge, south of Bruges. The Canadians got over the canal and were subjected to a series of vigorous counter-attacks, but they were not driven off.

The Germans suffered heavy casualties at Moerbrugge, with the loss of 700 killed and wounded and 150 prisoners. Amongst those captured near Bruges was Major Eberhard Furst von Urach, commander of the 505th Reconnaissance Battalion. 'It is now intended to hold out here', he told his interrogators, 'until the

THE ESCAPE OF ZANGEN'S 15TH ARMY, 4–23 SEPTEMBER 1944

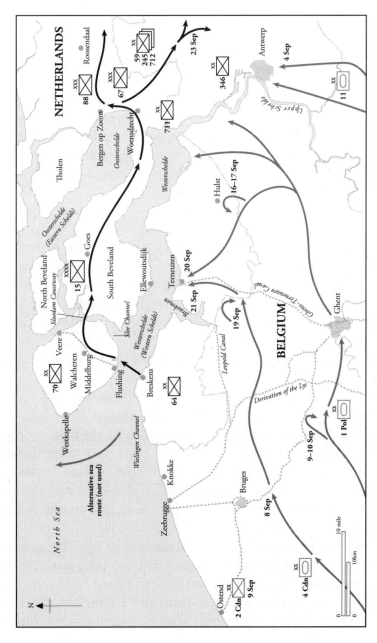

maximum possible number of troops have been shipped away.' When asked where they were going he said that he 'did not know'.[13]

Just as Bruges was being liberated, the isolated German garrison holding Ostend was overrun. 'The port of Ostend', noted Zangen, 'of which the enemy radio speaks frequently, is completely destroyed.'[14] News from Colonel Eberhard Wildermuth's headquarters at Le Havre was not encouraging either. The British launched a full-scale assault at 1745 hours on 10 September following two days of intensive bombing by the RAF and shelling by the Royal Navy. Thousands of tons of high explosive had fallen on the city.[15] Wildermuth was instructed to resist to the last man, but privately he doubted his garrison could hold for more than a few days. Zangen felt sorry for them; they were a long way from home and from help. There was nothing he could do.

While most of the journeys across the Scheldt Estuary were made at night-time, speed was of the essence and Schwalbe risked a few daytime crossings. 'Allied planes constantly harried the ships', he said, 'and a number of them, laden with troops, received direct hits.'[16] Zangen also noted that the evacuation had to endure 'up to six air attacks' a day.[17] The evacuees rightly feared being out on the open water and now knew how the British had felt at Dunkirk in 1940.

Schwalbe decided to risk another daylight crossing on 12 September. The ferry skippers were not happy, but what could they do? One of the Dutch freighters had just left Breskens harbour and half a dozen smaller boats were on their way back from Flushing when there was an ominous droning noise overhead. Then the bombs began to fall on Breskens town and the waterfront. Those captains heading for Breskens immediately took evasive action, frantically veering to the left, knowing that it was not safe to put into the harbour while the attack was under way. The men on the freighter looked back and were thankful they had cleared the harbour before the bombers arrived.

First came the shock waves, followed by the sound of the exploding bombs. The blasts forced great clouds of dust and debris up into the sky. The crews on the boats and the men being evacuated braced themselves, waiting for great geysers to erupt around them. They did not come. Thankfully the bombers had struck from the landward side and by the time they were out over the estuary had expended their bombs.

Huddled in his command post, Schwalbe realized that timings mattered little, because Allied medium bombers struck Breskens, Flushing and Terneuzen day and night. During daylight hours their agile fighter-bombers mercilessly hounded the ferries whilst in transit. Moving under the cover of darkness or low cloud offered the best protection. He requested that Zangen's headquarters seek help from the Luftwaffe's fighters, but none was forthcoming. Instead he had to rely on the Luftwaffe's anti-aircraft batteries, which at least were able to claim 40 enemy aircraft.[18]

Not long after, a tired and dirty Brigadier Karl Rheim received orders to ship the remnants of his 331st Infantry Division over. The division had arrived in France early in the year from the Eastern Front, having left all its combat veterans behind as they were reassigned. Some 10,500 strong, it had fought in Normandy from mid-August, losing about 1,500 men.[19] After reaching Flushing, Rheim and his men were deployed to the northeast of Antwerp, where they were combined with the remains of two other divisions.

Next went Major-General Walther Poppe's 59th Infantry Division. His officers oversaw the loading of their men, horses, vehicles and guns ready for the one-hour journey. Once under way, Poppe recalled, 'in completely darkened ships, exposed and defenceless, was a most unpleasant experience'.[20] They were followed by the 345th Infantry Division. In an effort to prevent overcrowding at Flushing, Schwalbe directed some units to Terneuzen. Amongst these was the 17th Luftwaffe Field Division under Major-General Hans Hocker. His unit had been deployed in the Le Havre area before D-Day and had been mauled trying to stop the Allies from crossing the Seine at Rouen. The survivors formed into an *ad hoc* battle group and then retreated north with Rheim's 331st Infantry.[21]

The phone rang in Zangen's headquarters on 12 September, and he was informed that Le Havre had fallen to the British with the loss of 11,300 prisoners. It seemed such a terrible and pointless waste of manpower. The only upside was that Colonel Wildermuth's garrison had completely destroyed the port, ensuring the Allies could not use it for some considerable time. Also the garrisons in Boulogne, Calais and Dunkirk were still holding out. Zangen was displeased by the news and appreciated that Model would be angry. Le Havre was considered one of the strongest fortresses of the so-called Atlantic Wall. The divisional-sized garrison was well stocked with ammunition and food. In reality, though, the troops were a combination of army, Luftwaffe and naval personnel, many of whom were of doubtful combat value.

When Zangen enquired how Le Havre's strong defences had been overcome, he was informed that the defenders had not responded fast enough following the British bombardment. The men had been down in their shelters and many had not emerged in time to reach their firing positions. In consequence many of the formidable strongpoints had been outflanked. Zangen could easily guess Model's response when he learned that Wildermuth had surrendered at Fort de Tourneville that afternoon, wearing just his pyjamas and his medals![22] It was certainly not the heroic last stand that Hitler had in mind.

The fighting around Zangen's defensive perimeter continued. The men of the 245th Division had to fend off the Canadian 4th Armoured Division again on 13 September. They had dug in on the double line of the Canal de Dérivation de la Lys and the Leopold Canal at Moerkerke. Once again the division was heavily shelled, and while they had their heads down the Canadians got across in assault boats. Once the dust settled, the defenders responded with artillery and mortar fire, catching Canadian engineers trying to build a bridge and sinking their supply boats. Also that day the 67th Corps was ferried over the estuary, with orders to reinforce General Student's newly formed 1st Parachute Army.

The following morning the 245th Division counter-attacked with such vigour that the Canadian bridgehead was overrun. The Canadians lost 88 killed and wounded, with 60 captured. A few escaped by swimming back across the canal. Much to the relief of the 245th Division, which had expended most of its ammunition, no further attacks were launched by its tough foe.

Overhead, the Allied air forces did all they could to make things difficult for Zangen and Schwalbe. 'Heavy air attacks on the Scheldt ferries, considerable bombing of Breskens and the railway installations on Walcheren and South Beveland', noted Zangen: 'the bulk of the ferry boats were put out of action; the passage out of Terneuzen harbour was blocked by sunken boats.'[23] Flushing was not spared either, with bombs falling on the Merchant's and Fisher's Docks, the Scheldt Shipyard and Spuikom. In the Scheldt yard there was a very large vessel known as '214', which could have helped with the evacuation, but it was not finished.

Luckily for Zangen and his men, the Allies' heavy bombers kept away. During this time, they were busy flattening the unfortunate German city of Darmstadt. Technically their target had been its factories, but the bombs killed up to 12,000 people.[24] Frankfurt, Kiel and Stuttgart likewise suffered. RAF Bomber Command was also directed to attack the Channel ports. Nonetheless, from 15 September it became impossible to cross the Scheldt Estuary except at night. That day the remains of General Daser's 70th Infantry reached the safety of Walcheren. They were to form the garrison of Scheldt Fortress North. Two days later the gunners manning the batteries near Biggeskerke, Flushing and Westkapelle were blasted by attacks from almost 100 heavy bombers taking a brief break from pounding Germany. Bremerhaven and München-Gladbach were next on their list. They would be back, however, and by the end of October had dropped 10,219 tons of bombs on Walcheren.

To the south of the Scheldt Estuary, 15th Army was slowly squeezed into a small pocket running in an arc north of Bruges and Ghent to just east of Axel. Preparing for the worst and to protect

Schwalbe's operations, Zangen instructed Major-General Kurt
Eberding's 64th Infantry Division to dig in north of the Leopold
Canal to create Scheldt Fortress South. This unit was made up of
convalescent combat veterans from the Eastern Front and their job
was to hold the Breskens Pocket.[25] They were joined by the 245th
Division, which was then ferried over the estuary and moved to
Tilburg to join the 1st Parachute Army.

Much to Zangen and Schwalbe's displeasure, the Poles
reappeared on the eastern flank of the Breskens Pocket. Their
tanks got over the Hulst Canal to the east of Axel and Terneuzen.
Zangen knew that this posed a very real threat to his evacuation
operations from Terneuzen, which lay just five miles away from the
enemy advance, and he ordered a counter-attack. This crushed the
Polish bridgehead, but the Poles crossed again and their engineers
built a bridge.

On 19 September Zangen relocated his headquarters from
Middelburg to the northeast to Dordrecht on the river Waal,
content that most of his army had now been saved. The Poles
breached Terneuzen's defences the very next day and captured the
port. In the process the Germans lost many of their surviving ferries
and 1,175 prisoners. Breskens, though, remained firmly occupied
by Zangen's forces.

Zangen ordered General Eberding to hold for as long as possible,
as this would delay any Allied seaborne assault on Walcheren and
South Beveland. Without control of the latter, Model and Zangen
knew the Allies would be unable to resupply their armies via
Antwerp. 'In this hour, the fortifications along the Scheldt Estuary
occupy a role which is decisive for the future of our people', said
Zangen. 'Each additional day it will be vital that you deny the
port of Antwerp to the enemy.' Just to make sure his commanders
were under no illusions, he added 'we must hold the Scheldt
fortifications to the end'.[26]

Eberding had every confidence in his defences. His left flank
was protected by the Braakman inlet, his right by the North Sea,
while much of the land to the north of the Leopold Canal was

flooded, making it wholly unsuitable for the Canadians' tanks. Eberding's garrison numbered around 11,000 men, supported by some 200 anti-tank and anti-aircraft guns and 500 machine guns and mortars. Eberding had six naval batteries deployed between Breskens and Knocke-sur-Mer to the north of Zeebrugge covering the mouth of the Scheldt, thereby ensuring the Allies could still not use Antwerp.

An exhausted Schwalbe had done an outstanding job. 'In sixteen days we managed to evacuate the remnants of nine infantry divisions', he said with pride. 'By 21 September my task was completed and the bulk of the 15th Army had been rescued from encirclement.' Rundstedt was delighted and reported to Hitler that 'the total number of personnel and equipment ferried across the Scheldt by 15 Army totals 82,000 men; 530 guns, 4,600 vehicles; 4,000 horses and a large amount of valuable material'.[27] There was clearly an element of inflated propaganda with the numbers, because Schwalbe recorded 65,000 men, 225 guns, 750 trucks and wagons and 1,000 horses.[28] It may be that his numbers reflected only the evacuation from Breskens. Whatever the case, these troops could easily be reorganized into seven or eight divisions.

So pleased was Zangen with Schwalbe's efforts that he gave him another equally important task. It was vital that the road along the Beveland isthmus be kept open as this was the resupply and escape route for those units still trapped in northeastern France and Belgium. The only way to do this was to prevent British tanks from advancing north of Antwerp. Schwalbe was given command of the 719th Infantry Division, consisting of just three battalions. When Schwalbe contacted his Corps headquarters demanding it be 'brought up to strength', he was told to round up whatever was available.[29]

In short order he was soon able to muster local Luftwaffe air crews, who were fighting as infantry, organized into two battalions, a local defence battalion, a Dutch SS-battalion, a railway security battalion and the '36th Stomach Battalion'.[30] With a total of nine battalions, Schwalbe put together a credible defence. Zangen tried to impress upon 15th Army how vital it was the Scheldt was held, otherwise 'the English would be in a position to land great masses of material [in Antwerp] and deliver a death blow at Berlin before the onset of winter'.[31]

What Zangen and Schwalbe did not know in mid-September was that the British and Americans were planning to strike north to Arnhem, not northwest towards Beveland or Rotterdam. Model, though, was reassured that with his right flank anchored on the Scheldt Estuary and 15th Army rescued to fight another day, he would be able to reinforce his left flank beyond Antwerp. He was grateful that Montgomery had made a great mistake by ignoring Zangen's withdrawal.

Far to the west in Brittany, General Bernhard Ramcke and the remains of his 35,000-strong garrison in the port of Brest surrendered to the Americans on 19 September. Since early August the Americans had maintained pressure on the trapped defenders and by 5 September they had suffered over 5,300 killed, wounded and missing. This then turned into an all-out attack. In the face of American infantry and British flame-thrower tanks, the paratroop battalion holding Fort Montbarey held out for three days. The rest of the garrison lasted another three. This was a severe blow, as it meant the loss of the 266th and 343rd infantry divisions, along with the 2nd Parachute Division. However, Ramcke's men managed to thoroughly wreck the port facilities, thereby denying it to the Allies. Also, German resistance at Brest was such that the Americans decided simply to lay siege to the remaining Breton ports of Lorient and St Nazaire until the end of the war.

Zangen heard the news on 22 September that another Channel port had been lost. Major-General Heim and his garrison at Boulogne surrendered to the Canadian 3rd Infantry Division. The attack there opened six days earlier when bombers pounded Mont Lambert. Some German defences survived, but the defenders were steadily rooted out by the Canadians, supported by British flame-thrower tanks and other specialized armour.

Heim had emerged from his headquarters looking decidedly dejected. There was no escape for him this time. His only solace was that he was out of Hitler's reach, so he could not be punished for his failure. However, he had followed Zangen's orders to the best of his ability. The Canadians did not take Calais until the end of the month, by which time only Dunkirk was still in German hands. Like Le Havre, the ports at Boulogne and Calais were comprehensively wrecked before the garrisons gave up.

3

Six and a Quarter

For the Germans it was vital that they held the southern Netherlands. This was in order to keep open their supply lines to the forces blocking the approaches to Antwerp and to protect the V-2 rocket launch sites in The Hague. The German grip on the Netherlands was always very firm. This had in part been facilitated by German intelligence penetrating the Dutch Resistance very early in the war.

In the Netherlands, as in Belgium, the Germans were able to call on various Dutch collaborationist militia units. The Germans had successfully co-opted the Dutch Nationalist Socialist party under Anton Mussert.[1] His organization controlled defence sections recruited and trained along military lines. Hitler had been impressed by Dutch loyalty, remarking, 'the idea of Germanic solidarity is making more and more impression on the minds of the Dutch'.[2]

There was also a Dutch branch of the SS, which raised five infantry regiments, plus a police regiment. They supposedly reported to Mussert, although in reality actually answered to the German chain of command. When the Germans had attempted to form an SS division using both Dutch and Scandinavian volunteers, Mussert objected and insisted that his countrymen form a national unit of their own. This resulted in two weak Dutch divisions. The first had been sent off to fight the Russians.

The most significant Dutch fascist collaborationist forces were the Landstorm and Landwacht Nederland, which had come into being in 1943. These two units could muster over 10,000 men. Initially they wore black uniforms that were slowly changed for field grey ones. The Germans also reorganized the Dutch police along paramilitary lines. In September 1944, elements of the Landwacht were designated the 34th SS Grenadier Division Landstorm Nederland. This consisted, on paper, of two grenadier regiments with supporting anti-tank and anti-aircraft units.[3] Although still little more than a police unit, it was available for immediate deployment.

Reichsführer Himmler kept Mussert on a very tight leash. 'For territorial defence', said Himmler, 'he has no need of a Federal Dutch Army, since after the war this defence will be exclusively our business.'[4] Then Himmler, who liked the sound of his own voice, added, 'Nor is it necessary to maintain an important Federal Army for show purposes'.[5] 'I am pleased', said Hitler, 'that there exists neither in Holland nor in Belgium, any government with which we should have to negotiate.'[6] Hitler had no intention of granting the Netherlands autonomy as part of Greater Germany. Both Hitler and Himmler even considered annexing Dutch Friesland. To divide and rule, Himmler encouraged Rost van Tonningen, another leading Dutch socialist, to work against Mussert. Now, though, Hitler's generals, in desperate need of manpower with which to stem the swift Allied advance, were left with a hodge-podge of Belgian and Dutch collaborationist forces.

Mussert had little option but to acquiesce to Hitler's plans to deploy his new V-weapons around the Dutch capital, from where they would be launched against England. Secretly Mussert must have hoped that these weapons would not be used on the Dutch people as well. Inevitably the launch sites would attract the attentions of Allied bombers and they were not famed for their accuracy. Amongst those German units now in the Low Countries that were of special interest to the Allies were Flak Regiment 155W and Battery 444. They were responsible for launching Hitler's V-1 flying bombs and V-2 rockets. Intelligence from the Dutch

Resistance was warning that The Hague had become the epicentre for Hitler's V-weapons.

Colonel Wachtel, commander of Regiment 155, and Major Sommerfeld had been given the task of setting up fixed launch sites along the north coast of France and Belgium in the summer of 1943. Thanks to the French Resistance, the Allies knew all about Wachtel. His preparations were constantly attacked by Allied bombers in the run-up to D-Day. Wachtel, concerned by the breach in his security, abandoned his headquarters at Doullens and established a new one at Creil north of Paris in early 1944.

He was so alarmed at the prospect of British Prime Minister Winston Churchill sending commandos to kill him that he grew a beard, dyed his hair and assumed the name 'Max Wolf'. His men changed their uniforms and transport in an effort to throw spies off their trail. Wachtel also instructed that over the telephone his unit was to be referred to as Flak Group Creil. All this subterfuge did him no good. 'Colonel Wachtel himself will not be in continual residence at his HQ', reported a French agent after the move, 'for he goes on inspection missions in Belgium and also makes frequent journeys.'[7]

Owing to the bomber attacks, Wachtel and his boss Lieutenant-General Walther von Axthelm opted for using more temporary sites. By the end of August 1944 they had launched 8,554 V-1s, most of which were aimed at London. Although about a third proved faulty and a third were shot from the skies, a large enough number were still hitting the British capital to please Hitler.

RAF raids on the V-2 base at Peenemünde persuaded Hitler to relocate the programme to Nordhausen. Likewise, the launch sites built in France in early 1944 were attacked before they could be completed. To oversee mobile launches two units were formed, Battery 444 and Group North. These had been deployed to create the launch sites around The Hague. Battery 444 conducted its first V-2 combat launch on 8 September 1944, when a rocket was fired at newly liberated Paris. Shortly afterwards Group North targeted London. Mussert was thoroughly alarmed by reports that subsequent launches had resulted in the rockets falling back onto The Hague. The Germans seemed in no hurry to offer apologies or restitution.

After the German collapse in Normandy, Colonel Wachtel's men withdrew from France and Belgium into the Netherlands and Germany. When the Allies overran Creil, they captured all his launch data. They learned that the Luftwaffe had conducted no photographic missions over London from 10 January 1941 to 10 September 1944. This indicated they had little idea of how their V-weapons were actually performing.

The largest V-2 rocket base in northern France was at Méry-sur-Oise. On 24 August the Germans abandoned it in the face of the Allied advance. Amongst those who escaped was Lieutenant Joseph Enthammer. The plan was to withdraw through Belgium and the Netherlands and into Germany to continue their work. Enthammer was separated from his unit after a road accident left him unconscious. When he recovered he was told to report to the Dutch city of Nijmegen. After a journey involving both a horse and moped, he reached his destination and learned that his V-2 rocket unit had established itself in a school in the northwestern suburbs of Arnhem.

Whereas the V-weapons had initially been used as a strategic tool against England, the Germans increasingly saw them as tactical weapons, and plans were rapidly drawn up to target Antwerp, Brussels and Liège. Himmler was also developing the V-4 rocket, which could bombard Antwerp. Elias, Mussert and the other collaborationists would soon regret their dalliance with Hitler, especially as the V-weapons now constituted a very real threat to Belgian and Dutch civilians.

The German Reichskommissar for the Netherlands, Dr Arthur Seyss-Inquart, fearing for his administration, on 1 September ordered all Germans to relocate to the eastern half of the country. He and Mussert abandoned The Hague and took up residence in Apeldoorn, some 15 miles north of Arnhem. This evacuation had been conducted calmly until the fall of Antwerp and Brussels, after which it turned into a mass panic.

While the German armed forces were fleeing the Allies, Reichskommissar Seyss-Inquart, Luftwaffe General Friedrich Christiansen and SS-General Rauter had their hands full guarding against Dutch saboteurs. This was easier said than done, because Seyss-Inquart and Rauter did not like each other. Seyss-Inquart characterized his police chief as 'a big child with a child's cruelty'.[8] Rauter much preferred working with Christiansen and Model, whom he saw as proper soldiers and not jumped-up bureaucrats.

Regardless, Seyss-Inquart really enjoyed being the supreme political authority in the Netherlands. It was a post he had held since 1940. Prior to that, he had been the Austrian chancellor and then deputy to Hans Frank, the brutal governor general of occupied Poland. Apart from the detested Rauter, he was assisted by Hans Fischböck, Willi Ritterbusch and Friedrich Wimmer, who were responsible for finance, propaganda and justice respectively in the Netherlands.

Seyss-Inquart always tried to reassure the Dutch that Hitler's occupation of their country was purely a military necessity. Germany had no imperial designs on Dutch overseas colonies. What this really meant was that Hitler lacked a fleet with which to seize them. In 1941 the Dutch East Indies had been occupied by the Japanese, creating a new problem for the Dutch. In the meantime, in the Netherlands the political parties and the civil service carried on as normal, largely unhindered by their occupiers.

Not all Dutch were happy with this state of affairs, especially the defeated military. The Orde Dienst, created by former army officers, appeared in 1940. Its goal was mainly to prepare for the day when the Germans were driven out. The Dutch Communist Resistance was far more active, but its small numbers left it ineffective. After the Orde Dienst was penetrated by German intelligence, the Resistance was brought to its knees during 1943.

A resistance council, called Raad van Verzet, tried to bring the various factions together as a Dutch home army, but it had insufficient manpower. In contrast, Rauter was able to deploy some 15,000 Dutch militia on anti-resistance operations. The Dutch SS was divided into five regional regiments, with bases in Amsterdam, Arnhem, Eindhoven, Groningen and The Hague. In theory each was supposed to be 500 men strong, but in practice each had little more than 130. The more ardent Dutch Nazis were taken to fight on the Eastern Front with the Waffen-SS. On top of this there were another 35,000 Dutch collaborators.

Thousands of Dutch had every reason to hate the German security forces, especially the Gestapo and the SS. Families and friends were ripped apart. Rauter was preoccupied deporting 117,000 Dutch Jews to the camps in Poland; by mid-March 1944 he considered his work was done. Another 400,000 Dutch were conscripted as slave labour. Almost three-quarters of them were shipped to Germany by Fischböck to work in Hitler's factories and mines. Others had been forced to work on Hitler's Atlantic Wall defences. The latter became redundant after D-Day, but construction of the defences along the Scheldt was a new priority. Some 65,000 people were displaced as part of the Germans' coastal defence preparations.

By the summer of 1944 there remained the problem of the concentration camps at Amersfoort, Westerbork and Vught. Although these acted as transit facilities, they were still very much operational, with Dutch SS guards under German officers. Karl Peter Berg, the SS-commandant at Amersfoort, had a reputation for being a brutal sadist. Hans Hüttig in charge of Vught was little better, having served as deputy to Karl Otto Koch at Buchenwald. Security was provided by SS-Captain Paul Helle in command of six companies of Dutch camp guards. Rauter, Seyss-Inquart and Mussert knew that the Allies would hold them personally responsible for the camps. 'I was very nervous', admitted Rauter.[9] Mussert, rightly fearing for the safety of his family, sent them to Twente on the frontier with Germany.

Like all Reichskommissars, Seyss-Inquart lived in dread of suffering the same fate as Reinhard Heydrich in Prague – assassination. He knew that some Dutch mocked his name behind his back, by calling him 'zes en een kwart' or 'six and a quarter'. This was not only a silly rhyming play on his name, but also, by using 'quarter', was a derogatory reference to the fact that he suffered from a limp. The only place he felt really safe was in his brick and concrete bunker complex at Apeldoorn. This had been built in front of a two-storey villa, which he used as offices. He knew that the safest place for his wife, Gertrud, and three children, Ingeborg, Richard and Dorothea, was back in Austria.

The security situation in the Netherlands was further hampered when exiled Queen Wilhelmina broadcast a call to arms from London in early September. She announced that Prince Bernhard, her son-in-law, was commander-in-chief of the free Dutch forces and would be responsible for the Resistance. The latter would now be known as the forces of the interior. Bernhard also made a public announcement cautioning the Resistance to bide their time. Once the British were in Antwerp and Brussels, Rauter expected trouble, but instead their advance came to a halt. The situation in the Netherlands by this stage was understandably very tense.

Seyss-Inquart and Rauter were mindful of how swiftly things happened in Belgium. Some 3,500 members of the Belgian Resistance assisted the Allies in securing Antwerp. In particular, they prevented the Germans from damaging the docks. German security had scored a success at the end of August, when they arrested Colonel Norbet Laude, head of the Belgian Resistance.[10] This move cut communication with London until 3 September. It did not, though, prevent the Resistance from capturing the German port commandant and his entire staff.

Next, German radio monitors gritted their teeth when General Dwight Eisenhower, the Allied supreme commander, promised that the liberation of the Netherlands was at hand. He was followed by Pieter Gerbrandy, the prime minister of the Dutch government in exile, who said the Allies had crossed the Dutch frontier. German intelligence scoffed at the latter claim as it was untrue. What made them uneasy was the creation of what the Dutch were calling the Binnenlandse Strijdkrachten, or forces of the interior. The Dutch regular army on its own constituted little threat, as there was only a single brigade fighting with the British.[11] German intelligence was also aware that by 5 September the German withdrawal from Belgium and France had reached such a crescendo that the Dutch dubbed it 'Dolle Dinsdag' – 'Mad Tuesday'.

Many tired and dirty German soldiers trudging back through the Netherlands could feel the contempt as Dutch civilians stared on impassively. Mussert reassured Seyss-Inquart that his Dutch SS would keep order. This he managed to achieve, but he could do little to stop the Resistance from spying on German troop movements and defensive measures. In turn Seyss-Inquart promised, 'resistance against the occupying forces will be broken'.[12] He feared that the Dutch Resistance might rise from the ashes and orchestrate a general uprising similar to that in Poland. To head this off, he instructed that Amsterdam, Rotterdam and The Hague be fortified. This was in keeping with Hitler's obsession with creating strongpoints or fortresses.

Unlike Seyss-Inquart, Rauter could see little point in tying the German defence of the Netherlands to its key cities. However, he was alert to the threat posed to German lines of communication. On the morning of 16 September, he issued orders that no civilians were to 'halt on or near bridges, any sort of bridge approach and underpasses'.[13] This rather made life difficult for the bridge guards, who constantly had to stop civilians to check their identification cards.

One young man German security missed was Jan van Hoof, who was monitoring German demolition preparations on the Nijmegen bridges.[14] He was exactly the type of saboteur they needed to guard against. Instead, Rauter's headquarters were being inundated with more banal problems. The police were reporting the theft of bicycles by German soldiers on a mass scale. It seemed as if the entire German Army was redeploying on stolen bikes. The problem was so epidemic that many Dutch had given up bothering the police with such matters. Besides, some two million bicycles and tens of thousands of cars and buses had already been sent to Germany.

Rauter was determined to ensure the Dutch were not in a position to conduct an insurrection. 'I had to paralyse the Resistance', he said.[15] His security forces arrested anyone on the slightest hint that they might have a connection to the Resistance. The German armed forces, SS and police units were instructed by Rauter to fire on groups of more than five. In the first week of September they shot 133 people. A curfew was introduced and travel between the Dutch provinces stopped. Civilians were pressed-ganged to dig defences for the Germans.

Rauter was greatly helped in his work by Lieutenant-Colonel Hermann Giskes, head of German counter-intelligence in the Netherlands, and his deputy Major Friedrich Kieswetter. At every step they thwarted British intelligence-gathering efforts. Agents in Arnhem and The Hague were caught and successfully turned. For example, everything the Dutch spy Thys Taconis did in Arnhem was reported directly to Giskes.

From late 1941 to late 1943 Giskes conducted Operation *England Game*, with which he completely wrecked the efforts of the British Special Operation Executive (SOE) and the Dutch Resistance. All weapons and supplies dropped by the RAF fell directly into German hands, as did 450 local activists and SOE agents. As a result, the Resistance had neither the manpower nor the weapons with which to assist the advancing Allied armies. Their greatest success was killing General Hendrik Seyffardt in February 1943, the former Dutch Army chief of staff who had sponsored the Dutch SS. However, the hated Rauter later escaped an attempt on his life.

Dutchman SS-Colonel Johannes Hendrik Feldmeijer, leading a special unit, helped the Germans destroy the Dutch Resistance. His Sonderkommando-Feldmeijer was responsible for the deaths of some 20 Resistance members during September 1943. The civilian population was punished for any 'terrorist' attacks. The general German policy was that for every German killed, one hundred hostages would be executed. In the Netherlands, Rauter was much more 'lenient', ordering the execution of three Dutch for every German; this resulted in the deaths of up to 3,000 people.

After running circles round the British and the Dutch, Lieutenant-Colonel Giskes could not resist signalling SOE in London. 'Whenever you will come to pay a visit…' he messaged on 1 April 1944, 'you may be assured that you will be received with the same care and result as all those sent us before.'[16] By this stage the Dutch Resistance was largely beyond help. Giskes knew that the Dutch government-in-exile's Bureau Bijzondere Opdrachten would try to salvage something from the wreckage. He also knew that the Orde Dienst and the rival Landelijke Knokploegen did not have the men or the arms. The greatest threat was a general strike by Dutch railway workers, who numbered some 30,000. Bringing the trains to a halt would impede the movement of German troops and supplies.

Among Giskes' double agents was Christiaan Antonious Lindemans, who had turned that March in return for the release of his younger brother and his mistress. He had since ingratiated himself with British and Canadian intelligence. Giskes considered him a wholly reliable source. Lindemans brought warning of an Allied attack on Eindhoven, but this information did not reach Giskes in time. Major Kieswetter did pass a report through to SS-Brigadier Walther Schellenberg, head of the SS foreign intelligence service. Schellenberg, questioning its accuracy, chose not to disseminate it any further.

Unfortunately for Giskes, who was away, Lindemans took five days to reach his headquarters at Driesbergen. The Dutchman left Allied lines on 10 September and had been picked up by a German patrol near the Belgian-Dutch border. He was wearing a British uniform, so his captors naturally assumed that he was a soldier. Eventually he was moved to Valkenswaard, where to their surprise he insisted that he report to Lieutenant-Colonel Giskes. His interrogators decided to make some enquiries and were instructed to send their captive immediately to Driesbergen. Yes, the man was a double agent, known as 'King Kong'.

What no one could work out was the credibility of his claims that there was to be an airborne landing at Eindhoven. Lindemans' handler, a Canadian intelligence officer, would hardly be privy to detailed operational plans. Furthermore, if the information was true, what was the goal of such an operation? It mattered little, as Bittrich's 2nd SS-Panzer Corps was already at Arnhem.

4

Student's Paras

Hitler was under enormous pressure by mid-1944. Strategically, the war could not be any worse. He had been severely shaken by the failed assassination attempt on 20 July 1944 and he took to his bed. Hitler's retribution for the betrayal had been swift and terrible. 'Now I finally have the swine', he declared 'who have been sabotaging my work over the years.'[1] His health took a dive in early August 1944, when the fainting fits worsened. By the middle of the month there was some improvement and he was able to attend the daily briefings. He soon regretted this.

His armies in Normandy had been outflanked and were in danger of being trapped against the Seine. Even worse, on the Eastern Front the Red Army had been severely mauling his armies since late June and his Hungarian and Romanian allies were wavering in their loyalty to the Nazi cause. News that the Russians were over the Vistula in Poland was equally alarming. By the end of August, they were at the gates of Bucharest, which meant Budapest would be next.

Then in early September the Russians marched into Bulgaria, threatening German forces deployed in Greece and Yugoslavia. Only in Italy were his generals holding their ground. In the West, Britain and America had made it known they were prepared to sign a separate peace treaty, but not with Hitler still in power. Hitler was not prepared to step down and convinced himself it was only a matter of time before the Americans and the British fell out with the Russians. The issue of an unconditional surrender was also a serious stumbling block for the German military.

Owing to all the stress, the Führer's ill health soon flared up again. 'Hitler suffered severe stomach and intestinal problems', noted his secretary Christa Schroeder. 'He put himself to bed but did not improve... Hitler lay apathetic for several days'.[2] This meant that he was far from focused on directing his two-front war. 'Neither in the West nor the East had any attempt been made to prepare fortified positions', grumbled General Heinz Guderian, Chief of the General Staff: 'in the former theatre Hitler had believed he could rely on the Atlantic Wall'.[3]

Even Hitler, after the German collapse in France, had to concede he needed to prepare the defences of the Siegfried Line or Westwall to protect Germany. Field Marshal von Rundstedt assessed that this would take six weeks. Whilst it was being done, the Allies would have to be held back. Model signalled Hitler's chief of operations, Colonel-General Alfred Jodl, on 4 September 1944 with his dire assessment of the situation. To defend a front line from Antwerp along the Albert Canal, the Meuse and the Westwall to the Franco-Luxembourg border would require 25 new infantry divisions, backed by half a dozen Panzer divisions. Model warned if these were not found, then 'the gateway into North-West Germany will be open'.[4]

Hitler, scrabbling around for something to reinforce the Western Front, suddenly remembered his airborne forces, thanks to Reich Marshal Hermann Göring, commander of the Luftwaffe. Hitler had been a strong advocate of airborne operations until the costly Crete campaign.[5] At the time British intelligence reported, 'in some places, four-fifths were killed as they swung in the air'.[6] Ever since, Göring's paratroops had fought as infantry. On 4 September 1944, Göring grandly announced he could put together a force of some 20,000 men, comprising eight parachute regiments, six of which were currently being re-equipped. These could be reinforced by up to 10,000 Luftwaffe personnel.[7] Hitler's eyes lit up. Jodl pointed out that their tough parachute divisions had fought well in Normandy and were currently being refitted.

They needed someone to command Göring's new-found force, and they had just the man for the job. Kurt Student, the leading light of the airborne assault and the early Blitzkrieg campaigns, had been consigned for three long years to an office job in Berlin. Once one of Hitler's favourites, Student fell from grace after Crete. Hitler had been content with the occupation of southern Greece, but it was Student who had persuaded him to go after the island using just airborne forces.

Afterwards, angry at their heavy losses, Hitler was adamant that 'the day of the parachute troops is over'.[8] 'Cyprus was then our next target, which was going to be used as our base for air-raids and paratroopers' operations against the Suez canal', recalled Student. 'But Hitler did not give his permission to go due to the high losses we experienced in Crete.'[9] Student was dismayed at Hitler's short-sightedness. 'He would not believe reports that the British and Americans were developing airborne forces.'[10] Hitler was forced to change his mind when the Allies deployed them over Sicily in 1943. He ordered an expansion of German parachute divisions, but by that stage the Allies had air superiority. The Allies had then used their airborne troops to great effect in Normandy.

To some, Student gave the appearance of being rather dim-witted. His slow, deliberate way of speaking contributed to this inaccurate impression. Few appreciated that this was the result of a serious head wound, which he had received during the paratroop drops on Rotterdam in 1940. However, there was nothing wrong with his brain. The man who had created Hitler's airborne forces was clearly capable of thinking outside the box. He was popular with his staff and was known for his attention to detail. Student had also proved himself extremely calm when under fire. During the early days of the war he was known for his 'brusque good humour'.[11] The last three years, though, had made Student much more cynical.

Student was sitting at his desk when at 1500 hours on 4 September 1944 he received a call from Jodl. The Führer wanted him to form the 1st Parachute Army. Look, said Jodl, you have to close the gap in the region of Liège–Maastricht and Antwerp by 'holding a line along the Albert Canal'.[12] This represented a front some 60–100 miles long. From their discussion, it was evident to Student that 'the sudden penetration of British tank forces into Antwerp took the Führer's Headquarters utterly by surprise'.[13]

Student, understandably, had mixed feelings about returning to an operational command. From Berlin he had continued to champion airborne operations with Hitler. 'I pressed the idea on him repeatedly', said Student, 'but without avail.'[14] He stared into space for a moment. Student had never really forgiven Hitler and Göring for sidelining him during the height of the battle for Crete. The campaign was full of 'bitter memories'.[15] Over 5,000 Iron Crosses had been awarded to those involved. Student got nothing but ingratitude. Hitler and Göring had been so incensed that they had not spoken to him for almost a year. Nonetheless, he knew that he had only himself to blame. 'I miscalculated', Student admitted: 'it meant the end of the German airborne landing forces which I had created'.[16] Now his country needed him and he had to heed the call. It seemed that Hitler wanted him again. However, this time he was to command a ground force.

Student was very proud of the German airborne ethos: 'You are the elite of the German Army. Know everything for yourself; don't leave it to your officers.' The part he particularly related to was 'Support your comrades always'.[17] On the eve of the attack on Crete he had shaken the hand of each of the glider pilots and wished them good luck. The young lads being sent to form the 1st Parachute Army might not be jump trained, but he could not let them down. They were going to need someone to look after them and it might as well be him. He cast his mind back to the youngsters lost on Crete. There had been reports 'the bodies of the parachutists turned a vivid green a few hours after death. The colour suffused the dead men's cheeks and arms and chests.'[18] If he could, Student wanted to prevent such a tragic and senseless loss of life being repeated amongst the new airborne force.

What, he asked Jodl, would this new army consist of in the light of Germany's manpower shortages? It transpired it was initially to be created from some 10,000 paratroops drawn from depots, training units and any combat forces available. They were to be bolstered by two whole infantry divisions and whatever the Luftwaffe and the navy had to offer. Armoured support would comprise 25 tanks and self-propelled guns, but there would be no artillery.[19]

Student was not sure how essentially what amounted to a corps could be construed as an army. To him, 'it was a rather high-sounding title for a force that did not exist'.[20] When did this so-called parachute army have to be in the line? asked Student – immediately, was Jodl's response. After coming off the phone he began to make enquiries. His first port of call was Lieutenant-General Paul Conrath, the inspector of parachute troops. Who was available? Just Erdmann, Hermann, Hoffman and Heydte, came the reply. Most of these men were colonels; where were all the divisional commanders? The parachute generals were in Italy, in Russia, or dead. He urgently needed to find General Eugen Meindl.

Meindl was another veteran of the campaign on Crete, where he had been seriously wounded. Although he was supposed to land by glider, he had insisted on parachuting to prove his prowess. Recovering from his injuries, he first commanded a battle group and then an *ad hoc* division on the Eastern Front with distinction. Afterwards he was sent to Germany to oversee the creation of Göring's controversial Luftwaffe field divisions. Following this he had commanded the 2nd Parachute Corps in Normandy. Meindl was not a big fan of Student, remarking caustically, 'he had big ideas but not the faintest conception as to how they were to be carried out'.[21]

It soon transpired that Lieutenant-Colonel von der Heydte's reconstituted 6th Parachute Regiment and a single battalion from the 2nd Parachute Regiment, in all around 3,000 men, were the only combat ready units available to Student. His jaw dropped. Not only was this not an army, it was not even a corps. But having Heydte on board was good news. He was likewise a tough Crete veteran, who had saved his regiment from destruction in Normandy. It had almost been trapped twice, but each time had escaped under his leadership. However, the 6th Parachute Regiment had gone into action with 4,500 men and suffered 3,000 casualties. By the time they pulled out of the line for refitting, Heydte had only just over a thousand men left. This meant that over half of his manpower was now made up of new recruits. Heydte, unlike Meindl, greatly admired Student.

The 2nd Parachute Regiment was being newly formed from whoever was available. Highly experienced combat veteran Adolph Strauch, with 2nd Battalion, recalled: 'Standing alongside young volunteers were old NCOs, Luftwaffe men taken away from their company office desks and from headquarters duties. The nucleus of the company consisted of just eight trained paratroops.'[22] He had fought with the regiment in its first incarnation on Crete, so was understandably despondent. Looking around, Strauch, recalling Battle Group Shrimer's role in taking Heraklion, appreciated only too well that these new recruits were of a much lower calibre.

'At that moment I had only recruit and convalescent units', grumbled Student, 'and one coast-defence division from Holland.'[23] That very same day the German High Command rather grandly announced:

> The defence of the Albert Canal was assigned to the newly created 1st Parachute Army (General Oberst Student). For this purpose, all of his units in the Fatherland and 3rd, 5th and 6th Parachute Divisions were assigned to him. In addition he was assigned 48th Infantry Corps with two divisions, ten battalions and forty flak batteries, new activations of the replacement army, security units and combat groups from the northwest.[24]

Student was unimpressed by such propaganda. All three of these parachute divisions had suffered very badly in France.

The 3rd Parachute Division, which was the best, had been almost completely destroyed in the Mons Pocket. Student found that good replacements were hard to come by because of this. In Normandy the division had been granted first call on the recruits from the jump schools and training centres, so its decimation was doubly damaging. The few survivors were sent to Enschede in the Netherlands and fleshed out with 17- to 18-year-old draftees of August 1944. Many had come from Luftwaffe units, where they expected to be pilots, aircrew and ground crew, not infantry. Their replacement officers and NCOs were also of an inferior quality, because they were not trained as infantry commanders. They were all to find their training period in the Netherlands was very short.[25]

The poorly trained and equipped 5th Parachute Division had been considered of little combat value while in Normandy. By 1 September 1944 it could muster only 4,000 men. The under-strength 6th Division had come into being only that summer and was assigned to 15th Army. It lost its better units fighting the Americans, particularly at Mons. Student's investigations showed that the division now largely consisted of a single training regiment, under Lieutenant-Colonel Hermann.[26] This could scrape together a training battalion and a field replacement battalion, with possibly a third available. He was also told that the survivors of the 2nd Parachute Corps, who had escaped from the Falaise Pocket with General Meindl, were currently in Cologne refitting. Meindl's divisions were scattered to the four winds and his corps units had suffered over 1,500 casualties in Normandy. In other words, it was not operational.

A fourth unit, Ramcke's 2nd Parachute Division, was trapped in Brest. The 6th Parachute Regiment belonged to the latter, but had been detached to fight in Normandy.[27] Student hoped to form a 7th and 8th Parachute Division, but they would simply not be ready in time.[28] Were any of the Luftwaffe's field divisions available? No, came the reply. However, the Hermann Göring Reserve and Training Regiment was being refitted and could be in the line by the middle of the month.

Some of the recruits sent to this regiment were forcibly press-ganged. The parents of those who refused their call-up papers often received a visit from the Gestapo or the SS. When two men, an Austrian and a Frenchman, deserted to the Dutch Resistance on 10 September they brought with them a tale of woe. The man from Lorraine had reported to the regiment in Utrecht only after his parents had been threatened. Over 300 fellow draft dodgers hiding in a wood in Lorraine were massacred by the SS.

The reluctant recruit from Lorraine arrived at Utrecht on 13 June. Owing to the German authorities being concerned about airborne attack, the following day he was sent by train to Berlin, along with 1,000 men. However, by 1 July they were back in the Netherlands at Hilversum. During the summer they were provided with infantry training and instruction in gas warfare. Up to 20 per cent of the regiment's 2nd Battalion were Austrians and they were given a hard time by their German instructors. This did not bode well for regimental morale.

News regarding the regular army units assigned to Student was not encouraging either. The 176th and 719th infantry divisions were all but useless, consisting of the elderly and semi-invalids. These included an 'ear battalion' and a 'stomach battalion'.[29] Student quickly concluded 'we had no disposable reserves worth mentioning on the Western Front or within Germany'.[30] He also discovered he had no transport for his men and would have to rely on the trains. Student did not even have a chief of staff until the appointment of Lieutenant-General Wolfgang Erdmann.

Student enquired whether any of the German armies in the west could help out. He was informed that Zangen's 15th Army was in the process of organizing an evacuation across the Scheldt. In a few weeks' time some of his divisions might become available, though their priority was holding the area north of Antwerp. The 5th Panzer Army and 7th Army, savaged in Normandy, had all but ceased to exist. Both had very few divisions under their command and those desperately needed to be withdrawn and refitted. The two armies belonging to Army Group G, in southern France, were busy making a dash for the German frontier.

It would take up to five days to get Student's ragtag forces to the front. Some of his paratroops, who were used to rapid deployments, were able to get to the Albert Canal within 24 hours. He quickly issued orders to the 2nd Parachute Battalion, which was to be followed by the 6th Parachute Regiment, then three battalions from the 6th Parachute Division, plus a further two regiments. 'We were soon to go into action so there was little time', recalled Adolph Strauch, 'a few days at the most, in which to give them weapon training.'[31] Known as Adi by his friends, he had been injured on the Eastern Front and his wounds still prevented him from operating a weapon. 'On 5 September, we moved out.'[32]

Student selected a cottage near Vught, which lay some 16 miles northwest of Eindhoven, as his headquarters. In the town of Oss, to the northeast, he set up a large supply depot full of bacon, butter, cheese and meat. Oddly, it was placed under the control of a Dutchman.[33] While ammunition, heavy weaponry and transport were a problem, at least his men would not go hungry.

5

Chill on the Albert

Student knew it was vital to hold the ground to the east of Antwerp, between the Albert and Meuse–Escaut canals, which was an old mining area. This region was ideal for defence, consisting of open heathland divided by small streams and marshes. His positions could be anchored on the villages built on the main crossroads, comprising Bourg-Léopold, Beeringen, Helchteren and Hechtel. These would be difficult to bypass and would force the British to make costly head-on attacks with their tanks. Beeringen in particular offered a good defensive position. Two high slag heaps from the local mines some 300 yards to the north of the canal meant that German observers could overlook the crossing and the town. Troops dug in on the reverse slopes and for good measure they damaged the nearby bridge.

He was unaware that one enterprising general had taken the initiative and was already trying to cobble together a defence along the Albert Canal. General Kurt Chill's 85th Infantry Division had come into being only at the start of the year. It had been assigned to 15th Army on the Channel coast, but at the beginning of August was sent to Normandy. Elements of the division saw combat on the northern part of the Falaise Pocket before retreating east. By the beginning of September, Chill had only about 3,000 men remaining. It is unclear if they had managed to retrieve their anti-tank guns and artillery from Normandy.

Chill was ordered back to Germany to refit and had reached Turnhout when he heard that Brussels had fallen. Fortunately for Student, he was an experienced soldier, having seen combat in Poland and in Russia. Without orders, Chill turned round and directed his men to dig in on the canal. He also set up roadblocks on the northern exits over the canal and began to round up stragglers, who were turned around and put back into the line.

It is possible that Chill was inspired by Model's order of the day issued on 3 September, which had exhorted everyone to 'Take thought then that at this moment everything adds up to the necessity to gain the time the Führer needs to bring into operation new troops and new weapons... Soldiers, we must gain this time for the Führer!'[1] While Model was exhorting his men to face the enemy, Himmler took a much more simplistic and brutal approach to rallying the troops. 'Every deserter... will find his just punishment', he warned. 'Furthermore, his ignominious behaviour will entail the most severe consequences for his family'.[2]

When Student arrived he was very pleased with Chill's enterprising efforts, as it meant he was not starting completely from scratch as he had feared. Chill soon cobbled together elements of the 84th, 85th and 89th divisions, which created a battle group around 4,250 strong. Student also promised him elements of the Hermann Göring Training Regiment and Heydte's 6th Parachute Regiment.

Student and Chill had no real way of knowing the fate of many of the German infantry escaping from France. The 84th Division suffered high casualties covering the withdrawal from Falaise and by 1 September had only 2,500 men on its roll call. Similarly, the 89th claimed it had 3,000 remaining. Added to the survivors from the 85th, Chill should have been able to muster around 8,500 men, but he had less than half this. Many had been lost in the chaos of the retreat, along with all their anti-tank guns and artillery. But as far as Student was concerned, Chill's forces were better than nothing.

Student could not understand why the British had not quickly secured the bridges over the Albert Canal on the northern edge of Antwerp. If they had, they could have been sweeping north westwards towards Woensdrecht and blocked the Beveland isthmus. They did establish a small bridgehead over the canal on 6 September, but this was vigorously counter-attacked, preventing them from ferrying over any anti-tank guns or building a bridge. However, the British were soon probing German defences to the east of Antwerp along the canal. They crossed at Beeringen, south of Gheel, on 7 and 8 September, but were met by Student's vanguard and the rearguard of 7th Army.

The British, thinking the Germans had abandoned Beeringen, thanks to intelligence from local civilians, got across the damaged bridge. A few German prisoners were rounded up, while British engineers built a replacement Bailey bridge. Just as this was completed and British tanks began to cross, the Germans, assisted by their observers on the slag heaps, opened up with artillery and mortar fire. One brave artillery officer took position in a bucket dangling from the overhead cable strung between the heaps. However, the British armour took no notice and headed east towards Helchteren and Hechtel.

By 7 September elements of the German 2nd Battalion, 2nd Parachute Regiment had arrived at Helchteren, about ten miles to the east of Beeringen. This opening engagement was a disaster for the battalion. 'For the next few days the British attacked again and again but each assault was beaten back', said Adolf Strauch.[3] Then without warning an 88mm gun that had been protecting their position was withdrawn. Strauch's company was equipped with machine guns and mortars, but had very few anti-tank weapons. 'We were attacked constantly, and were practically wiped out.'

They found themselves fighting off British flame-thrower tanks, bulldozer tanks and infantry on 11 September. Without proper heavy weapons, courage alone was not enough. Their bazookas, known as the Panzerschreck, were out of ammunition and they had only a few single-shot Panzerfausts. There was no way of stopping the tanks from burning them out of their positions. If they tried to run, they were cut down by rifle and machine-gun fire. Inevitably losses were heavy. Strauch's company commander was wounded, so he took charge. 'We evacuated the wounded, putting them into very small, two wheeled, horse-drawn carts.'[4]

To cover their retreat, the battalion commander and one of the other company commanders grabbed the last of the Panzerfausts. They bravely went off to hold the British tanks at bay and were killed in the process. Strauch and just five of his comrades managed to reach battalion headquarters. 'There we learned our company and one other had been destroyed', recalled Strauch, 'and I was told to collect little groups of men and regroup them.'[5]

The German troops holding Helchteren did have some anti-tank and self-propelled guns, but they were not sufficient to fend off the British armour. The intensity of the fighting was such that the Germans suffered 500 dead and 300 captured.[6] 'I led the remnant of the battalion battle group back', recounted Strauch, 'and late in the night reached a bridge across the Maas-Schelde [Meuse–Escaut] Canal.'[7] Their sacrifice had slowed the British advance on Hechtrel. Strauch and his comrades, though, were not out of the fight. 'A General to whom I reported ordered me to take the men back to Kinrooi', Strauch said, 'where he proposed to regroup our battalion's surviving members.'[8] They would soon be redeployed against the Americans at Son and Veghel.

In the meantime, Student appreciated that if he could feed more men into the fight at Beeringen, then he stood a slight chance of cutting off the British advance. Shelling of the enemy was increased and five Panther tanks moved forward to launch a counter-attack. Their advance was short lived. British observers in a nearby convent called down artillery fire and two tanks immediately caught fire and the rest quickly withdrew. A German officer, with 40 paratroops, decided to make one last-ditch attempt to wreck the bridge at Beeringen. Moving along the canal bank, they bumped into a British column and managed to destroy 30 lorries before most of them were captured.

Student's paratroops, supported by a few tanks and self-propelled guns, still held Bourg-Léopold and Hechtel. Both these isolated garrisons were soon lost. Although at Hechtel the British had almost surrounded the town, Student continued to reinforce it until defended by around 1,000 men. They were shelled and mortared and then overwhelmed. Over 150 were killed, 200 wounded and 500 taken prisoner.[9]

To compound Student's woes, the British, using boats, slipped over the Albert Canal south of Gheel, some 15 miles west of Beeringen, in the early hours of 8 September. The local German units, having destroyed the nearby road bridge, had lulled themselves into a false sense of security and were caught napping. During the night the British created a bridgehead without them realizing. At daybreak all hell was let loose when the Germans realized the British were in their midst. They did all they could to prevent more British troops from getting over the canal. Despite laying down heavy fire, they could not stop this from happening, nor prevent the British from bringing up a replacement bridge.

For four days the Germans tried to dislodge the Gheel bridgehead. Units of the 2nd Parachute Regiment and a Luftwaffe regiment, backed by tanks, were thrown into the fight. On 12 September the German paratroopers' final attack was driven off. Under heavy fire they withdrew beyond the Meuse–Escaut Canal, leaving behind large numbers of dead.

Now that the British were firmly established over the Albert Canal, Student and his commanders knew it was only a matter of time before they seized a bridgehead over the Meuse–Escaut Canal. Sure enough, on 10 September the British exploited a gap in Student's defences between Bourg-Léopold and Hechtel, dashed north and grabbed the De Groot bridge, to the west of Neerpelt. Student was not happy, especially as the crossing was defended by four 88mm guns. A factory building obscured the view of the approaches and the British had engaged the guns at point-blank range for 20 minutes. When the defenders did not blow the bridge, British tanks rumbled across it.

Both of Student's main defensive lines had been breached in a matter of four days. The following morning, German troops cut off to the south of the Meuse–Escaut Canal counter-attacked the British at De Groot bridge, aided by armour and self-propelled guns. Although they inflicted heavy losses on the British, they could not budge them. A German counter-attack conducted to the north of the canal was also defeated. Student had to content himself with trying to contain the British bridgehead using Colonel von der Heydte's paratroopers.

Not long after, Student was thoroughly alarmed by the news that a British patrol had got as far as Valkenswaard, just five miles south of Eindhoven. Two scout cars had reportedly dashed right through German lines and parked up by a local café to spy on the bridge over the river Dommel. German guards had been alerted when the Dutch, thinking they were being liberated, started celebrating and slapping the British crews on their backs. The patrol had then returned the way it had come and, despite being shot at, made it safely back. What was particularly irritating was that the British had witnessed a Panzer crossing the bridge, which meant they knew it would take the weight of a tank.[10] The German guards, incensed by this incursion, went to the café and shot three civilians for collaborating.

Student resolved to strengthen his defences along this road. He appointed Lieutenant-Colonel Hoffman, commander of the newly arrived Parachute Training Regiment von Hoffman, commandant of Eindhoven. His regiment was placed astride the Valkenswaard road, along with the Luftwaffe's 6th Penal Battalion, facing the centre of the British bridgehead. The latter unit was made up of convicts promised a reprieve if they fought well. Few were under any illusions about their reliability.

Hoffman's regiment was a parachute unit only in name. It had been organized at the beginning of the month and consisted largely of Luftwaffe personnel. He had no real paratroops, jump trained or otherwise. It was fleshed out by former air force ground crews from the Eastern Front and members of Luftwaffe ground units who had been wounded in Italy, as well as some armed forces personnei from Russia and Finland. Although the regiment consisted of three battalions, only Major Helmut Kerutt's 1st Battalion was of any value. The latter was reinforced by the welcome addition of some tank destroyers from Tank Hunter Group Roestel from the 2nd SS-Panzer Corps.

By mid-September, Student had the equivalent of five divisions strung along the Albert Canal, linking up with the reconstituted 7th Army, which was responsible for the Westwall area. However, his centre had been pushed back to the Meuse–Escaut Canal between Gheel and Maastricht. On his right, near Antwerp, Student had the 719th Division, then Battle Group Chill made up of the remains of Chill's 85th Infantry, Battle Group Walther, Lieutenant-General Erdmann's Parachute Training Division and the 176th Division. He also had the weak 59th and 245th infantry divisions from 15th Army and had been promised a Panzer brigade, plus the support of the 2nd SS-Panzer Corps refitting near Arnhem. Initially the units from the 2nd and 6th parachute regiments were assigned to Battle Group Walther, but these were later transferred to Chill. The battle groups were placed under the direction of General Hans Reinhard and the 88th Corps, on loan from 15th Army. Erdmann's command consisted of three of the new parachute regiments.

The Hermann Göring Training Regiment was deployed in the Turnhout area, northwest of the Meuse–Escaut Canal. When its commanding officer reported to Student, he was pleased to learn this unit consisted of three battalions, equipped with some artillery and anti-aircraft guns, plus a few tanks and assault guns. What was not so encouraging was the newest recruits had been called up only in July and received just four weeks of basic training. None had received parachute training. Less than half of their officers and NCOs had combat experience, with the rest being composed of instructors. Ready or not, the regiment went into action on 14 September. Gathering at 's-Hertogenbosch, in the southern Netherlands, were various parachute training units, which amounted to several thousand men. Student sent veteran Major Hans Jungwirth to co-ordinate their organization.

Remarkably, in less than a week, Student had managed to cobble together a new defensive line. Out of necessity his men had been committed to the battle in a piecemeal fashion, and it would be only a matter of time before the British made a concerted effort to breach his defences. It was clear to him that Valkenswaard lay firmly in the firing line.

THE WESTERN FRONT, 14 SEPTEMBER 1944

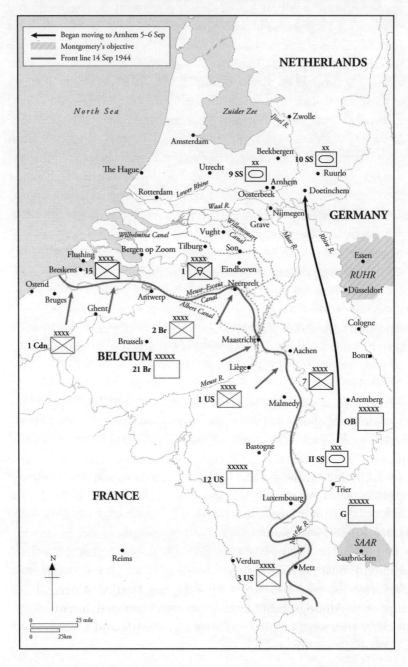

6

The Devil Lies in Wait

Luftwaffe General Friedrich Christiansen, on the morning of 17 September 1944, had gone for a leisurely lunch at a nice country restaurant. After four years of German occupation, many Dutch people were subsisting on potatoes, but this restaurant was always able to conjure up culinary delights for senior German officers. It was a beautiful day and a Sunday come to that. However, his tranquillity was soon disturbed by the news of Allied air attacks and airborne landings across the Netherlands. Reluctantly he was forced to return to his office.

The German administration in Arnhem, headed by Major-General Kussin, found itself targeted by Allied bombers. Seyss-Inquart had a provincial headquarters in the nearby Angerenstein park. The building was hit and caught fire. Rauter's mansion at the Velperweg was only just spared when the bombs accidently fell on the neighbouring block of houses. The Willems barracks, used by the SS, did not escape. 'Some 250 young SS "machos", as my parents called them', remembered local resident Harry Kuiper, who was five years old at the time, 'were said to be killed instantly. The billowing smoke of the burning barracks was visible in most parts of the city.'[1] A nearby restaurant, frequented by Germans, was also hit, scattering the startled diners in all directions. Amongst other targets that were damaged, intentionally or otherwise, were a church, a hospital, a theatre and a warehouse.

At Deelen airfield, north of Arnhem, Luftwaffe personnel braced themselves for attack. Two weeks earlier they had been the recipients of 580 tons of bombs dropped by the RAF. This rendered the airfield temporarily unusable. Deelen was the Luftwaffe's largest night-fighter and bomber base in the Netherlands. It also hosted a radar station, with a second one near Arnhem's road bridge. Following the air raid the night-fighters had been withdrawn to Germany, along with most if not all of the anti-aircraft guns. Some of the latter did not get very far. They were loaded onto a train, along with ammunition and other supplies, operating on the branch line between Deelen and Wolfheze Station. The train got to Wolfheze when it was pounced on by Allied fighters and all the guns were destroyed.[2]

Those units which remained at Deelen understandably felt very exposed. The airfield was host to the headquarters of the 3rd Fighter Division. Its command post, constructed in some nearby woods, soon came under attack by enemy fighter-bombers on 17 September. Such was the fury of the raid that the Luftwaffe personnel found themselves trapped in their bunkers. This and news of airborne landings caused a state of panic, and the staff were soon making plans to evacuate to Duisburg in the northern Ruhr.

The abandoned flak train at Wolfheze was attacked again, along with the local asylum. North of the station there were some 200 explosions. Reports came in of attacks on military facilities in Ede, Cleve, Nijmegen and Wageningen. At Ede a barracks was bombed, with Dutch SS concentration camp guards and German marines suffering casualties. The latter had been undergoing infantry training. American heavy bombers struck a flak battery at Wageningen. Barracks were also bombed at Cleve and Nijmegen. In all instances, there were civilian casualties.

That morning the Luftwaffe reported that 117 flak sites had been attacked. During the night five airfields had been hit and the Luftwaffe struggled to get any fighters in the air to meet the Allied air forces. Just 15 challenged the Americans near Wesel and seven of these were shot down. The German radar stations still operating indicated that the Allies had flown over 2,600 bomber and fighter sorties, and that they were maintaining up to 1,000 fighters in the sky at any one time.

In the meantime, Christiansen's headquarters became a hive of activity. He had the grand-sounding title of Commander German Armed Forces Netherlands. What this meant in practice was that he had authority over all the rear echelon units. His phone had been ringing off the hook, with field commanders wanting to know what reserves he had available to help counter the Allied landings. As far as he was concerned that was a damn fool question, as everyone knew there were no reserves in Belgium or the Netherlands. What was he supposed to do, conjure them up from thin air?

Christiansen summoned Major-General Hans von Tettau, his senior staff officer, and tasked him to establish exactly what was in their area of responsibility. When Tettau reported back, his response was not altogether encouraging. In all, there were just three units, which consisted of SS-Major Eberwein's SS depot battalion, SS-Major Krafft's SS-Panzergrenadier training and reserve battalion and the staff of SS-Colonel Lippert's non-commissioned officer's school: essentially a bunch of clerks, teachers and teenagers.

There were also a number of rather dubious locally raised units available. The Luftwaffe was offering up a Flemish flak brigade and there was a so-called division of Dutch SS, commanded by German police officers. It was a stretch of the imagination to consider the latter a military unit, as its volunteers had been recruited for second-line security and guard duties. Hanns Rauter was keen to see his Dutch Nazis in action, but Christiansen was of the view that they would run away at the first opportunity.

Austrian SS-Captain Paul Anton Helle was in the Amersfoort region, with a Dutch battalion some 600 strong. It included men who had enrolled with the SS rather than be sent to Germany as workers. They were employed as concentration camp guards. Helle had no combat experience and was reliant on a disabled Eastern Front veteran, SS-Lieutenant Albert Naumann. SS-Lieutenant Wilhelm Fernau, another of his officers, had reportedly served in the household staff of the late exiled Kaiser at Doorn.

Tettau explained only Krafft's unit was capable of immediate combat. It was well led and reasonably equipped with anti-tank and flak guns as well as flamethrowers, machine guns and mortars. He highlighted that he had recently dined with Krafft and had found him a competent officer. The only snag was that Krafft's men had already been committed to the fight in the Oosterbeek–Arnhem area.

What other stragglers were available in Arnhem? queried Christiansen. At St Joseph's School there was a company of artillerymen, numbering about 120, which included Lieutenant Joseph Enthammer. Gunners could easily fight as infantry. They were part of a V-2 rocket unit that had withdrawn from Méry-sur-Oise and it was imperative that they did not fall into enemy hands. This meant they could not be deployed as fighting troops and had been ordered to move to Emmerich in Germany as soon as possible. Enthammer was placed in charge of the poorly armed rearguard ready for their departure.

Located at Deelen was a Luftwaffe signals company under Captain Willi Weber. At a pinch they could be issued with rifles and ordered to attack the British landing zones. Along with Krafft, Weber could conceivably help hold any British northern advance on Arnhem. Christiansen and Tettau knew that they were grasping at straws using these units. Tettau then smiled and pointed out that two SS-Panzer divisions had arrived on their patch just ten days earlier, belonging to SS-Lieutenant-General Willi Bittrich's 2nd SS-Panzer Corps. They just happened to be deployed north of Arnhem at Hoenderloo, Apeldoorn, Zutphen and Ruurlo. In that case, said Christiansen, Tettau was to muster the training battalion and assist Bittrich in overrunning the British drop and landing zones immediately.

There was only one problem, said Tettau, they were not exactly Panzer divisions. When Christiansen demanded to know quite what he meant, Tettau explained that at their authorized strength the two units should have totalled around 30,000–40,000 men. Unfortunately, they had suffered extensive losses in Normandy. Well, asked Christiansen, how strong were they now? The answer was less than 10,000. SS-Lieutenant-Colonel Walther Harzer's 9th SS-Panzer Division could field about 6,000 men and around 20 tanks, not all of which were in running order. These were backed by some armoured cars and self-propelled guns. SS-Brigadier Heinz Harmel's 10th SS was in an even worse condition and had at best 3,500 men and a few tanks.[3]

This was a very sobering report. The 2nd SS-Panzer Corps had first gone into action against the British in Normandy in late June 1944. The well-equipped 9th SS deployed to France with 18,000 men, over 200 tanks, self-propelled guns and armoured cars, 287 armoured half-tracks and 3,670 trucks. In contrast, although the 10th SS arrived with 14,800 men, it was the weakest Panzer division in Normandy. Its Panzer regiment had only a single tank battalion with just 80 tanks and assault guns. The latter had been commanded by SS-Colonel Otto Paetsch, who was now serving as Harmel's chief of staff. The division had also been supported by about 20 self-propelled guns.[4]

The Allies knew that Bittrich was at Arnhem. On 15 September 1944 the Dutch Resistance signalled London, 'SS Div Hohenstrufl [Hohenstaufen] along the Ijssel, sub units observed between Arnhem and Zutphen and along the Zutphen-Apeldoorn road… Along Ijssel work on field fortifications in progress.'[5] The British had off-handedly dismissed Bittrich's forces, doubting if he could muster anything more than a single weak armoured brigade and a motorized brigade.

Bittrich was angry at the way his exhausted divisions were being treated. They had fought with distinction and desperately needed to be refitted and brought back up the strength. To do that, they should be pulled out of the line. Instead they were being split up piecemeal. A battle group had already been sent off to help Student's 1st Parachute Army, in response to British tanks getting over the Albert and Meuse–Escaut canals. This included a company of tank destroyers under SS-Captain Roestel[6] and a battery of artillery under SS-Captain Karl Godau, both from the 10th SS. Neither officer was happy about this turn of events, as they had been anticipating returning to Germany to visit family and friends. The British bridgehead at Neerpelt, near the Dutch border, was particularly worrying. Another battle group had been sent south to help 7th Army fighting the Americans at Aachen.

Roestel's unit was equipped with the Jagdpanzer IV, which was not strictly a tank, as it was turretless. This was a relatively new piece of kit that had gone into production at the beginning of the year. It was a development in the German Army's highly successful series of assault guns. Armed with a 75mm gun, the Jagdpanzer IV was a very efficient design, intended to stalk enemy tanks. Limited numbers had seen combat in Normandy with a handful of Panzer divisions, serving with the tank destroyer battalions. For defensive operations along the Valkenswaard road, it was an ideal weapon. Roestel knew that it was armed with a more powerful gun than that on the Panzer IV, which gave it greater stopping power against British Sherman tanks. In light of the Neerpelt bridgehead, it was self-evident that a British ground attack into the Netherlands was imminent.

Bittrich's faith in the German high command had been severely shaken by Hitler's refusal to give ground in Normandy until it was too late. His vocal criticism of Hitler soon reached Berlin. Reichsführer Himmler was 'eager for me to return to Germany for a little talk', noted Bittrich.[7] Model, who had better use for Bittrich's talents, refused to let him go. However, Model could not keep hold of the 9th SS. Bittrich had gathered together Harzer and Harmel on 10 September and explained that the 9th SS was to be shipped by train to Sigene, northeast of Koblenz, by 22 September to be refitted. The 10th SS had drawn the short straw and was to remain in the Netherlands, where it would supposedly be reinforced. Understandably Harmel was not pleased at this. 'It always seemed to work out that the Hohenstaufen got the cushy jobs', he grumbled.[8]

WAFFEN-SS UNITS, LUFTWAFFE AND REGULAR TROOPS IN THE ARNHEM AREA, 17 SEPTEMBER 1944

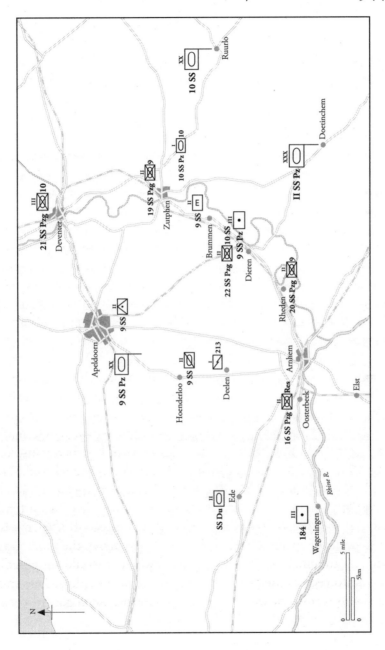

It was clear that the 9th SS was the more viable division, and was therefore to be saved. For Harzer this would mean promotion. Harmel was at a loss to see how his 10th SS would not be dissipated and then disbanded. He also suspected favouritism: Bittrich had once commanded the 9th SS and Harzer had served as Bittrich's chief of staff. To add to Harmel's displeasure, he was ordered to go to Berlin on the evening of 16 September to plead their case for reinforcements at Waffen-SS headquarters. Paetsch was to assume temporary command in his absence.

The smile soon vanished from Harzer's face when he was told to leave all his heavy equipment behind for Harmel. Model said that while this exchange was going on both divisions should put together rapid reaction forces or 'alarm units' that could respond to emergencies. It was a logical move, but Harzer quickly decided not to comply. 'I knew damn well that if I gave over my few tanks or the armoured personnel carriers to Harmel', he said privately, 'they'd never be replaced.'[9] Acting quickly, Harzer ordered his mechanics to remove the tracks from his tanks and half-tracks and the wheels from his vehicles and guns ready for shipment to Germany. He then told his chief of staff to list them as non-operational. His first units moved out on 12 September.

At Doetinchem on the afternoon of 17 September, Model and Bittrich discussed their options. Bittrich was already up to speed, as the Luftwaffe had reported the Allied airborne landings just five minutes after they commenced. From the intelligence coming in, it was clear to Bittrich that Arnhem and Nijmegen were the focus of American and British efforts. Before Model arrived, Bittrich had already instructed elements of the 9th SS to head for these two cities and Oosterbeek. The 10th SS was also ordered south to hold Nijmegen. Bittrich rightly reasoned that if Nijmegen could be blocked, then the British at Oosterbeek would be cut off. Model was pleased by Bittrich's decisive actions and saw no reason to make any changes. However, the pair disagreed over their assessment of the situation. Bittrich believed that Arnhem was the objective of the British, with a view to thrusting into the Ruhr. As far as

Model was concerned, the situation was too fluid to come to any immediate conclusions.

It was vital that the 9th SS occupy the Arnhem area and hold the road bridge and nearby rail bridge. No one had been able to raise General Kussin, the Arnhem commandant, after he had headed for Wolfheze, and no one seemed to have a real grasp of what units were in the city. SS-Major Krafft had a company in Arnhem, but he had ordered that west to Oosterbeek. Holding the road bridge was a unit of just 25 elderly men.[10] It was obvious to Model and Bittrich that the southern end of the bridge must be secured, as that would prevent British ground forces from getting over it.

Major Krafft did not hang about. The trees around Wolfheze concealed the size of the British landings, so he sent several patrols to gauge quite what was happening to the west. Meanwhile, he instructed one company to conduct a fighting reconnaissance through the woods towards the British, while another set up defensive positions around the Wolfheze Hotel, to await his third company from Arnhem.

It was at this point that Major-General Kussin turned up in his staff car demanding to know what was going on. Krafft briefed him as best he could: reports indicated that the nearby heath was 'jammed with gliders and troops'.[11] What was equally alarming was the rate at which the enemy was assembling ready to attack. Kussin promised reinforcements and then sped off towards Arnhem. Krafft doubted very much they would reach him in time. He appreciated that 'it was up to me to stop them from getting to the bridge – if that's where they were going'.[12]

Krafft had intended for his men to approach the British from the north, but instead, after getting lost in the woods, they blundered into the centre of their landing zone. The German machine-gunners opened fire on gliders coming in to land, damaging at least four. In light of the British strength the company had little option but to withdraw towards Wolfheze, and Krafft fell back towards Oosterbeek. Krafft was not confident that he and his men would survive the British onslaught. He summoned his driver, Private Wilhelm Rauth, and instructed him to load his personal effects in the car and head for Germany. When Rauth looked quizzical, Krafft said, 'I don't expect to get out of this alive'.[13]

To prevent the British from reaching Arnhem, Krafft deployed his soldiers to the north on the Ede–Arnhem railway cutting and to the south on the Wageningen–Arnhem road. He ordered his machine-gun platoons to hold these two points, while the rest of his men took up positions in the woods in between. Near the Johannahoeve farm, Krafft's men established ambush positions overlooking a track that led to Arnhem, which was dominated by the nearby railway embankment. His soldiers had just dug their defensive scrapes or shallow trenches when they heard the sound of a vehicle roaring up the track.

A British jeep suddenly appeared and the Germans opened up, swiftly killing all on board. The sound of their MG42 machine gun and rifle fire echoed along the railway; then there was a brief silence. The gunners adjusted the weapons against their shoulders, while the loaders checked the belt feeds to make sure there were no stoppages. For a brief moment it seemed as if the vehicle was on its own. Then a second jeep came down the track; it was also hit and the wounded occupants captured. The presence of these vehicles suggested the force was a *coup de main* intent on breaking into Arnhem. More British then appeared and a firefight soon developed.

North of the railway, German armour, on the Ede–Arnhem road, also held up British attempts to push eastwards. Captain Weber's Luftwaffe personnel put in a brief appearance, attacking over the Amsterdamseweg road. Weber had only 90 lightly armed signallers and soon withdrew back towards Deelen airfield. His actions, however, further alarmed the British over German strength in the area and enabled the German air traffic control staff to evacuate Deeleen. At Oosterbeek, just east of the Hartenstein Hotel, German mortar fire likewise hampered British efforts to break through.

To the south, there were insufficient troops to stop the British from reaching the Arnhem railway bridge. A few desultory shots were fired, but this did not matter because the bridge had been rigged for demolition. Just as the British were about to cross, at 1800 hours, the sappers detonated their explosives. The blast left 'the southernmost span lying half in and half out of the water'.[14] The route was cut and thwarted British attempts to reach the Arnhem road bridge via the southern bank of the river. For some reason, the British ignored the Heveadorp ferry to the west of the railway bridge. A German pontoon bridge farther east had been partially dismantled, leaving just the Arnhem road bridge open. This left the British stuck on the north side of the river.

Krafft was amazed at what his battalion had achieved; he was proud of 'the courageous impetuosity of my young lads'.[15] Not all his men had stood fast, though, as one of his lieutenants was wanted for desertion. Increasingly Krafft was worried that he had been left out on a limb. There had been no further word from General Kussin, nor any sign of his promised reinforcements. Krafft did not know that Harzer's 9th SS were hastening to his aid and preparing a new defensive line.

SS-Captain Helle's Dutch SS also went into action against the British at Groote Heide or Ginkel Heath on the Ede–Arnhem Road. Helle briefed his officers, SS-Lieutenants Bartsch, Bronkhorst, Fernau and Hink and SS-Drum Major Sakkel, that they were to tackle the most western end of the British landing zones. His battalion lacked transport; there were only enough vehicles to move the quick response unit and a single company. Helle should have concentrated his battalion first before attacking, but he was under pressure from General von Tettau to act straight away.

Helle's operation was a shambles from start to finish. The battalion's bandsmen formed the quick response unit and at about 1700 hours arrived to patrol the woods bordering the heath. Sakkel immediately led his men into an ambush and was fatally wounded. Most of the survivors ran away. Bartsch's company did not set out until 2100 hours and in the dark blundered into British positions.

His men, illuminated by British flares, came under fire and taking casualties were forced to withdraw. When Hink's company arrived on the right, they committed the same error. Helle decided to set up his headquarters in the Zuid-Ginkel restaurant and await the arrival of the remainder of his battalion. What he did not know was that the rest of the British 1st Airborne Division was going to land right on top of him the following day.

7

Bittrich's Quick Reaction

SS-Lieutenant-Colonel Harzer was at the Hoenderloo barracks to the north of Arnhem and Deelen on the morning of 17 September, holding a parade for some of the survivors of his division. 'It was a sunny day', he recalled, 'a typically quiet and peaceful Sunday.'[1] He stood before SS-Captain Paul Gräbner and with great pleasure gave him the Knight's Cross. Gräbner was in charge of the reconnaissance battalion and the award was in recognition of his exploits in Normandy. Beforehand Harzer had made a brief speech commending 'the bravery of the troops and their commander'.[2] There was a sense of relief amongst the 500 men attending the ceremony. They were going home. 'We believed the war was probably over', said veteran SS-Lance Corporal Wolfgang Dombrowski. 'Life's deeper issues did not concern us too much.'[3]

Harzer was looking forward to getting back to Germany to celebrate his birthday. SS-Brigadier Harmel was due to return from Germany that night. 'As the troops were moving off to their quarters and the officers and myself were making for the officers' mess for lunch', said Harzer, 'we saw the first British parachutes in the sky over Arnhem.' He was not unduly alarmed and decided not to change his plans. 'It could not be deduced at this stage', he reasoned, 'that a large-scale operation was under way and we sat quietly down to lunch.'[4] Such was the unflappable ethos of the Waffen-SS.

It was not long before he received a call from Bittrich, who ordered him to set up headquarters in Arnhem's northern suburbs in a school building. As far as Harzer was concerned, the key to holding Arnhem was the Utrecht–Arnhem road and the Ede–Arnhem road, both of which approached from the west. If he created a defensive arch astride these two highways, he could deny the city to the British airborne forces. Crucially, he missed a third route running parallel with the river. This oversight would allow the British to reach the Arnhem road bridge.

Harzer knew he needed to get men down to Oosterbeek to block the British advance as quickly as possible. The problem he had was that it was going to take hours to reassemble all his vehicles, which had been deliberately taken apart for shipping to Germany. He needed to react immediately, so called his artillery commander SS-Lieutenant-Colonel Ludwig Spindler, who was billeted to the northeast of Arnhem. Harzer instructed him to create a defensive line between the Lower Rhine and Arnhem railway station. Spindler was to use men from his artillery regiment and the division's two SS-Panzergrenadier regiments. SS-Captain Hans Möller, commander of the pioneer battalion, was given similar orders and told to hold the area east of Den Brink Park near the station. The railway line curved round the western outskirts and provided a useful defensive barrier. Den Brink dominated the ground behind it.

Harzer then contacted SS-Captain Klaus von Allworden, who was in charge of what remained of his division's tank destroyer battalion. This was deployed to the northeast of Hoenderloo at Apeldoorn. Allworden reported he could muster about 120 men, several self-propelled guns and a few towed 75mm anti-tank guns. Harzer told him to get his force to the north of Arnhem. Understandably, SS-Lance Corporal Dombrowski was disappointed not to be returning to Germany, but noted with pride, 'We were prepared to fight on'.[5]

Harmel was at Bad Saarnow, near Berlin, with SS-Major-General Hans Juttner, chief of Waffen-SS operations, when he received an urgent recall message from Bittrich. He dashed outside and leapt into his car. 'Back to Arnhem and drive like the devil', Harmel instructed his driver, SS-Corporal Sepp Hinterholzer.[6] Frustratingly, they faced an eleven-and-a-half-hour journey.

In Harmel's absence, SS-Colonel Paetsch tried to help by mobilizing the 10th SS. His best unit was SS-Major Brinkmann's reconnaissance battalion. This, though, was the farthest of all 2nd SS-Panzer Corps units from Arnhem. Brinkmann's men were billeted to the east of Harmel's headquarters at Ruurlo, in the villages of Borculo and Eibergen. Paetsch was understandably concerned about what might happen to the east of Arnhem and ordered Brinkmann to send some of his men to screen Emmerich and Wesel. This left just one company under Karl Ziebrecht free to head west to Arnhem.

General von Tettau set up his headquarters at Grebbeburg, some ten miles to the west of Arnhem. He received conflicting reports about enemy drops, but thanks to dummy paratroopers coming down southeast of Utrecht, none of them was regarding Arnhem. In The Hague, SS-General Rauter, once word reached him of the landings, decided to help Tettau. He immediately called SS-Captain Helle, the commander of the Dutch SS guard battalion at Amersfoort concentration camp.

At the time Helle was with his Dutch-Javanese mistress and had no wish to be disturbed. When SS-Lieutenant Naumann answered the telephone, Rauter told him that Helle was to report to General von Tettau at once. Helle reluctantly left the arms of his lover and made contact with Tettau's headquarters. He was instructed to get his battalion to Ede to the northwest of Oosterbeek. When Helle's men were told that they were deploying, morale immediately plummeted. Once on the road, many took the opportunity to slip away.

Tettau signalled SS-Major Krafft, who was holding the area west of Oosterbeek, at 1620 hours and informed him of landings reportedly at Driel and Nijmegen. Krafft soon filled him in on what was happening at Wolfheze and said that he needed reinforcements. Tettau responded that these would be supplied by Christiansen's Netherlands command, in the shape of Battle Group Eberwein, the Hermann Göring Reserve and Training Regiment and an SS-Training School from Rauter's SS security command. The snag was that they would not reach Krafft until the following morning.

SS-Colonel Hans Lippert had also been ordered to report to Tettau at Grebbeburg. His NCO school personnel were reinforced to regimental strength, with at least three battalions. Thanks to the confusing reports of Allied landings at Utrecht, Veenendaal, Dortrecht and Tiel, Tettau did not give Lippert his marching orders until the end of the day. Lippert was a veteran from the 9th SS and most of his trainee NCOs had already done a year's military service. For many this had been on the Eastern Front, which meant the regiment should perform well. Likewise, Lippert's instructors were veterans. SS-Staff Sergeant Erwin Heck had served since 1938 and thanks to a wound he had received that summer in Russia walked with a limp. Unfortunately, Heck and most of his trainees were on the Dutch coast when they heard of the landings.

Harzer visited Major Schleifenbaum around 1700 hours, who was trying to co-ordinate the defence of Arnhem bridge in the absence of Major-General Kussin. So far the British had not reached the city. It was decided that all units in the vicinity of the railway station, either just arriving or about to depart, were to be thrown into the fight. Everyone was to be rounded up, assigned to a company and armed. Amongst them was SS-Squad Leader Alfred Ringsdorf, who had just arrived, and Master Sergeant Emil Petersen of the Reich Labour Service, who was due to ship back to Germany. Petersen and his 35-man platoon were hungry, as they had not eaten for 24 hours. Bittrich also visited Arnhem, calling in on the command post of SS-Captain Möller in the Den Brink area. The railway line was covered by machine guns and snipers, while the approach roads were patrolled by armoured cars. These defences seemed encouraging.

In the meantime, Harzer's mechanics worked all afternoon to reassemble the division's disabled equipment. By about 1830 hours the 40 vehicles of SS-Captain Gräbner's reconnaissance battalion were ready to drive south from Hoenderloo. His orders were to scout towards Nijmegen to ascertain the enemy's strength and intentions. Gräbner found Arnhem largely deserted and just before

1900 hours his column crossed the vast expanse of the road bridge. A mile on he came to a halt and signalled divisional headquarters, 'No enemy. No paratroopers'.[7]

However, chaos reigned in Arnhem. Major Schleifenbaum was unable to warn all the German units entering the city, with predictable results. A Luftwaffe flak unit, comprising 80 men with a 20mm and 88mm gun, came under British fire upon arrival. Coming to a halt, they leapt from their vehicles and began to engage their antagonists. Elsewhere, four lorries carrying German assault pioneers, including SS-Corporal Dombrowski, were amazed to see tracer rounds flicking across the road. 'Idiots!' thought Dombrowski. 'They are on exercise!'[8] Suddenly an angry major yelled at them from across the road, 'That's live ammunition – the Tommies have landed!'[9] Piling out of their trucks, Dombrowski and his comrades joined the battle.

Sergeant Petersen and his men found themselves assigned to a company some 250 strong. There was only one problem: few of them were armed. Petersen and just four others had submachine guns. They were taken to an SS barracks and given very old carbines. Even once armed, Petersen was not happy at the thought of fighting alongside the Waffen-SS. At dusk they were marched through Arnhem and got to within 300 yards of the bridge. Suddenly they became aware that they were moving alongside British paratroopers. The moment the mistake was realized, both sides began shooting. Falling to the ground, Petersen managed to crawl to a small park where he found the others taking cover. The British had occupied the buildings on both sides and the German company was caught in a deadly crossfire.

Lacking specific instructions to do so, Gräbner failed to strengthen the guard on Arnhem's highway bridge. A single armoured vehicle remained in support of a machine-gun team manning a pillbox.[10] Less than 30 minutes after he crossed, the British seized the northern end of the bridge. They soon silenced the pillbox. The young SS soldiers defending it were inexperienced and failed to conduct foot patrols. Their post offered them security, or so they thought. As a result, they had failed to notice the British vanguard coming along the riverbank. They also failed to appreciate that the British would inevitably bring up heavier firepower to deal with their bunker. This error cost them their lives.

The pillbox machine-gunners were first alerted by the sounds of fighting going on below the bridge. Twice the British approached their position and twice their MG42 drove them off. The Germans then launched a counter-attack against the British positions on the bridge embankment. This was preceded by flares and mortar bombs, but they were driven off. Once it was dark, the men in the pillbox decided it was best to stay put. Suddenly at around 2200 hours they and the surrounding area were bathed in bright orange flames. These engulfed a nearby shed containing ammunition. In an instant it exploded, destroying the pillbox and setting fire to the bridge's paintwork. It burned all night long.

Perversely the loss of the pillbox actually helped the German defence. Just as the British were about to cross, four lorry loads of Panzergrenadiers drove over from the south side. The lead driver, seeing the flames, slowed down to take a closer look and as he did so the British opened fire. Within seconds the lorries were also ablaze, blocking the road, and many of their occupants jumped screaming into the river. The dazed survivors were taken prisoner. These additional flames from the wrecked vehicles further illuminated the bridge and, along with the heat, deterred the British from trying to get to the southern end.

Other German units were caught up in the confusion in Arnhem. These included SS-Captain Karl-Heinz Euling's battalion from the 10th SS, which had been instructed to reinforce the garrison at Nijmegen. At the northern end of the bridge, his advance guard came under fire. Also heading for the bridge was a company from the 21st SS-Panzergrenadier Regiment, likewise from the 10th SS. SS-Corporal Rudolf Trapp with the latter unit had found himself comically pedalling from Deventer to Arnhem on 'requisitioned' Dutch bicycles.

When he and his comrades reached the outskirts of Arnhem, they dumped the bikes and walked towards the bridge. 'It must have been about 20.00', recalled Trapp, 'and it was getting dark.'[11] They were tasked with clearing the houses below the bridge ramp and soon started taking casualties. He and the others, short of equipment, resorted to using weapons taken from British dead and wounded. 'Later we received some panzerfausts and ammunition.'[12] It was clear that the British were well entrenched around the northern end of the bridge, having established a defensive perimeter in the surrounding buildings.

Karl Ziebrecht's company from the 10th SS Reconnaissance Battalion also arrived on the scene. He had been instructed to reconnoitre the approaches to the bridge. When his armoured cars drove forward, they came under fire and it was evident the British had fortified the area. Ziebrecht's gunners shot back, but his force lacked the strength to do much else. Getting on the radio, he reported his findings to Paetsch.

It was now that Lieutenant Enthammer's luck ran out. He and 17 soldiers had just left St Joseph's School when their truck was stopped by the British. They had only a handful of rifles, so surrendered on the spot. 'What could we do?' asked Enthammer.[13] They were herded from their vehicle and placed under armed guard in a nearby house. Enthammer was thankful his artillery uniform gave no indication that his unit was involved with Hitler's top secret V-weapons.

British possession of the northern end of the bridge meant that Harmel would have to find another way to get his men over the river. He held Gräbner responsible for this state of affairs. 'If only Gräbner had left a few soldiers behind to reinforce bridge security', Harmel grumbled, 'then it would have been a different story.'[14] It was Harzer, though, who had instructed Gräbner to focus on Nijmegen. The real culprit was Kussin, who had left his headquarters at the very moment he was needed. The result was that the battle was fought in a very *ad hoc* way, with no one knowing who exactly was responsible for the defence of the bridge. Schleifenbaum was only a major, so was not of sufficient rank to take charge. This meant that no one was really in overall command of the various battle groups and disparate units that had turned up in the city.

While all this was going on, SS-Colonel Lippert instructed his lead battalion, under SS-Captain Schultz, to make its way via Leerdam, Rhenen and Wageningen to Oosterbeek to help Krafft. This was easier said than done. Schultz's men lacked transport and they were forced to commandeer anything with wheels. This resulted in a rather comical convoy ranging from bicycles to fire engines. SS-Staff Sergeant Heck managed to get his hands on a motorbike and got to the front before his pupils. Lippert's other two battalions under SS-Captains Mattusch and Oelker were to deploy as soon as they had gathered.

A very tired Harmel, commander of the 10th SS, arrived back from Berlin at 2330 hours. When his staff car pulled up at his headquarters at Ruurlo, which lay to the east of Hoenderloo and north of Doetinchem, he discovered that it had been relocated. Driving on, he found Paetsch, his chief of staff, at Velp some three miles northeast of Arnhem. Paetsch was exhausted and there seemed to be an air of panic. This was worrying, because Paetsch was Harmel's former Panzer commander, and was not a man easily alarmed.

'Everything seemed confused and uncertain,' said Harmel. 'The gravity of the situation was such that I called Bittrich and told him I was coming to see him.'[15] At Doetinchem, Bittrich, who was also extremely tired, proceeded to brief Harmel on the day's developments. 'In my opinion', he said, 'the objectives are the bridges. Once these are secured, Montgomery can drive directly up the centre of Holland and from there, into the Ruhr.'[16] He went on to explain how Harzer was currently countering the British to the north and west of Arnhem.

When Harmel asked what reinforcements they could expect, Bittrich responded that General Christiansen was sending what he had under the command of Major-General von Tettau. They were to assist Harzer. Bittrich told Harmel that his men were to hold the Nijmegen bridges at all costs, as well as the area south of Arnhem. However, there was a problem, explained Bittrich. 'Harzer failed to leave armoured units at the north end of the Arnhem bridge. The British are there now.'[17]

This meant that Harmel would have to use the ferry at Pannerden, around eight miles to the southeast of Arnhem. This crossed the Pannerden Canal, which linked the Rhine and the Waal. Such an operation would be a time-consuming process. Surely, reasoned Harmel, it would be easier just to blow the bridge at Nijmegen. 'Model has flatly refused to consider the idea', said Bittrich. 'We may need it to counter-attack.' Harmel looked aghast and asked, 'With what?'[18]

On his way to Pannerden, Harmel saw the road was jammed with vehicles and troops. When he arrived, he found makeshift ferries using rubber rafts were taking forever to get his men and equipment across. When Harmel pressed Paetsch on their rate of progress, the latter said a battalion had got over and was heading for Nijmegen. However, by Paetsch's estimate it could take until 24 September to get the whole division into the Arnhem–Nijmegen area. Harmel knew that there was only one way to speed things up. Arnhem bridge must be recaptured as soon as possible.

Spindler's battle group had joined Krafft's blocking force too late to stop the British from reaching Arnhem bridge. Nonetheless, Krafft in the meantime had halted the advance of two other British parachute battalions. Then at 2130 hours, fearing he was going to be outflanked, he withdrew northeast to meet Spindler's forces. This went smoothly on the whole, though British mortar rounds falling through the trees caused a few casualties. 'We met the battle group "Spindler" from the SS Panzer Division "Hohenstaufen" on the Ede–Arnhem road', reported Krafft, with some relief.[19] It had been a long day. At 2245 hours, he officially came under the command of the 9th SS. Thankfully, he was no longer on his own.

8

Panzers at Valkenswaard

General Student, commander of 1st Parachute Army, was at Vught on 17 September 1944, feeling a little foolish. If anyone should have anticipated an airborne assault in the Netherlands, it was him. Four years previously, he had led the daring German airborne attack on Rotterdam. Now his ragtag command was holding the Meuse–Escaut Canal in an infantry role. Gone were the glory days of his parachute and glider operations.

The day before, his intelligence report to Model had simply noted, 'increased motor transport activity and confirmed armoured preparations strengthen the appreciation… that a heavy attack must be expected very shortly'.[1] He made no suggestion that this might be backed by a large-scale airborne assault. Student should have been suspicious that since D-Day the Allies had refrained from using their quite considerable airborne forces. He must have pondered, what were they planning to do with them? What he did not know was that the rapidity of the Allies' advance had resulted in a whole series of operations being continually cancelled.

No one, including Model, Rauter and Kieswetter, had seen fit to warn Student of their concerns about an Allied airborne drop in the Netherlands. He was in his study sifting through paperwork at midday on 17 September when the sound of aircraft drew him out onto his balcony. He was 'completely surprised'[2] by what he saw: 'nobody in the German command knew anything about the attack until it happened.'[3] Looking up, Student exclaimed, 'Oh, how

I wish that I had ever had such powerful means at my disposal!' His chief of staff, Colonel Reinhard, joined him and the pair watched the crowded skies. 'Wherever I looked I saw aircraft; troop-carriers and large aircraft towing gliders', said Student. 'I was greatly impressed but during those minutes I did not think of the danger of the situation.'[4]

The pair clambered on to the roof to get a better look and saw airborne forces heading for Eindhoven and Son, as well as Grave and Nijmegen. 'On the grounds of the headquarters, our clerks, quarter masters, drivers and signalmen', noted Student, 'were out in the open, firing with all their weapons. As usual there was no sign of our own fighter planes.'[5] Reinhard said to his boss, 'We've got to do something!'[6] Student quickly concluded that the enemy were going after the bridges at Eindhoven, Grave and Nijmegen. These were all prepared for demolition, so that was fortunate, although they could not be blown without Model's express authorization. It did not occur to him that they might also be going after the bridge at Arnhem over the Lower Rhine.

Worryingly, when Reinhard tried to call Model's headquarters, he found that the line was dead. Despite the risk of the Dutch Resistance eavesdropping, the German armed forces in Belgium and the Netherlands relied on the local telephone system, because it was a lot more reliable than their radios. When Reinhard then tried 1st Parachute Army's various forward command posts, they could not be reached either except by radio. Student was not pleased about this; not only was he unable to communicate effectively with his command, but it was being cut in two by the airborne landings.

By 1330 hours the skies over Arnhem, Nijmegen and Veghel were full of enemy transport planes and gliders, so it was fairly obvious what was going on. Everywhere German units blasted away at them. 'The troops baled out from a very low altitude, sometimes as low as sixty metres', observed German war correspondent Erwin Kirchhof. 'Immediately after that the several hundred gliders started to land. In those first few minutes it looked as if the downcoming masses would suffocate every single life on the ground.'[7] The Dutch were equally taken by surprise; many, having been to Sunday church, were heading for the local cinema, or out for a bicycle ride with friends and family along the canal pathways.

Shortly after, Student received an unexpected intelligence windfall. He could not believe his luck: 'a few hours later the orders for the complete airborne operation were on my desk.'[8] These had been found in the wreckage of a glider. Student was amazed. 'They showed us everything – the dropping zones, the corridor, the objectives – even the names of the divisions involved.'[9] He was surprised that the Allies could be so foolhardy with their operational security. Nonetheless, it could easily happen. 'It was the same as in 1940 during the 1st German Airborne operation in Holland', observed Student, 'when a German officer, despite the strictest injunctions, carried operational orders in person. It fell into Allied hands.'[10]

Ironically, this intelligence about Allied intentions did him no good, as he was unable to communicate it to Model. It would take Reinhard almost ten hours to translate and then transmit the captured plans in three sections to Model at Terborg. They were so detailed that Model refused to believe that they were not a ruse. 'If we are to believe these plans and are to assume that the Arnhem bridge is the true objective', reasoned Model, 'why were not troops dropped directly on the bridge?'[11]

Student slammed the phone down just after 1400 hours. Yet more bad news. The British were heavily shelling his forward positions and conducting counter-battery fire against his artillery across a mile-wide front. About 40 minutes later, he was informed that British tanks were advancing under the cover of their supporting artillery and prowling rocket-firing fighter-bombers. Directly in the path of the British tanks lay elements of Battle Group Walther, while to the east deployed south of Weert were elements of the 7th Parachute Division.

After the British patrol had reached Valkenswaard, Student gathered six battalions in the woods immediately bordering the road. The route was blocked 500 yards north of the Dutch border, but because the road was made of concrete it was largely impossible to mine it. These units consisted of two battalions from the 6th Parachute Regiment on his right, with one from the 9th SS and one from the 10th SS on the left, plus the 6th Penal Battalion in the centre.[12] The Luftwaffe convicts were bolstered by Major Kerutt's battalion, from Regiment von Hoffman, which deployed on their right. The former criminals were considered a 'suicide battalion'[13] and placed directly across the road, because they were suitable only for defensive combat. These forces came under Battle Group Walther, also known as 'Division Walther'.

Once in the woods, Student's men dug in. If there was one thing the Germans had learned on the Eastern Front, it was how to prepare good defensive positions. The veterans showed the new recruits how to cut logs to protect and camouflage their dugouts. Although the wood would not shield them from direct hits, at least it was shrapnel proof. Even for the veterans, though, facing down tanks was never easy. It took courage not to run when a 35-ton metal box was bearing down on you, shelling and machine-gunning everything in its path at the same time.

'Instead of selecting the major road to Valkenswaard as the main effort of the defence', observed Battle Group Walther's chief of Staff, 'it was designated as a boundary between units. Consequently nobody really wanted to feel responsible for the road.'[14] Nonetheless, Lieutenant Heinz Volz, with Regiment von Hoffman, felt 'we were able to impose a decisive block, because the terrain to the left and right of the road was not suitable for tanks, being boggy'.[15] On 17 September their work had been interrupted. 'At about midday we suddenly discerned an unearthly droning noise', recalled Lieutenant Volz. Looking up, he saw 'a huge stream of transport aircraft and gliders... This enormous swarm was escorted by countless fighters'.[16]

Student had no idea how he was supposed to fend off General Brian Horrocks' armoured thrust towards Valkenswaard when he lacked anti-tank weapons. In the case of the Hermann Göring Reserve and Training Regiment, it had only two or three Panzerfausts per rifle company. Its 2nd Battalion had two weak companies of tanks, but the crews were largely made up of new recruits and instructors. How he wished he had the Hermann Göring Panzer Division, the Luftwaffe's elite armoured unit, but it was fighting on the Eastern Front. This tough division had served in North Africa, Sicily and Italy. Instead he had ended up with the training regiment, which was supposed to be supplying replacements for the Parachute Panzer Corps forming in Prussia.

Over the last few days Student had received reinforcements, but they were not up to much. The Hermann Göring Regiment had arrived in the Turnhout–Riel sector. However, Student had been informed that they were scheduled to redeploy to West Prussia to fight the Russians at the end of the month. In other words, he could use them for two weeks. The 245th Infantry Division came under his command on 16 September 1944, although it was nowhere near at full strength. The following day, he had been assigned the remains of Major-General Walther Poppe's 59th Infantry Division. Again, it was a division only in name. Student was informed that it could barely muster 1,000 infantry, supported by 30 guns and supplemented by a replacement battalion. In total he had about 30,000–40,000 paratroops, Luftwaffe personnel and assorted soldiers with which to stop the British 30th Corps.[17] He desperately needed more manpower and most of all he needed tanks.

Student had been promised a regiment from Schwalbe's old outfit, the 346th Infantry Division. This was to be strengthened by the 279th Replacement Battalion, currently at Eschwege in Germany. There were two problems with this. Firstly, this was an ill-health 'stomach' battalion, and although it could muster 1,150 men, almost all of them had intestinal complaints. Secondly, as a result, only a company of 250 men would be available at the end of the month.[18]

At most, Student had about half a dozen 75mm and 88mm anti-tank guns protecting the road barricade. The Panzerfausts were divided up amongst the tank hunter teams, whose job was to shoot and scoot. Kerutt had emplaced just over half a dozen field guns behind the Luftwaffe convicts. The SS, grouped into Battle Group Henke, on the eastern flank could call on just six 105mm howitzers. In stark contrast the heavy opening British

THE BRITISH BREAKOUT, 17–18 SEPTEMBER 1944

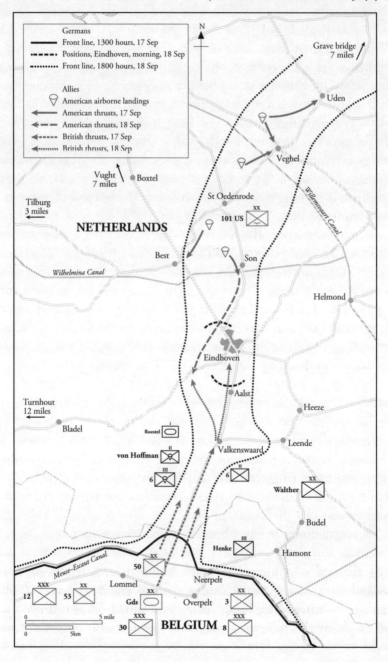

Germans
— Front line, 1300 hours, 17 Sep
- - - Positions, Eindhoven, morning, 18 Sep
····· Front line, 1800 hours, 18 Sep

Allies
⛳ American airborne landings
← American thrusts, 17 Sep
←- American thrusts, 18 Sep
←-- British thrusts, 17 Sep
←··· British thrusts, 18 Sep

Grave bridge
7 miles

Uden

Veghel

Willemsvaart Canal

Vught
7 miles   ● Boxtel

Tilburg
3 miles

St Oedenrode

NETHERLANDS   101 US   XX

Best   Son

Wilhelmina Canal   Helmond

Eindhoven

Aalst

Turnhout
12 miles   Heeze

Bladel   Roestel   I

von Hoffman   II   Valkenswaard   Leende

6   III   6   II   XX
    Walther

Budel

Henke   III

Hamont

Meuse–Escaut Canal   50   XX

XXX   XX   Lommel   Neerpelt   XX
12   53   Gds   XX   Overpelt   3

0   5 mile   XXX   XXX
0   5km   30   **BELGIUM**   8

bombardment employed 350 guns. 'The front, which had been relatively quiet from about midday', recalled Lieutenant Volz, 'suddenly erupted into a hell.'[19]

Student's men weathered the British barrage, but were too stunned to react when the enemy tanks began to roll forward. Firing back was made difficult when the British guns were dropping their shells in a rolling barrage 100 yards in front of their tanks. The RAF's Typhoon fighter-bombers were delivering their rockets at almost zero feet from all angles, some 200 yards in front of the British advance. Added to this appalling din was the sound of tank and lorry engines and the clatter of machine guns. The noise, 'a sudden, deafening roar', was described 'as though an express train was passing overhead'.[20]

Lieutenant Volz and his men endured this ordeal, which he called 'an unearthly crescendo... the soil shook time and time again... Captain Brockes was killed by a direct hit from a mortar round'.[21] For ten minutes, the defenders struggled to respond and it seemed as if nothing was going to stop the British Guards Armoured Division. By then, though, the German gunners had reached their concealed anti-tank guns and began to pour fire into the leading British vehicles rumbling up Highway 69. 'A large number of English tanks were soon knocked out by Panzerfausts', said Lieutenant Volz, 'firing from five to ten metres away.'[22]

The gunners were impressed by the British tankers' bravery, as they were driving up the road in single file. There was no cover for them, apart from the odd shrub and small trees. These did nothing to obscure the distinctive outline of the British Sherman tanks. It was as if they were on parade, but the truth was they had no option, because the route was only wide enough for one tank at a time.

In the space of just two minutes, the defenders successfully blocked the road by knocking out nine enemy tanks.[23] They managed to catch three tanks of the lead squadron as it drove by, and six from the following one. The gunners also engulfed two scout cars in flames. There was chaos as the British struggled to barge the damaged vehicles out of the way. The gunners had now revealed their positions and they were soon bombed, rocketed and shelled. One young German paratrooper exposed himself to fire his Panzerfaust and was promptly cut down by a tank's machine gun. Just to be on the safe side, the machine-gunner put an entire belt of bullets into the corpse.

One German anti-tank gun crew, having knocked out an enemy tank, found a Sherman Firefly bearing down on them. They jumped clear just as a 17-pounder shell smashed their weapon. The Sherman rolled forward and the gunners threw their hands up to surrender. British infantry, furious at being shot at, surged forward into the woods. Several of the German tank hunter teams were flushed out, killed or captured. German snipers started taking pot shots at the British, who in response showed no mercy by spraying the trees with light machine-gun and rifle fire.

The British had no way of getting their captives to the rear, so ordered them to mount the tanks. The Germans, frightened at the prospect of being fired on by their own side, immediately gave away the positions of the rest of their gun battery. One prisoner, the crew chief of the destroyed anti-tank gun, even climbed onto a British tank and helped direct its fire against two other guns. Shortly after, British artillery and fighter-bombers pounded the rest into oblivion. Several of SS-Captain Roestel's Jagdpanzer IV tank destroyers were also destroyed.

While this was going on, the British brought up an armoured bulldozer to clear the road. Unceremoniously the burnt-out British tanks were shunted into the verges. Minutes earlier they had been deadly weapons. Now they were discarded heaps of scorched junk. Only as long as they could kill were they valuable tools of war. This was how their usefulness was measured.

It was not long before the positions of Kerutt's command and the Luftwaffe battalion were overrun. The British were amazed at the large number of different units the prisoners came from. Some of the captured Germans resolved to resist to the last. As a column of prisoners was briskly marched back down the road, one of them suddenly produced a grenade, which he threw into an open-top tracked carrier. The blast caught a British sergeant, who lost both his legs. The culprit was immediately gunned down by angry British soldiers. Another tried to make a run for it and was also killed.

Colonel von der Heydte's paratroopers avoided the worst of the British assault. However, he found himself cut off from the rest of Division Walther and headquarters. 'The enemy airlandings on 17 September and the break through by the Guards Armoured Division seemed to spread panic', complained Heydte: 'communications and logistics appeared to be largely paralysed.'[24] No one seemed to be co-ordinating the defence.

Heydte had been in many tight spots before, and he had no intention of being trapped now. The British bombardment at Valkenswaard reminded him not only of overwhelming Allied firepower in Normandy, but also the terrible shelling he had experienced in Prison Valley on Crete. Heydte had suffered heavy casualties there. He was not easily flappable and was generally a cool customer. Frustrated by a lack of orders, Heydte now took matters into his own hands. He assumed control of the 2nd Battalion, Regiment von Hoffman, as well as any Luftwaffe survivors, and ordered a withdrawal. This immediately opened up his left flank, leaving Major Kerutt and SS-Captain Segler to the east of the road on their own.

Outside Valkenswaard, the remaining tank destroyers from the 10th SS, under SS-Captain Roestel, tried to stop the British tanks. He had started the day with a force of 15 Jagdpanzer IVs but was now reduced to just eight. They had taken up position in some woods, but every time they fired they drew attention to themselves. It was not long before they were silenced by a combination of artillery, tank fire and circling fighter-bombers.

At 1700 hours, Student was informed that the British were on the outskirts of Valkenswaard, halfway to Eindhoven. There was nothing to stop them from taking possession of the town. There was also nothing to stop them from getting to Eindhoven, so Colonel Hoffman was put on alert. Apart from the remaining tank destroyers, Student's defences before Valkenswaard were now very sparse. Defending the bridge over the Dommel, just to the south, were four 88mm guns and some infantry in the nearby woods. Upon the arrival of British tanks, the frightened gun crews fled and their headquarters was hit by a tank round. The German infantry contented themselves with sniping at the armour, but made no counter-attack. It was now dark and British artillery soon honed in on any points of resistance, setting light to some buildings in the town.

By 2140 hours, British tanks were in the centre of Valkenswaard, illuminated by four large fires. In the post office, which had been used as the German headquarters, the Dutch town clerk greeted his liberators. He then answered a telephone call and a German voice barked down the line. They had a message for the garrison: 'they were to hold on at all costs and that reinforcements were on their way'.[25] The clerk did not have the heart to inform the caller that Valkenswaard's occupiers had already fled. The British, fearing a counter-attack, took up defensive positions in the northern outskirts and hunkered down for the night.

Student was very relieved that the British had stopped at Valkenswaard. He was also puzzled about why they had called a halt. SS-Captain Karl Godau, of the 10th SS, was also relieved. At 1400 hours his battery of four guns had been ordered south to protect the Eindhoven road. On the way they had been set upon by fighter-bombers and lost some of their vehicles. Once deployed, his guns had soon targeted British tanks heading their way. He knew at close range he could not miss. Godau was very reluctant to open fire, however, because once they had done so, they would be unable to escape. He hurriedly contacted the headquarters of Battle Group Walther and remarkably was given permission to redeploy farther north. 'We had so little', Godau noted. 'If they had kept going that night, there was nothing worth mentioning between their halting place and Eindhoven.'[26]

Over the next two nights, Student received worrying reports of attacks on his left and right by the British 8th and 12th Corps. This suggested that British ground forces were making for Helmond, Eindhoven and Turnhout. Fortunately, there seemed no urgency with these flanking operations. On the right 12th Corps crossed the Meuse–Escaut Canal near Lommel late on 17/18 September, while on the left 8th Corps did not get over the Meuse–Escaut Canal until 19 September. This was two whole days after 30th Corps had commenced its attack on Valkenswaard and the Allied airborne drops at Eindhoven, Nijmegen and Arnhem. This state of affairs made Student wonder just what the British were playing at.

9

Airborne Stepping Stones

By 18 September, Colonel von der Heydte's 6th Parachute Regiment had withdrawn until it made contact with General Chill's 85th Division, on the western side of the British corridor. Together they would have to try to block the road at Aalst, midway between Valkenswaard and Eindhoven. To the east lay the remains of Battle Group Walther, along with Roestel's forces. Either side of the road the countryside was not conducive to a wider British attack, as there were many waterways and the local bridges were incapable of bearing tanks. This meant that the British would be unable to expand their narrow corridor.

Not surprisingly, Heydte's actions the previous day made him very unpopular with the chain of command. Chill was told in no uncertain terms that he must keep tight control of the wayward colonel. He was instructed that 'Heydte was not to be allowed to exercise any initiative when it came to withdrawing.'[1] Chill smiled at the rebuke. Heydte had made a decision to save his command; there was no shame in that. Besides, what they really needed was sufficient reinforcements, which could counter-attack every time the enemy outflanked them.

The area certainly favoured Chill's defence. Beyond Valkenswaard the road traversed thick pine woods for several miles, which was good ambush country. After that the ground was flat and sandy, exposing anything using the road. Two miles outside Valkenswaard, the Germans deployed a Panther tank and two self-propelled guns ready to greet the British. The defence of Aalst was in the hands of Major Kerutt, who was now the surviving senior officer of Regiment von Hoffman. He commanded the remains of the 1st and 3rd battalions, supported by 11 75mm anti-tank guns and a platoon of 20mm anti-aircraft guns. Some of these forces were dug in south of Aalst, with further defences prepared about a mile to the north of the village along the Tongelreep stream. These would provide a second stop line.

In the early morning of 18 September, both the Germans and the British found themselves hampered by the weather. A thick ground mist reduced visibility to only about 400 yards. This was good for Kerutt and his men, as it meant the Allies' fighter-bombers were grounded. It was not so good for his gunners. Just after 0530 hours the British advance recommenced and a scout car surprised the tank crew, who were sitting on top of their Panther. After firing on them with a machine gun, the British withdrew, and the German tank and the self-propelled guns drove off towards Aalst. Luckily for them, because of the woods, the British infantry were leading the attack, not the tanks, and their follow-up was delayed.

To Kerutt's relief, the enemy advance was very slow. Fortunately for his men, the British had been struggling with an almighty traffic jam around Valkenswaard. He reported to Chill's headquarters 'contact with enemy armour in front of Aalst' at around 1020 hours. By this he meant armoured cars, as it would be another two hours before he signalled 'under attack by tanks'.[2] From the shelter of the pinewood forests his troops, supported by a single self-propelled gun, poured fire into the struggling British column. The latter vehicle was swiftly knocked out.

Once the British tanks were brought up, they attacked, supported by field artillery. Kerutt's men withdrew to their next defensive line. Their ambush, employing anti-tank guns and the remaining self-propelled gun, was triggered prematurely by the appearance of agile British armoured cars that promtly escaped. The British, unable to call in close air support, contented themselves with shelling German defences until the defenders were again compelled to retreat.

Student knew that Eindhoven was now all but lost. The city was defended by a single company of men, made up of rear echelon and Luftwaffe personnel. They were supported by Anti-Tank Group Grünewald, a few self-propelled 88mm anti-tank guns, plus some 88mm anti-aircraft guns belonging to the 18th Flak Brigade. These troops, trying to defend Eindhoven, were now trapped in a pincer attack, with British tanks pushing north from Aalst and American paratroopers approaching southward towards the northern suburbs. Most had escape on their minds, rather than some last-ditch heroic stand. Many of the clerks and administrative personnel did not know where to go, as there was no discernible front line.

The northern approaches were protected by a few machine-gun positions that proved unable to repulse the American airborne forces or even slow them. Once inside the city, it did not take long for the Americans to overrun most of the 88mm guns. One battery, of two weapons, was outflanked thanks to the assistance of the Dutch Resistance. The gunners and their supporting infantry were taken by surprise. After a brief firefight, the Germans suffered 13 dead and 41 captured. At 1230 hours, the British Guards Armoured Division drove into Eindhoven heralding its liberation.

'Enemy has penetrated into the north of Eindhoven. Street Fighting,' reported the 18th Flak Brigade's headquarters at 1318 hours. 'Further contact with units not now possible; the insertion of infantry reinforcements has been ruled out.'[3] It was clear that the German chain of command had broken down in the city, because army units were asking the Luftwaffe for instructions. Flak headquarters went on to say 'Grünewald requests further orders'.[4] Before they could get a response, the telephone line was severed. The Luftwaffe staff officers stood staring at each other; they were on their own. As the remaining garrison was marched into captivity, they watched a column of British vehicles being mobbed by jubilant Dutch civilians.

North of Eindhoven, as the reports poured in, it was evident to Student and Model that men of the US 101st Airborne Division were seeking to take the bridges over the river Dommel at Eindhoven and St Oedenrode, the Wilhelmina Canal at Best and Son, as well as the Zuid Willems Canal and the river Aa at Veghel. The presence of an American divisional landing zone to the northeast of Son posed a threat to the German position at Eindhoven and Veghel. There were also reports of smaller landings to the northwest and southwest of Veghel.

The US 82nd Airborne had created another stepping stone for the British ground forces, with airborne landings near Nijmegen. These included forces coming down to the southwest of the city, in the Grave area, with the intent of taking the bridges over the river Maas and the Maas–Waal Canal. Others had landed to the southeast, between the Groesbeek Heights and the vast Reichswald forest. The latter forces, it was assumed, would march on the rail and road bridges over the river Waal at Nijmegen. To the north, the British 1st Airborne were firmly in Oosterbeek and Arnhem.

When the Americans first landed in the Nijmegen area, veteran Sergeant Major Jakob Moll was serving with a company from the German 39th Replacement Battalion. They were acting as field police, rounding up reluctant waifs and strays from Belgium and France. Moll and his inexperienced lieutenant were patrolling the woods to the south of Groesbeek hunting for deserters. When they heard the drone of aircraft, they moved forward and looked out beyond the trees. 'The field was covered with gliders', noted Moll, 'and paratroopers were dashing about.'[5] His lieutenant was all for attacking, but when Moll pointed out how ill-trained and ill-equipped their company was, for the moment battle was prudently avoided.

Elsewhere, German troops were not so lucky. At the Hotel Berg en Dal, near Beek to the east of the Groesbeek Heights, when four gunners manning a 20mm flak gun tried to surrender they were shot by paratroopers angry at being fired on in the sky.[6] As it was a Sunday afternoon, many Germans were off duty. Caught unawares, 400 were soon captured, some of whom were reportedly drunk and placed under armed guard with the Dutch Resistance.

Student and Christiansen had practically nothing with which to defend Eindhoven and Nijmegen from the Allied airborne forces, or the British ground attack. In the Best area, to the northwest of

Eindhoven, there was a weak battle group from the 59th Infantry Division. They were supported by the 3rd Police Regiment, which consisted of men in their early 40s, who had not expected to be fighting as infantry. Other units were equally unsuitable for combat. In early September, the German labour service sent a 200-strong company to Nijmegen to dig an anti-tank ditch. It consisted of 17-year-olds, half of whom were Poles. Although issued with rifles, they were given only ten rounds of ammunition. Around the same time, elderly members of the German air raid protection service, essentially air raid wardens, were sent to the Dutch border village of Wyler, southeast of Nijmegen, to dig an anti-tank ditch across the Nijmegen–Wyler road.[7]

Student was very fortunate, as the Americans had no idea that his headquarters was a mere ten miles from the 101st Airborne's drop zones. Nor did they know that elements of Zangen's 15th Army were nearby at Tilbury. These included Major-General Poppe's 59th Infantry Division and a large quantity of artillery.

Model and Student were baffled by American logic, because just as the British had done at Arnhem, the 82nd Airborne came down eight miles from the Nijmegen bridges. To get to them, the Americans would have to move through a very densely forested and in places built-up landscape. Both types of environment greatly hampered the deployment of close air support. The trees would provide welcome respite for German forces from Allied air strikes.

Student sent Colonel Henke, with his regimental parachute training staff, to organize about two battalions to take charge of the defence of Nijmegen. The core of these were to be three companies from the 6th Replacement Battalion and a company from the Hermann Göring Reserve and Training Regiment. They were supplemented by Luftwaffe personnel, some police reservists and some railway troops to form a battle group. This force, though, was woefully inadequate for Henke to hold both of Nijmegen's bridges.

German guards managed to blow up the bridge just to the south of Son, with American paratroopers only 50 yards away. This served to delay the 101st Airborne's entry into Eindhoven. Men of the

59th Infantry Division also held the second bridge over the canal at Best to the west of Son. However, farther north the crossing over the Dommel at St Oedenrode was lost to the Americans. They also took the Veghel bridges.

News filtered in from Nijmegen that the Americans had captured the vast road bridge over the Maas to the southwest of the city at Grave. At the time it was Europe's longest bridge, at almost 450 yards. It was supposedly well protected by sentries and two 20mm anti-aircraft guns, mounted in small flak towers either end of the crossing. A local garrison was billeted nearby in Grave. Alerted to the American landings, the Germans had sent two lorries full of infantry to secure the bridge. Meanwhile, four guards were killed and one wounded on the southern approaches by American paratroopers. In response, the flak towers opened fire over their heads.

It was at this stage that the German reinforcements arrived on the scene, only to run straight into trouble. The driver of the first lorry was shot and his vehicle came off the road and crashed down the embankment. The second screeched to a halt just in time. The infantry piled out of the back of both and fled towards Grave. The 20mm gunners on the southern end of the bridge were unable to depress their weapon low enough to engage their attackers. The exposed crew were promptly dealt with by three bazooka rounds, which killed two and wounded another.

To their alarm, the gunners on the northern end soon found themselves on the receiving end of the captured flak gun. Also, there were reports of enemy paratroopers approaching from the east. Sure enough, American paratroopers appeared at the Nederasselt end of the bridge. The flak crew had exactly the same problem of being unable to shoot low enough. The only real resistance came via German fire from Grave and several snipers who had tied themselves to the bridge girders. The bridge and Grave had been lost by early evening. To the east, the Americans captured the lower of the Maas–Waal Canal bridges at Heumen, but the two farther north near Malden and Hatert had been blown. Likewise, the rail bridge at Honinghutje was brought down.

In Nijmegen, the small German garrison found they had been granted a welcome breathing space on 17 September. The US 82nd Airborne concentrated mainly on securing the Groesbeek Heights to the east of the city and the open glider landing zones to the east of Groesbeek ready for the arrival of reinforcements. Some three and a half hours after the American landings, reports indicated that they had moved into a suburb a mile and a quarter southeast of Nijmegen called De Ploeg. This straddled the Nijmegen–Groesbeek highway. The American battalion deployed there showed no signs of marching on the city.

The first American patrol did not reach Nijmegen until the early evening. Then at 2200 hours some American units, having made their way through the city's suburbs, tried to secure the road bridge. Dutch Resistance counted just 19 German soldiers protecting it.[8] Alert German machine-gunners opened up on the advancing paratroopers a few blocks before they reached the defences on the Keizer Karel Plein roundabout. In the darkness, a confused firefight broke out and several buildings caught fire. Both sides resorted to brutal hand-to-hand combat.

Above the din, German vehicles could just be heard manoeuvring in the side streets, heralding the arrival of reinforcements from the 2nd SS-Panzer Corps. A German half-track traversing the road was hit by a bazooka and the surviving Panzergrenadiers escaped into the night. An SS-Captain was not so lucky and was shot trying to climb a nearby fence. Their presence clearly indicated that the Dutch Resistance had been wrong about the strength of local German defences. The Germans then brought up a self-propelled gun, which proceeded to shell the Americans. As the fighting progressed, the Americans anchored their defence on a brick schoolhouse.

The German garrison also found itself under attack to the east of the roundabout. Seven men were erecting a roadblock when they were killed by American fire. When the Americans reached a hill south of the road bridge, the Germans repulsed them using small arms, artillery and mortar fire. The defenders had successfully held the Americans at the Keizer Karel Plein, leaving the road bridge firmly in their hands.

Another American patrol seized Nijmegen's main post office after shooting the guards. The Dutch reported German demolition charges on the road bridge were to be detonated from there. The Germans quickly laid siege to the building, trapping the men, until they were finally rescued by the Guards Armoured Division. The garrison was heartened that it had dealt with these weak probing attacks, but once British tanks arrived, fending off the Allies would be a much tougher task.

Fierce Counter-Attacks

Beyond Eindhoven, one of the best places for Student to stop the Allied advance was between Son and Veghel. The latter was the northern point of the US 101st Airborne's drop zones, with the division stretched south through St Oedenrode, Son and on down to Eindhoven. Student knew he needed to concentrate all available forces either side of this exposed corridor. To the west he started gathering the 59th Infantry Division, Battle Group Huber, the 6th Parachute Regiment, and the 712th Infantry Division. On the eastern side he soon had available the tanks of the 107th Panzer Brigade and Battle Group Walther.

At Best a unit from the 18th Flak Brigade, supported by some 300 infantry from the 59th Division, had held the Americans to the east on a road junction at the edge of the Son Forest on 17 September, while at Son a battle group from the Hermann Göring Regiment managed to delay the Americans long enough to blow the bridge.

Amongst Student's reinforcements arriving from 's-Hertogenbosch was Major Hans Jungwirth's Parachute Training Replacement Regiment. The first unit, Battalion Ewald, was directed against St Oedenrode via Schijndel, which lay to the west, and another against Veghel. A regiment from the 59th Division was tasked with attacking Son via Best. Jungwirth's paratroopers were thrown into an attack towards Veghel astride the Willemsvaart Canal at 0200 hours on 18 September. This involved 300 men. They succeeded in pushing the Americans back beyond the railway bridge. This was subsequently recaptured, but Jungwirth conducted more attacks on the Americans' western perimeter.

The opening attack on the railway station at Eerde, to the southwest of Veghel, did not go so well. The force lacked heavy weapons and the inexperienced recruits blundered into the Americans in the darkness. 'The light infantry companies', recalled German military pastor Willi Schiffer, 'walked straight into the machine gun fire of the Americans who were hiding in the station.'[1] They were eventually driven out, and, supported by some flak guns, the Germans succeeded in pushing the Americans to the west of the railway bridge. Pressure was maintained throughout the night and by the afternoon they had taken the bridge. However, British armoured cars attacked Schijndel to the west and the forces at Veghel bridge were ordered to withdraw.

German reinforcements arrived at Best, to the west of Son, during the night under Major Klauck. His force, totalling 150 men, was from the 347th Infantry Division. It formed part of the 88th Corps stationed in the Netherlands under the control of 15th Army. Klauck had been stopped at Boxtel and redeployed on the personal orders of Student. 'There was quite a bit of shooting', recalled Klauck, 'as artillery arrived and registered on the enemy.'[2] Under the cover of darkness the Germans moved forward artillery, mortars and flak guns. These weapons opened up at 0520 hours on 18 September and during the morning the Germans launched two determined counter-attacks against the Americans. Both were driven off with heavy losses. The German artillery caused numerous American casualties by dropping shells onto the Son Forest where they were sheltering. The Germans also conducted aggressive patrolling, which infiltrated American positions, resulting in confused close-quarter fighting.

When American reinforcements began moving across some open farm land, Klauck thought this was a counter-attack. He sent Staff Sergeant Dorn to steady their men in the forward positions. At 1100 hours, the Germans blew the Wilhelmina Canal bridge at Best. The explosion was such that it rained debris down on nearby Americans sheltering in their foxholes. While this denied the bridge to the Allies, it also meant that Student could not reinforce the Eindhoven garrison.

The morning mist now cleared and Allied fighter-bombers materialized in the skies to pound German positions around Best. The Germans watched with amusement as these also strafed their own men. There was worse to come, as at 1450 hours Klauck saw American glider-borne reinforcements coming in. 'From knowing we were to win this battle', he lamented, 'in a moment were destined to be losers.'[3]

That afternoon, Battle Group Rink, cobbled together from trainee soldiers, flak personnel and police, gave ground at Best. General Hans Reinhard, in charge of 88th Corps, now one of the 1st Parachute Army's subordinate commands, was furious. He ordered them to take part in a counter-attack with the 59th Infantry Division. At 1700 hours the Americans renewed their efforts to get to the Wilhelmina Bridge, unaware that it was down. They advanced to within 1,000 yards, but were driven off by shelling from 88mm guns positioned on the opposite bank.

On 19 September both sides reinforced their forces, ready to renew the ongoing battle for control of Best. The American paratroopers were now backed not only by glider-borne infantry but also by British tanks and self-propelled guns. The Americans struck first, followed by a German counter-attack. Also that morning, 200 German troops were spotted marching south towards Best. Realizing they had been seen, the column moved as fast as they could, but lost 75 captured or killed by a pursuing American airborne battalion.

Major Klauck had been rattled the day before by the arrival of American gliders, and he was even more rattled by the arrival of British tanks. 'Soldiers were looking to their rear and we had radio reports from forward elements', he said, 'telling us that the front was breaking and soldiers were surrendering.'[4] These reports were correct. When British tanks began shelling a building on the main road, German soldiers started waving white flags up and down their front line. Klauck watched as tanks headed south towards the canal, while others began to shell his positions.

Other than machine guns, Klauck and his men had nothing with which to hold the enemy armour at bay. When he ran forward to try to stop one of the neighbouring platoons from surrendering, he was captured. The 59th Division, unable to stand up to the enemy's armour, crumpled at 1400 hours. German resistance in the bridge area had ceased by 1730 hours and around 550 men had been captured. When a German artillery battery opened up from the far bank of the canal, the British tanks moved to silence it. Farther east, surviving German infantry in the Son Forest were rooted out.

After three days, around 800 of the 2,500 German troops defending the Best area were dead and 1,042 captured. Amongst those captured were the doctors and orderlies from a German field hospital. They lost 15 88mm guns and other pieces of artillery. The Americans and British, though, did not press home their attack on Best, and it was left occupied for another month.

Apart from manpower, Student was critically short of tanks. While his forces had a few Panzers, tank destroyers and self-propelled guns, they did not provide him with much punch. It therefore came as welcome news that he had been assigned Major Freiherr von Maltzahn's brand-new 107th Panzer Brigade. Farther north, the first of seven infantry battalions belonging to the 2nd Parachute Corps had moved into the Reichswald on the right flank of the US 82nd Airborne. Although these were the usual pick-and-mix units, they included two tough parachute battalions – or so it was thought. To help Bittrich at Arnhem, more armour was on the way, in the shape of the 208th Assault Gun Brigade and the 506th Heavy Tank Battalion.

Despite the Allies' attack in the Netherlands, fighting was continuing all along the Western and Eastern Fronts, so there were few German armoured units to spare. Most of the mauled Panzer divisions had been withdrawn for refitting, and Hitler's newly created Panzer brigades had been sent south to counter General Patton's US 3rd Army in Lorraine. These brigades were formed using units salvaged from the destruction of Army Group Centre on the Eastern Front that summer. Three had already been destroyed in France during September. Although called brigades, the first ten such units were really little more than regimental strength. In theory, each had 36 Panthers, 11 Jagdpanzer IVs and four Flakpanzers.[5]

The Panther was an awesome piece of kit. After the Russian T-34, it was the best tank of the entire war. However, it was only awesome in trained hands. In untrained hands, it was like any other weapon of war – a death trap. The new Panther crews needed first to train together at battalion level, and then at brigade level with their supporting Panzergrenadier battalion in order to fight effectively. Often, neither type of training took place, or was wholly inadequate.

Nevertheless, Student rubbed his hands together with enthusiasm at the thought of the 107th Brigade. It comprised a battalion of Panther tanks, a battalion of motorized Panzergrenadiers transported in armoured half-tracks, a self-propelled gun company and a company of engineers. The gun company may have been equipped with armoured cars armed with a close support 75mm howitzer, similar to those issued to the 106th Panzer Brigade sent to Lorraine. This force offered Student a real chance to cut off the British advance. He wanted Maltzahn to strike westwards along the Wilhelmina Canal to attack Son, where the Guards Armoured Division had built a replacement bridge. If the brigade could then cut its way to St Oedenrode, this would completely sever the British push on Grave, southwest of Nijmegen.

No one had told Student this brigade was actually a very poor-quality unit that had been formed from the ashes of the 25th Panzergrenadier Division. The remains of the latter had been withdrawn from the Eastern Front after being crushed by the Red Army.[6] Using the few survivors and the 215th Panzergrenadier Training and Replacement Battalion, the brigade had come into being in mid-July 1944 at Mochove in East Prussia near Mielau. Training had not gone well, owing to sabotage and the late arrival of equipment. Lubricants had been deliberately contaminated by Czech workers, which caused engine problems. Despite these issues, the brigade was deemed fully combat ready on 15 September.

Maltzahn's command was sent to Helmond to the northeast of Eindhoven. By the afternoon of 19 September, some 40 of his Panthers were gathered in Molenheide Woods to the east of Son. Despite Student's orders, Maltzahn was unenthusiastic about his mission. The Dutch countryside was not conducive to the mass deployment of his armoured brigade, as it consisted either of woods or open soft, sandy ground, neither of which was good tank country. He was anticipating assistance from the 59th Division, but it was stuck at Best. Crucially, intelligence regarding his enemy's location and intentions was not forthcoming. As a result, he was essentially operating blind. These three factors mitigated against the success of his operation, and Maltzahn knew it.

Furthermore, with the British at Eindhoven, it would not be long before their tanks were pushing on Maltzahn's left flank, so he would have to protect that. Likewise, he would need to safeguard his right flank by getting some of his tanks over the Wilhelmina Canal. This he could do by using the bridges north of Molenheide. Both requirements meant dissipating his attack on Son. In the centre, though, the American airborne forces, equipped only with bazookas and 57mm anti-tank guns, would be almost powerless against his Panthers. His hope was that the lightly armed Americans, once under pressure, would give ground and abandon Son.

Maltzahn decided first to probe American defences at Son from the southeast, using half a dozen tanks supported by dismounted infantry from the 1034th Grenadier Regiment. The biggest problem he faced was that to attack Son from the south, he would have to get over the Dommel and the canal. His best hope was a subsidiary bridge to the east, but he soon discovered that this had been blown up by a German unit days earlier. His only other option was to trundle his tanks along the canal towpath towards the British Bailey bridge, which would expose them to fire from the far bank and enemy fighter-bombers once they emerged from the cover of the trees. There could be little element of surprise when deploying a 45-ton tank, belching out petrol fumes from its powerful and very noisy V-12 engine.

At 1700 hours two Dutchmen on bicycles spotted the approaching tanks and rode off to warn the Americans, who had only a platoon of infantry and some engineers protecting the Bailey bridge. Just 15 minutes later, a high-explosive 75mm tank round from a Panther with the northern flanking force crashed through the local church tower. The explosion showered debris everywhere and shook the whole village. At the same time, the Germans began shelling the school building, located between Son and the bridge. Maltzahn ordered the destruction of the church on the grounds it was being used as an observation post and the school as it was likely to be an enemy headquarters.

In the meantime, on the canal path Maltzahn's lead tank had got within range of the Bailey bridge. The gunner zeroed in on an ammunition truck just as it was crossing and fired. The vehicle immediately exploded into a ball of flames, blocking the bridge with burning wreckage. It was round one to Maltzahn. However, his supporting grenadiers, who should have been dealing with enemy anti-tank teams, were pinned down by fire coming from a school. Suddenly two bazooka rounds shot past the lead tank, while a third bounced uselessly off its sloping frontal armour.

Although exposed out in the open on the towpath, the Panther tank commander rotated his turret and fired five high-explosive rounds in quick succession into the school. His tank then juddered as an American 57mm round tore into the wheels, disabling it. The crew, with their Panzer now completely stranded, had no option but to bale out. Just as they did so, several more rounds hit their stricken tank. The hull caught fire, and as the ammunition 'cooked off' the turret was blown up and forward off the turret ring. The 75mm gun was left pointing uselessly down towards the ground. The towpath was now blocked.

When a second Panther was knocked out by a bazooka, it was evident that the Americans were determined to hold their ground. The lack of support from the grenadiers left the remaining Panthers vulnerable and the crews were loath to press on. The Panzers began withdrawing, along with the grenadiers, with both groups unhelpfully heading in opposite directions.

To complicate matters for Maltzahn, British tanks and American paratroopers had reached Nuenen to the south and bumped into his screening force. This consisted of some Panthers, supported by 88mm guns, well concealed amongst the trees and bushes. Despite a warning from the Americans, the gung-ho British tankers were taken by surprise. A German tank hit the first British Cromwell, turning it into a blazing inferno. The crew frantically baled out, leaving the tank in gear, and it continued to roll forward. Foolishly, a second British tank advanced and received the same treatment. Then the hidden German guns opened up. In total four British Cromwell tanks were swiftly destroyed and the rest of the force withdrew towards Eindhoven.

That night the Luftwaffe hit the city with 70 bombers, thereby hampering the Guards Armoured Division's advance even more. Their target was a British supply column, and when they met no flak they made a number of unopposed bombing runs. In the process their bombs were scattered widely, killing 227 civilians and wounding 800. Eindhoven was left badly damaged. Student's fierce counter-attacks had yet to produce positive results.

11

Reichswald Assault

German forces in the Nijmegen area, although confused by events, were not idle. The Americans had got into the town of Groesbeek southeast of the city on Sunday 17 September with little difficulty. They had also set up blocking positions to the east facing the Reichswald Forest, which formed the German border. These were out of the range of small arms fire, though German snipers made their presence felt. The German authorities in Nijmegen and the Reichswald seemed to have little idea of the extent of the American landings or their obejectives. During the night, a German train caught the Americans napping and barrelled right through Groesbeek towards Nijmegen before they realized what was happening. When a second train attempted this, it was stopped by an American bazooka team and the dazed occupants were rounded up and taken away.

While there were no forces available to oppose the Americans' western perimeter, to the east units were rapidly summoned from Germany. Major Rasch, the adjutant of the 406th Infantry Division, had been minding his own business at their headquarters near Krefeld on 17 September. His division was little more than an administrative office, overseeing training units and replacement battalions. It was certainly not a combat command, and work was mundane. Rasch knew that trouble was brewing because the 6th Replacement Battalion had signalled, 'Nijmegen detachment surrounded, support urgently requested'.[1]

His telephone rang at 2100 hours, and after Rasch had taken the call from his commander, General Gerd Scherbening, he stood mouth agape. They were to move to Nijmegen in the next six hours. 'Only an expert in such matters can appreciate what it means to change from a barracks-based staff organization, with no equipment or vehicles', said Rasch, 'and turn it into a mobile field headquarters.'[2] He then set to work conjuring an infantry division from thin air.

Scherbening called an urgent staff meeting at 0200 hours. The 406th were to counter-attack the US 82nd Airborne Division at Nijmegen as soon as possible. First his headquarters was to relocate to Geldern, and a tactical headquarters was to be established on the Kranenberg–Nijmegen road at Kreugers-Gut. They were to come under the command of General Kurt Feldt's *ad hoc* Corps Feldt. The news from Nijmegen was not good, and Rasch warned, 'the three companies in Nijmegen must be regarded as write offs'.[3] Colonel Henke's forces, numbering about 750 men, could do little more than hold the two enclaves south of the rail and road bridges.

Although General Feldt was promised manpower, there was the problem of transport for ammunition and rations. Rasch solved this by requisitioning every vehicle he could lay his hands on. By 0630 hours the following morning, Scherbening and Rasch found they miraculously had four battle groups numbering some 2,650 men ready for the attack. These forces had been created from infirmary cases, NCO instructors, World War I veterans and surplus Luftwaffe staff. The bulk of them were infantry, armed with old rifles, though they were supported by 130 machine guns and 24 mortars, as well as three detachments of howitzers and some flak guns. Heavy support was provided by Captain Freiherr von Fuerstenberg's five armoured cars and three half-tracks, armed with quad 20mm anti-aircraft guns. They had no tanks, assault guns or self-propelled guns, though.

Feldt, on surveying the array of different uniforms belonging to convalescent soldiers, signallers, medical orderlies, sailors and Luftwaffe personnel, called them a 'motley crowd'. Including blocking forces to hold a line behind the battle groups, Feldt's command totalled around 3,400. They were completely inadequate to take on a combat-hardened American airborne division, and Feldt knew it. Nonetheless, three of the battle groups, dubbed Greschick, Fuerstenberg and Stargaard, were to strike the Americans between Beek through Wyler to Groesbeek. A fourth, Goebel, which included elements of the 39th Replacement Battalion, was to attack Mook to the southwest on the Maas. Morale of these units varied enormously.

'I had no confidence in this attack', confessed General Feldt. 'But it was necessary... in order to forestall an enemy advance to the east, and to deceive him in regard to our strength.'[4] Model promised Feldt that by the afternoon of 18 September he would be backed by the 3rd and 5th parachute divisions, tough Normandy veterans. In the meantime, Feldt's only hope was to overwhelm the Americans, who were stretched thin along their extensive 25-mile defensive perimeter, by sheer weight of numbers alone.

General Scherbening and his adjutant moved to a forward command post to watch the main assault on Groesbeek. They were not encouraged when they witnessed some of their men forming up, equipped only with old Czech machine guns that had been captured after the dismembering of Czechoslovakia in 1939. Likewise, the sight of Captain Gruenenklee's battalion, consisting of elderly World War I veterans, was extremely disheartening.

In places, the attack got off to a good start, especially in the Mook area. This was because the Germans infiltrated through the woods so close to the Americans' positions that they almost ambushed them in their own outposts. 'My men will soon kick you right off this hill', warned an angry German colonel captured during the opening stages.[5] For a time they swarmed through the 82nd Airborne's defences, overrunning their trenches, as well as ammunition and supply dumps.

Briefly, it seemed as if victory might be attainable. The sacrifice of the battle groups might just prevent a second American airlift. However, it was foolhardy to believe that low-calibre German infantry could prevail against experienced and determined American paratroopers. General Feldt's gloom proved well founded.

American glider-borne reinforcements were due to arrive at 1200 hours, so the 82nd Airborne threw everything it had into the fight to keep the Germans at bay. Scherbening's attempts to get farther onto the landing zones east of Groesbeek struggled to make any headway in the face of this stiff resistance. His men were shelled and mortared at every turn. The 12 guns of the 82nd's artillery battalion fired 315 rounds in the first 24 hours and the crews took 400 prisoners.[6]

A troubled Captain Gruenenklee radioed Scherbening to advise that his men were being shot at from both sides and were now pinned down. Their attack towards Groesbeek had stalled. Scherbening turned to Rasch with an exasperated expression. 'Take over his task', ordered the general. 'If we don't get Groesbeek inside half an hour, the whole attack will have had it!'[7] Rasch took with him a machine-gun section to try and boost Gruenenklee's attack. He found them taking fire on the boundary of some trees.

Major Rasch valiantly did his best to rally the World War I veterans. 'Can't you see', he yelled, 'that it's up to us old boys to run the whole show again.'[8] The 'old boys' who had gone to ground rose reluctantly to their feet and began to advance again. Luckily for them, the Americans were firing high and inflicted few casualties.

Not long afterwards, Rasch was informed that Field Marshal Model had arrived, demanding a situation report. He was summoned to headquarters and handed command back to Captain Gruenenklee. Midday came and went and the fighting continued for another two hours, during which time Feldt's battle groups expended the last of their ammunition and energy.

Bad weather delayed the American reinforcements, but they finally arrived at 1400 hours. Beforehand, those Germans on the landing zones were machine-gunned and bombed. 'Enemy aircraft formations covered the entire sky', said Rasch. 'Then gliders came down at every conceivable place... gliders were landing as if on a normal field.'[9] This show of strength was too much for the inexperienced German troops.

The Americans did not have it all their own way, however. Some German units inflicted significant losses. Men of the 1st Replacement Battalion operating in the Bruck–Horst area, supported by an anti-aircraft gun, shot up the incoming gliders. The surviving airborne infantry were forced back towards Groesbeek and their equipment captured. Corporal Kronenburg took a newly delivered jeep as booty and drove it to Wasserburg.

On the northern landing zone, the Americans, seemingly heedless of the Germans' anti-aircraft and small-arms fire, charged downhill to clear their tormentors. The Germans turned tail and ran, leaving behind losses that included 50 dead, 149 prisoners and 16 large-calibre weapons. In the meantime, to the south, Battle Group Goebel's attack towards Mook collapsed and the 39th Battalion panicked. Before long, all the battle groups were fleeing eastwards.

Feldt and Scherbening had great difficulty stopping their men from stampeding deep into Germany. The general himself narrowly escaped capture near Papen Hill. When some semblance of order was restored, they found that members of the 39th Battalion and the Viennese Luftwaffe 'fortress' battalions had fled far into the sanctuary of the Reichswald. For the moment, Corps Feldt had all but ceased to exist.

General Feldt, desperate for reinforcements, made his way to Emmerich to inspect the two divisions of General Meindl's 2nd Parachute Corps. Field Marshal Model's headquarters had informed him that they were combat ready. Instead, he was horrified to discover there were just two weak battalions, made up of logistical personnel, who had escaped from Normandy. They were hardly front-line troops and had few heavy weapons.

Shortly after, Model arrived at Kreugers-Gut for a conference with Feldt, Meindl and Rasch. Model likewise discovered that Meindl's corps was a shadow of its former self. During the Normandy campaign, apart from its assigned parachute divisions, it was also supposed to have almost 9,000 men in supporting combat units. In reality they numbered just under 3,400, and they had suffered over 1,500 killed, wounded and missing.

Meindl was reminded of the bad old days in 1942, when he commanded a division made up of Luftwaffe field regiments on the Eastern Front. There they fought as infantry. He lacked supporting weapons and his men improvised by using a battery of captured Russian field guns. He waited almost a year before he received any trained gunners. Nonetheless, Division Meindl's conduct was such that it got mentioned in dispatches. He now wondered if his latest recruits would fight with such vigour; deep down he doubted it. They were simply not ready.

Knowing that Eindhoven was lost and the fighting was ongoing at Arnhem, Model insisted they must attack at Nijmegen again on 19 September. Feldt refused in light of the weakness of their forces and because they were still rounding them up. Grudgingly Model conceded and said that only battle groups Becker and Hermann, drawn from the parachute corps, would attack in the Wyler–Zyfflich area the following day. At this point Meindl intervened, saying that Major Becker from the 3rd and Captain Hermann from the 5th parachute divisions needed more time to prepare. An exasperated Model acquiesced to delaying things for a day. Later Rasch took a call; Corporal Kronenburg had been killed in a road accident involving his new jeep and a bus.

Model's constant urging for action was understandable. He was worried that the Allies would realize just how weak his containment forces were and would renew their efforts to get to Arnhem. They must be held at Nijmegen, or, if the worst came to the worst, in the Betuwe, the flood plain between the Waal and the Rhine.

Remarkably, on Tuesday 19 September Corps Feldt managed to put together four battalions, around 2,000 men. This says much for the German officers and NCOs who succeeded in cajoling their dispirited men back into the line. Fighting during the day was to be localized, but in places was very intense. A hill overlooking the Wyler–Nijmegen road, east of the Hotel Berg en Dal, changed hands four times in 24 hours. It was hoped that such actions would help alleviate some of the growing pressure on the Nijmegen garrison.

Meanwhile, General Feldt prepared his attack for 20 September. Once again, he doubted that it had much prospect of success, and it was essentially a rerun of his previous operation. Nor was the quality of his troops any better. Nonetheless, Model insisted that these spoiling attacks were buying valuable time. Feldt planned to commence his three-pronged attack at 0630 hours.

In the north, Major Becker was instructed to take Beek and the nearby hills, with the aim of reaching the Maas–Waal Canal to the west of Nijmegen. Once there, he was to link up with Battle Group Hermann striking north from Mook. Becker's battle group, with over 800 men, consisted of the remains of the 3rd Parachute Division and some elements from the 406th Division. Heavy weaponry comprised a single 88mm and a few 20mm guns.

He opened his attack by mortaring American positions all along the line. A battalion of infantry, supported by Captain Fuerstenberg's self-propelled 20mm anti-aircraft guns, was thrown at Beek. The flak guns poured devastating fire into the houses held by the 82nd Airborne. The American defence consisted of just two platoons, and they were driven back after some tough street fighting. Both sides became so preoccupied with the battle that the Germans failed to sidestep into Nijmegen. By midnight, Becker's forces had been driven out of Beek and the Americans had again cut the Wyler–Nijmegen road.

To the southeast, straddling the Dutch-German border, was the village of Wyler. If it fell to the Americans, this posed an immediate threat to German soil. As part of General Feldt's renewed attack, infantry tried to occupy the Dutch half. They soon discovered the Americans had beaten them to it. When a lorry carrying a platoon drove up the road, it was hit by an American 57mm gun. Any survivors quickly scattered. During the afternoon, thanks to a more determined attack, the Germans managed to push the Americans back, but they then ran out of steam.

Albrich Zieggler, a 17-year-old with the 3rd Parachute Division, recalled, 'I had been mobilized two months earlier... I was so proud to be a parachutist.' Marching past Wyler, he saw dead and wounded lying in the streets. 'It was a shock to see the corpse of a senior veteran that we youngsters looked up to.'[10] Moving through the woods to their attack point, they came under fire. Zieggler was immediately wounded below the knee and captured. He had to endure German shelling for four days before he was moved to a hospital in Eindhoven.

Farther south, at 0800 hours, 350 men of the 526th Infantry Battalion attacked through Horst towards Groesbeek, forming part of Battle Group Greschick. This unit was fresh from Germany and had been formed only on 17 September. It included reluctant convalescents from the Eastern Front, pressed-ganged straight out of hospital, one of whom still had an open wound. The men were mainly armed with rifles, with just two light machine guns per company and no mortars. As only two companies were committed to the assault, with one held in reserve, it meant there were just four light machine guns to provide covering fire for over 200 men.

The battalion commander was told that his right flank would be supported by a flak division, but this in reality was thought to be only of company strength, with a few guns. In the face of American firepower, his attack soon petered out. Other elements of the battle group did reach the outskirts of Groesbeek. These consisted of two weak battalions, backed by 14 20mm flak guns. The latter at least forced the Americans to keep their heads down.

Battle Group Hermann, supplemented by Goebel, which had failed previously at Mook, also made good progress. This was in part because it was supported by an artillery battery with four 105mm howitzers from the 6th Parachute Division. It also had four anti-aircraft guns firing in a ground-support role. By late afternoon they had captured Riedhorst and Mook and were threatening the Heumen bridge over the Maas–Waal Canal. This was now in British hands. Hermman, though, could get no farther and an American counter-attack supported by British tanks drove them out of Mook.

Feldt reinforced his attacks, employing an assault pioneer battalion under Major Molzer, a parachute battalion under Lieutenant-Colonel Budde and a battalion-size battle group commanded by Captain Lewin. These forces numbered only about 900 men and made little difference to the outcome of the battle. At 2125 hours Scherbening signalled Feldt, trying to put a gloss on things. He said that although resistance had been met at Groesbeek and Mook, they had taken Wyler and Riedhorst. The reality was that the American perimeter remained intact. Model, though, was more concerned about events unfolding in nearby Nijmegen.

12

Resistance at the Valkhof

At Pannerden, a detachment of Harmel's anti-aircraft gunners deployed their weapons to protect the exposed ferry. It seemed unlikely the Allied fighter-bombers would leave them alone, and come daylight their fears were rapidly confirmed. Frustratingly for Harmel and Paetsch, 16 tanks arrived at the crossing, but they were far too heavy for the ferry. Engineers were summoned to construct a 40-ton raft, though that would take precious time. The crews of four Jagdpanzer IV tank destroyers, which were of a similar weight, decided to chance their luck with the ferry and got over the river.

The lack of tanks did not really matter. What the Germans really needed to prevent the British and Americans from getting over the Waal was artillery. Harmel's gunnery commander, SS-Lieutenant-Colonel Sonnenstahl, reported that he had 72 guns, some of which had been rounded up in Arras from an abandoned train. The ferry was more than capable of transporting these. Sonnenstahl already had two gunnery officers down in Nijmegen, SS-Captains Krueger and Schwappacher.

Once SS-Lieutenant Baumgaertel had crossed with his company of engineers, he was sent to Nijmegen first with instructions to prepare the road and rail bridges for demolition. He was cautioned that these were to be blown only on the explicit orders of Field Marshal Model. The engineers were also to help strengthen the defences at the southern end of the road bridge. They got there using the usual trusted combination of stolen bicycles and commandeered trucks.

At about noon, SS-Captain Karl-Heinz Euling arrived at Nijmegen with a hundred men. Having got out of Arnhem, he had not gone via Pannerden, but instead made use of a ferry at Huissen. He then moved through Elst and south. Euling joined SS-Captain Leo Hermann Reinhold at his command post in Lent, on the northern bank of the Waal. This village lay sandwiched between the railway and the road. Reinhold was charged with holding this side of the river, while Euling with Baumgaertel was to protect the south side and reinforce Colonel Henke's forces. The Jagdpanzers rumbled over the road bridge, but Allied fire was so heavy it was impossible to get the infantry across other than by armoured half-track. The paratroopers of Battle Group Henke were already engaged fighting Americans from the US 82nd Airborne Division in the southern suburbs of the city.

Euling and some of his men drove across the bridge as fast as they could, hoping for the best. When they pitched up on bicycles that afternoon, the rest of his battalion had to get across using rubber boats. Meanwhile, Euling and his forces, once over the bridge, veered to the southeast and into Hunner Park to link up with Battle Group Henke.

While the German defence was short of infantry, the 10th SS was clearly able to provide a reasonable level of artillery support. SS-Captain Schwappacher, who had been in charge of the 5th SS Artillery Training and Replacement Regiment, was instructed to arrange the fire-support plan for Nijmegen. He did this by traipsing the streets on foot, mapping the most likely entry routes that the enemy would take. Southwest and southeast of the bridges were two large traffic circles, which would provide chokepoints before the enemy reached their main defences. He also mapped out the immediate approaches to both bridges. The guns were deployed along the northern river bank, while SS-Captain Krueger set up an artillery observation post in the Belvedere tower, just to the southwest of the road bridge.

The challenge facing Euling was how best to defend Nijmegen. There were simply not enough troops to hold the entire perimeter of the city and in any case this had already been penetrated by the Americans. He decided his best option was to set up blocking positions in the gardens and ruins of an old palace known as the Valkhof and in the neighbouring Hunner Park. To protect the western approaches to the Valkhof, his men turned the police station into a strongpoint. Other buildings in the area were likewise barricaded and fortified.

The medieval chapel in the Valkhof gardens dominated both the southern and northern approaches to the road bridge. To the northeast of this building, a pillbox had been built into the old walls of the Valkhof. Its machine guns covered the western approaches to the bridge. These strongpoints would provide a fall-back position when the time came. The grounds of the Valkhof were separated from the Belvedere and Hunner Park by a road running through a cutting known as the Voerweg. They were linked by an ornamental footbridge accessible from the Kelfkenbosch. South of the park was the Keizer Lodewijk Plein traffic circle; from this ran the Arnhemseweg, leading to the bridge. Hunner Park extended either side of the Arnhemseweg. The northwestern part of the park was dominated by the Belvedere, beyond which was the Valkhof.

Euling's men entrenched themselves in and around Hunner Park as best they could, supported by the four Jagdpanzers, five light guns and an 88mm deployed at the traffic circle. The Valkhof and Krueger's observation post were defended by Baumgaertel's armed engineers. Colonel Henke's parachute forces were responsible for holding the rail bridge a mile to the west. The main route to it was from the Keizer Karel Plein along the Kronenburgsingel. On the eastern side of this, Battle Group Henke set up defensive positions in Kronenburger Park. Krueger sent SS-Sergeant Hotop to artillery spot for Henke's men. Sandwiched between the three parks, the traffic circles and the Waal was a huge sprawl of buildings that offered the Germans further defensive positions.

Understandably, Bittrich and Harmel desperately wanted to blow the Nijmegen bridges. Both felt it would be easier to mount a defence on the far bank. This would also seal the fate of the British 1st Airborne at Arnhem. However, Model was insistent that they were needed for a counter-attack, although quite where he thought the troops were coming from no one seemed to know. In Model's defence, he had been encouraged by the slow progress of the 82nd Airborne.

The fighting in and around the American Groesbeek landing zones greatly weakened the Americans' ability to take the Nijmegen bridges on 18 September. This did not stop them from trying to circle east towards the road bridge. They were pushing back the German police reservists when SS-Captain Schwappacher's artillery intervened. He noted 'the attack was brought to a halt with precise salvoes dropped amongst the leading waves'.[1] This shelling caught the American paratroopers by surprise and they were forced to take shelter or suffer the consequences.

The Germans then counter-attacked, using their newly arrived SS-Panzergrenadiers. 'Our own infantry now reinforced... supported by further artillery fire', said Schwappacher, 'were able to force the enemy well back to the south.'[2] Model convinced himself that his growing strength in Nijmegen meant that he did not need to demolish the bridges. The Americans would not be able to take them without the help of British tanks.

At 1445 hours on Tuesday 19 September, Model got the news he did not want to hear. Meindl's 2nd Parachute Corps reported enemy vehicles heading for Nijmegen from the southwest. It was not long before British armoured cars, tanks and artillery arrived in the city and soon made their presence felt. In support of the 82nd Airborne, they were involved in a shooting match with German 88mm guns in the Lent area on the far side of the river. When British artillery opened up, Schwappacher responded with counter-battery fire. This engagement lasted for 90 minutes and the city echoed with the sound of gunfire. The Germans braced themselves for the inevitable attacks on their bridge defences.

To the southeast, fighting erupted in the vicinity of the Keizer Lodwijk Plein when the British and Americans tried to force their way through to the road bridge. They were met by defences comprising trenches, barbed wire and strongpoints created from local buildings. For the loss of an anti-tank gun, the Germans destroyed three British tanks. The defenders also managed to stop British infantry from trying to outflank them. An 88mm gun was then used to hit a building the British were using to shoot down on German positions. Nijmegen began to burn.

Artillery observer SS-Sergeant Hotop reported to Schwappacher that he could see tanks to the southwest. This indicated the Allies were going to try and grab the railway bridge from Henke's battle group. Thanks to a Dutch guide, they had circled in from the west. As the column of British tanks and supporting American paratroopers approached, machine-gunners holed up in a house opened fire, with predictable results. The leading Sherman tank swivelled its 75mm gun and blasted them into silence. Just to the south of the bridge, the defenders in Kronenburger Park braced themselves for the armoured onslaught.

The methodical Schwappacher had already produced a fire plan for this area. The railway line and embankment heading north from the station towards the bridge provided an ideal killing ground. Hotop called in the coordinates with considerable accuracy. His shells landed just as the British tried to storm the embankment opening, successfully hitting two of their tanks. Two German self-propelled guns moved forward to engage the enemy column. The Americans fared no better, coming under machine-gun fire from all sides. Now that it was getting dark, the fighting died down, though the night sky was illuminated by burning buildings and tracer fire.

The defenders of the southern end of the road bridge came under attack again at 0800 hours on Wednesday 20 September. British tanks began to push up the ring road towards the Valkhof gardens. The fighting was bitter and close quarter. Euling and Baumgaertel consolidated their positions in Hunner Park and the Valkhof. To attack either strongpoint, British tanks would have to cross the open expanse of the Kelfkenbosch. Euling's headquarters, located in Haus Robert Jannssen, just to the east of the latter, was defended by about 150 men.

THE BATTLE FOR NIJMEGEN, 20 SEPTEMBER 1944

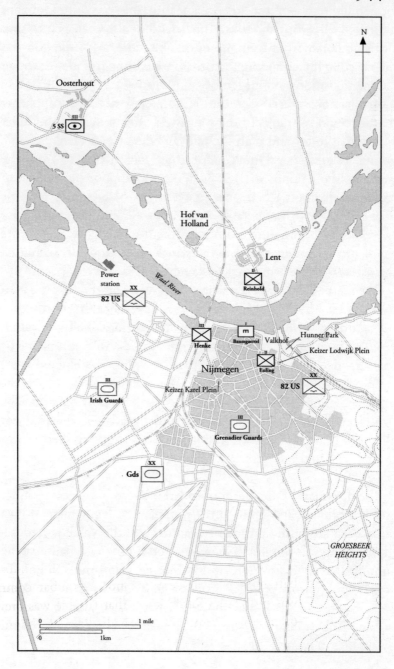

Field Marshal Walther Model was taken by surprise by the Allied airborne landings in the Netherlands on 17 September 1944. (Bettmann/Getty images)

Camouflaged Waffen-SS anti-tank gunners in France in the summer of 1944.
The German collapse there led to a swift retreat to the Low Countries. (Photo by
Keystone-France\Gamma-Rapho via Getty Images)

Belgian Resistance with a captured German self-propelled gun on the streets of
Antwerp. The arrival of the British in the city and in Brussels was a potential disaster for
the Germans in northwest Europe. (Photo by Hulton Archive/Getty Images)

General Gustav-Adolf von Zangen, to the left of Field Marshal Erwin Rommel, was tasked with rescuing the German 15th Army. (Photo by ullstein bild/ullstein bild via Getty Images)

Arthur Seyss-Inquart, the Reichskommissar for the Netherlands, with Adolf Hitler. (Photo by Heinrich Hoffmann/ullstein bild via Getty Images)

Zangen, centre, conducted a highly successful fighting withdrawal to Walcheren on the Scheldt Estuary. (Photo by ullstein bild/ullstein bild via Getty Images)

Anton Mussert, the Dutch fascist leader, meeting Hitler. (Photo by ullstein bild/ullstein bild via Getty Images)

General Kurt Student, founder of Hitler's airborne forces and commander of 1st Parachute Army. (Photo by ullstein bild/ullstein bild via Getty Images)

SS-General Wilhelm Bittrich's 2nd SS-Panzer Corps just happened to be recuperating in the Arnhem area at the time of the Allied airborne landings. (Photo by Heinrich Hoffmann/ullstein bild via Getty Images)

In the summer of 1944 the Arnhem road bridge had only just reopened, having been destroyed at the start of the war. (Photo by Picture Post/Hulton Archive/Getty Images)

Model, Student, Bittrich, Knaust and Harmel all played key roles in the German victory at Arnhem. (Photo by ullstein bild/ullstein bild via Getty Images)

Model being briefed by SS-Brigadier Heinz Harmel, commander of 10th SS-Panzer Division. (Photo by ullstein bild/ullstein bild via Getty Images)

A German soldier captured at Valkenswaard being questioned by members of the Dutch Resistance. (Photo by Jack Esten/PNA Rota/Getty Images)

Arnhem road bridge, showing the wrecked vehicles after SS-Captain Paul Gräbner's
column was ambushed on the northern ramp on 18 September 1944.
(Photo by Pen & Sword/SSPL/Getty Images)

German prisoners gathered on Nijmegen road bridge. (Photo by Hulton-Deutsch/
Hulton-Deutsch Collection/Corbis via Getty Images)

The devastation inflicted on central Nijmegen, where the fighting was intense.
(Photo by Hulton Archive/Getty Images)

German troops amongst British debris left behind in Arnhem.
(Photo by ullstein bild/ullstein bild via Getty Images)

A German self-propelled flak gun in Arnhem, mopping up the last pockets of resistance.
(Photo by ullstein bild/ullstein bild via Getty Images)

A dug-in German flak gun on the streets of Arnhem.
(Photo by ullstein bild/ullstein bild via Getty Images)

SS-Grenadiers with captured British paratroopers from 1st Airborne.
(Photo by ullstein bild/ullstein bild via Getty Images)

British airborne forces going into captivity.
(Photo by ullstein bild/ullstein bild via Getty Images)

A knocked-out German Panzer Mk III in the village of Oosterhout.
(Bettmann/Getty Images)

A British soldier guarding Nijmegen bridge. This was vital for maintaining the Betuwe bridgehead after the battle for Arnhem. (Photo © CORBIS/Corbis via Getty Images)

A sketch showing German demolition frogmen blowing up the Nijmegen railway bridge on 29 September 1944. (Photo by Universal History Archive/Universal Images Group via Getty Images)

An artist's impression of the German demolition frogmen captured at Nijmegen. They failed to destroy the road bridge. (Photo by Universal History Archive/Universal Images Group via Getty Images)

Arnhem road bridge being bombed by the Americans. It was destroyed on 7 October 1944. (Photo by Photo12/UIG/Getty Images)

British forces finally liberating Arnhem in April 1945. (Photo by Pen and Sword Books/ Universal Images Group via Getty Images)

On the far side of the Waal, west of the railway bridge, Reinhold's forces had burrowed into the dyke, which dominated the flat land along the river's edge. They had also taken over the old ramparts of Fort Hof van Holland, which was surrounded by a moat. Inside they deployed mortars, which were being used to provide fire support for the troops in Nijmegen. Just before 1500 hours on 20 September these defences were heavily shelled by the Guards Armoured Division. Its fire was concentrated on the trenches along the dyke. Afterwards smoke rounds began to drop along the river bank.

Then, to their amazement, the Germans watched as men of the 82nd Airborne began frantically paddling across the wide river towards them in flimsy assault boats. German manpower here was thin, comprising a few paratroopers, gunners, pioneers and Luftwaffe personnel. Realizing what was happening, they opened up with rifles, submachine guns, machine guns, mortars and 20mm cannon in a bid to stop this outrageous river assault. A flak gun deployed on the northern embankment of the railway bridge joined in, raking the water and the near shore.

Schwappacher's guns at Oosterhout, which had been firing into Nijmegen, were now redirected onto the Americans' departure and landing points. His gunners were given permission to fire 250 rounds. German shells and mortar bombs threw up great geysers that shot from the river's surface. In places some boats capsized, and their occupants were thrown into the water dead or wounded. Men were also hit in the surviving vessels and slumped back, no longer able to paddle. It seemed as if none could survive this deadly deluge.

However, despite this firestorm, the Americans did not stop or turn back. Miraculously, the soaked survivors reached the shore and began to engage the defenders behind the dyke. Their bloodlust was up and they offered little quarter. Regardless of German fire, more Americans crossed, along with their heavy support weapons such as anti-tank guns and mortars. 'The enemy reached the north side in regimental strength', reported Schwappacher despondently.[3]

The calibre of German soldiers in this area was not good, and most fled rather than come face to face with the tough American paratroopers. Reinhold's adjutant SS-Second Lieutenant Gernot Traupel observed 'they looked to me like children'.[4] At first, the German teenagers were surprised by the audacity and foolhardy bravery of their enemy. Rapidly that surprise turned to terror at the thought of those men once over the water coming to kill them. When a counter-attack was attempted, Schwappacher recalled, 'I never ever saw these troops again'.[5] His gunners now had to conduct an all-round defence at Oosterhout, while continuing to provide fire for the Valkhof directed by SS-Captain Krueger.

At his headquarters in the village of Doornenburg, east of Pannerden, Harmel was trying to cope with a never-ending stream of situation reports from his scattered units. He was handed one just after 1600 hours that caused him some alarm: 'a white smoke screen has been thrown across the river opposite Fort Hof van Holland'.[6] This indicated that the Allies were trying to get over the Waal by boat. He scoffed at the notion, as the river was far too wide nor did the Allies have the resources at Nijmegen.

Nonetheless, Harmel remained troubled by this news. What else could the smoke mean? Could it be that they were planning another airborne landing? He knew that it was his neck that was on the line. 'I had no intention of being arrested and shot by Berlin for letting the bridges fall into enemy hands', he said, 'no matter how Model felt about it.'[7] He decided perhaps he had better go and have a look for himself. Summoning his staff car, Harmel sped off towards Lent. By late afternoon he was in a bunker to the east of the road bridge. Having lost contact with Euling, he was agonizing over what to do with the bridges. Model had instructed Bittrich that they were not to be destroyed. Harmel knew if he let them fall into enemy hands he would be in trouble, but if he blew them he was disobeying orders.

The defenders of Hof van Holland were subjected to the British barrage, and while they were keeping their heads down the Americans stormed it around 1700 hours. The small garrison had been preoccupied firing their mortars when suddenly they found hand grenades abruptly landing in their midst. Unbeknown to them, Americans had swum the moat, clambered up the ramparts and started lobbing bombs into the interior. At this point, some others fought their way across the bridge over the moat and into the courtyard. The garrison promptly surrendered, having lost at least 75 men.

There was now no way of stopping the 82nd Airborne marching east towards the northern end of the railway bridge and Lent. Nonetheless, the bridge was protected by a considerable amount of firepower that included one 88mm gun, two 20mm anti-aircraft guns and 34 machine guns. The men assigned to protect it, though, were losing heart. The Allies were pressing in from both ends and they were having to watch a steady stream of dispirited stragglers crossing northward in a state of near panic. It was clear that things were not going well in Nijmegen.

By early afternoon the Germans, holding the perimeter around the southern edge of the railway bridge, had been slowly forced back. SS-Sergeant Hotop lost his radio to a direct hit and saw no point in staying at his forward observation post. Gathering his men, he joined an SS-company and hurried across to safety. When the American paratroopers finally arrived at the northern ramp, they began firing on the bridge and some panic-stricken Germans jumped into the river or off the ramp. Most were killed in this desperate bid to escape. At dusk about 200 German soldiers, caught in the middle of the crossing, surrendered. Others were not so lucky and 267 corpses were found on the bridge. Many had been caught in the crossfire trying to get away.

Over in the vicinity of the road bridge, an equally fierce battle was going on in the Kaiser Lodewijk Plein area. Both sides were tiring from the continual fighting. Just after 1600 hours the last of the Jagdpanzer IVs were overrun, denying the defenders their armoured support. Then at 1813 hours the 88mm gun on the Kaiser Lodewik Plein opened fire on a Sherman tank. The round deliberately or not bounced off the road and hit the tank with a ricochet. The tank crew quickly laid down smoke and beat a hasty retreat. As it did so, the 88mm targeted a second Sherman, but was promptly destroyed by high explosives.

About 45 minutes later, the Guards' tanks went roaring over the bridge with their machine guns blazing, scything German engineers and snipers from the girders. Others fled along the walkways and the road trying to reach the far bank. The tanks came under fire from an 88mm gun protected by sandbags some 100 yards from the northern end. A battle ensued between the gun and a Sherman, with both sides firing four rounds each. The Sherman's fifth shell silenced the 88mm gun crew.

Harmel, with a cigar clamped between his teeth, watched in horror from his bunker. Trying to calm his nerves, he said, 'when I first saw the British tanks I lit the cigar'.[8] To hell with Model, he thought. The tanks had reached the centre of the bridge when he gave the order. Nothing happened, so he gave it again. 'I waited to see the bridge collapse with the tanks into the river', he said. 'It failed to go up – probably because the initiation cable had been cut by artillery fire.' He watched as the tanks got closer and closer. Turning to his radio operator, he cried, 'My God, they'll be here in two minutes!'[9]

The Shermans, once over, rumbled round the concrete chicane at the end of the bridge. Behind them lay 180 dead Germans. On the bridge ramp were two anti-tank guns; the first was hit by high-explosive shells, the second was run over along with its unfortunate crew. By this point the 82nd Airborne had also reached the northern end. Still in his bunker, Harmel issued orders 'to block the roads between Elst and Lent with every available anti-tank gun and artillery piece because if we don't, they'll roll straight through to Arnhem'. Then as an afterthought he added, 'tell Bittrich. They're over the Waal'.[10] It was 1910 hours on 20 September.

Luckily for Harmel, the British tanks headed straight into Lent rather than taking the exit ramp and circling under the bridge. If they had, the road along the river would have taken them straight to him. Harmel knew that Model and Student would not be happy. First Valkenswaard, then Aalst, Eindhoven, Son, Grave and Nijmegen. It seemed that the game was up. Dashing from the bunker with his staff, Harmel drove northeast to Bemmel, where Reinhold had set up his new headquarters.

In Nijmegen, the remnants of the trapped garrison fought on. Baumgaertel's engineers had been taken by surprise when the British assaulted the Valkhof from the west and got behind them. They achieved this by capturing the police station, which enabled British machine guns to fire down into the gardens. While the defenders had their heads down, British infantry had attacked up the slope into the Valkhof, intent on clearing the German trenches.

Krueger's observation post was cut off. His radio had been destroyed, so he resorted to using flares to mark enemy positions. The defenders of the Belvedere had heard the Americans crossing the river to the west, endangering their route of escape. This had been sealed when they saw British tanks on the road bridge. They were also by now without artillery support. Schwappacher lost contact with Krueger by 1930 hours. However, resistance around the Belvedere continued for at least another 60 minutes. When the American attack came on their positions, they could not withstand it and about 30 men were captured. Two of them, SS-Corporal Kochler and SS-Lance Corporal Burgstaller, escaped their captors and reached Euling's hard-pressed positions.

Trapped at Haus Robert Jannssen, Euling fought on with 60 men, but he was running out of ammunition. When British tanks arrived outside and started shelling the building and surrounding trenches, he knew the battle was over. A soldier with a Panzerfaust managed to disable a tank, but another one appeared and shelled the communication trench, blowing in the front of the structure. Haus Robert Jannssen was extensively ablaze by 2230 hours.

The British, assuming all the occupants must be dead, lost interest and moved elsewhere. Euling and the survivors escaped by slithering in the darkness down the bank into the Voerweg cutting between Hunner and Valkhof. Making their way to the river, they turned east and under the ramp of the road bridge, where they briefly found sanctuary. Above them they could hear the rumble of the Guards Armoured Division as its vehicles headed into Lent. Despite brushes with several British patrols, they managed to cross the Waal at Haalderen and reached their own lines. Baumgaertel also managed to escape, but Krueger was not so lucky and was killed in the Belvedere. Nijmegen had fallen and the British were free to push on to Arnhem.

13

Creating Hell's Highway

While Field Marshal Model desperately sought to hold the Allies at Groesbeek and Nijmegen, he maintained pressure to the north of Eindhoven. Looking at the map, showing the Allied corridor, he convinced himself that Veghel was the key. However, on the flanks of Highway 69, which the Allies dubbed 'Hell's Highway', things were not going very well for him.

Student's initial attacks towards Eerde and Veghel had been repulsed. At Dinther and Veghel, a battalion from Major Hans Jungwirth's Parachute Training Replacement Regiment was left partially hemmed in along the Willemsvaart Canal by units of the 101st Airborne Division. This battalion was another poor-quality creation, made up of reluctant youngsters and pensioners. They had neither the training nor the willpower to take on aggressive American paratroopers.

The attack by General Poppe's 59th Division from Schijndel towards Veghel was no more successful either. On the afternoon of Tuesday 19 September, German artillery had opened up, trying to knock out American defences at Veghel and ending liberation celebrations by the Dutch. 'I watched... two large 88mm guns', recalled Student, 'shooting at American snipers who sat in the tall trees and hindered our attack from the flank.'[1] His operations at Best and Son had also proved ineffective.

At Son, on 20 September, Major von Maltzahn decided to repeat his unimaginative tactics of the previous day. Under cover of the British 30th Corps noisily rumbling northward and during the hours of darkness, he had rounded up his wayward forces. At dawn his Panther tanks and Panzergrenadiers once more pressed towards the vital bridge at Son. Once more, there was no element of surprise or adequate support for his operation.

An Allied patrol bumped into Maltzahn's advance elements and drove off sharpish to warn the 101st Airborne. Although the 1034th Grenadier Regiment overran some of the Americans' forward positions, anti-tank guns kept their supporting Panzers at bay. Once ten British Cromwell tanks and a battery of self-propelled guns arrived on the scene, the attack wilted under the shelling. Still lacking artillery or air cover, Maltzahn was unable to press home his attack. During the fighting, four of his Panthers were destroyed to add to the two lost on 19 September. Although he had again disrupted the flow of traffic, he failed to cut the bridge. It seemed that his brigade was simply not up to the job.

Northwest of Veghel, any plans Jungwirth had of trying to cut the highway were rapidly derailed. At 0930 hours that day, near Heeswijk and Dinther, the battalion from his battle group found itself under attack from all directions. Once the Americans, striking from Dinther, had reached the bridges at Heeswijk, the battalion fighting with its back to the Willemsvaart Canal was completely trapped. The inexperience of the new recruits soon began to show. After being under fire for 30 minutes, some 50 men from one company surrendered.

In the meantime, other American units were pushing east from Veghel up the Aa Valley and along the canal. Another 200 Germans belonging to the Jungwirth battalion were captured, but elsewhere they put up a stiffer fight. A machine-gun crew in a windmill and three 20mm anti-aircraft guns did all they could to slow the American advance. Nothing could move when confronted by such devastating firepower, although they were eventually silenced by small arms and mortar fire.

At 1500 hours the remaining soldiers tried to escape northwards, only to run into an American machine gun. Some two and half hours later the entire battalion had ceased to exist. It lost 40 dead, around the same number wounded and 418 captured. Student lamented that 'with their light weapons they could not prevent the... [Americans] from taking Dinther and Heeswijk'.[2] For the 101st Airborne the operation was a triumph, but for Jungwirth it was a farce and a complete waste of a battalion of men.

Despite these setbacks, Model was confident that with his steady flow of reinforcements, albeit rather poor ones, a concerted effort could crush the Allies' 50-mile-long corridor. He contacted Student, who passed on his instructions, saying, 'Field Marshal Model had ordered that the enemy columns marching on Nijmegen are to be attacked at the Veghel bottleneck on 22 September from the west and east'.[3] Plans were hastily put in place and ragtag units summoned to carry them out.

To the west, Battle Group Huber, formed from General Poppe's 59th Division supported by four Jagdpanther tank destroyers, was to strike towards Schijndel, Wijbosch, Koevering, Eerde and St Oedenrode. To the east, Battle Group Walther would attack towards Uden and Veghel. Student's immediate responsibility for the eastern side of the corridor was ended when Model formed the 86th Corps under the direction of General Hans von Obstfelder. He controlled Battle Group Walther, Division Erdmann and the 176th Infantry Division.

The Americans pre-empted Student at 1900 hours on 21 September by attacking south from Heeswijk towards Schijndel. The town was sparsely defended by a few anti-aircraft guns and these quickly withdrew. By 0150 hours it was in American hands. Another American force moved in from the east from the direction of Eerde. This overcame German defences in the railway station. In the confusion, German units kept arriving at Schijndel, only to be disarmed by the waiting Americans.

The German response was predictable. At 0715 hours on 22 September some 200 troops counter-attacked to the south, backed by two tanks, under cover of the morning mist. The men of the 101st Airborne outsmarted them. The Germans were caught in the flank, and ten were killed and 20 captured. Another attack from the east succeeded in infiltrating the town, but was too weak to remain. The arrival of British tanks and clear skies meant that the German force came under increasing fire.

German 88mm guns tried to hold the enemy tanks when they pushed south, but they were quickly dealt with by American bazooka teams. The Germans lost 125 prisoners and a similar number killed or wounded. Student was now facing a defeat if the British armour reached St Oedenrode. At that critical moment Battle Group Walther broke through northeast of Veghel. This forced the Allies to retreat from Schijndel and saved Huber's battle group, which was now reinforced by Heydte's 6th Parachute Regiment.

Battle Group Walther included a battalion of Panzergrenadiers from the 10th SS under SS-Captain Richter, supported by six of Maltzahn's remaining Panthers and three of Roestel's Jagdpanzer IVs. Another battle group drew on units from Maltzahn's brigade. Walther's goal was to take Veghel, blow the four bridges and block the highway, while the enemy divisions to the north were dealt with. Walther was unhappy about the short preparation time, which meant that his units would have to fight piecemeal as they arrived. The only hope was that the British were too strung out to respond effectively.

Walther quickly took Erp to the east of Veghel and his battle group sat astride two critical miles of road north of the town. He had successfully cut his way into 30th Corps' supply column, destroying many vehicles in the process. Everywhere were shot-up and burning supply lorries. Maltzahn's 107th Brigade, meanwhile, got to within two miles of Uden. This forced the British to turn part of the Guards Division south to deal with the problem, along with elements of the 101st Airborne. It was not long before artillery and fighter-bombers were helping to thwart the German attacks. 'Further progress through this marshy terrain was not possible', said SS-Lieutenant Heinz Damaske, Richter's adjutant. 'Moreover, the engineers and Panzergrenadiers came under well-aimed rifle fire delivered by the American paratroopers and were not able to take a further step forward.'[4]

GERMAN COUNTER-ATTACKS ALONG
'HELL'S HIGHWAY', 19–25 SEPTEMBER 1944

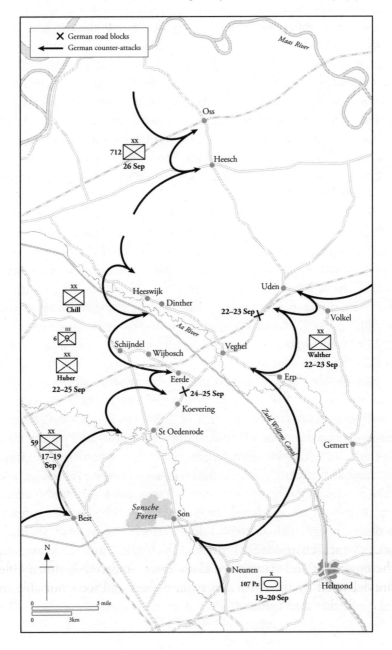

At dawn on 23 September, Heydte's reconstituted 6th Parachute Regiment renewed Student's attack from the west. He had been ordered to retake Eerde, then swing north to Veghel. Heydte was not pleased by this, noting sourly, 'the training and combat experience of the troops were inadequate… little hope of success'.[5] He was promised the support of an infantry battalion from the 9th SS under the command of SS-Captain Segler, and a dozen of Roestel's tank destroyers. They had not materialized. Supported by mortars, Heydte's two parachute battalions advanced, only for one of them to be quickly pinned down. He was forced to recall them and by 1200 hours his regiment was digging in. An hour later the SS renewed the attack, only to be halted by artillery fire.

The Americans counter-attacked at 1400 hours towards Uden and bumped into three of Maltzahn's Panthers. These let rip with their 75mm guns and their machine guns. The crews perhaps hoped that the lightly armed Americans would turn tail. They were wrong. In response, an American 57mm anti-tank gun returned fire. The driver of the lead Panther felt an almighty bang as the armour-piercing round struck his tank. The force was such that the Panther lurched to the left and into a field, where it promptly caught fire.

Meanwhile, the Germans came under pressure south of Uden and at Volkel. Major Maltzahn, faced with the prospect of fighting on two fronts, decided to withdraw. At Volkel, 88mm guns managed to keep British tanks and American paratroopers at bay for a while. However, a group of seven supporting Panthers unhelpfully retreated. The Panzergrenadiers holding the village did not give up so easily and had to be driven out house by house. It was firmly in British hands by 1500 hours. The fighting took a serious toll on Battle Group Walther, which lost 25 per cent of its infantry and 20 per cent of its armour.

To make matters worse, the British 8th Corps was now pushing north, threatening Walther's southern flank. It had got between Eindhoven and Helmond. German losses amounted to three tanks destroyed and 300 men captured. To the southeast the Germans were forced to evacuate Weert. Late on 23 September, 88th Corps signalled the battle group to withdraw to the Velno area. Frustratingly for the Germans, 'Hell's Highway' was once more open for business.

Although Model's eastern pincer had been removed, it was decided to persist with the attacks on the Allies' western flank. German intelligence had detected gaps in the 101st Airborne's defences. Notably, patrols had found that while Eerde was occupied, between Schijndel and Dinther there was no sign of the enemy. Likewise, north of St Oedenrode there were holes in the American line.

To ease his chain of command, Model decided to place all his forces to the west of the corridor under the control of Zangen's 15th Army, while those to the east would be the responsibility of Student's 1st Army. The latter now included Corps Feldt, 2nd Parachute Corps, 86th Corps and Battle Group Walther. Student also found himself in charge of the 2nd SS-Panzer Corps as well as Division Tettau, which had been under Model's direct command.

The enterprising General Chill deployed his battle group to Schijndel, with orders to attack the Veghel bridges at 0900 hours on 24 September. The bulk of his force consisted of 500 men belonging to Heydte's 6th Parachute Regiment. They were to strike via Eerde. Held in reserve were the remains of Battle Group Huber, now part of Battle Group Jungwirth, along with the 1035th Fusilier Regiment.

Some 200 of Heydte's men, supported by five assault guns, moved to the sand dunes northwest of Eerde. They were greeted by nine Sherman tanks and artillery fire and a counter-attack. This cost the Germans 15 dead and seven wounded or captured. However, two assault guns circling to the south destroyed three Shermans and then set about attacking the British vehicles on the highway. Within minutes, ammunition and other supply vehicles were exploding and ablaze. Drivers scattered in all directions as debris rained down around them. The lucky ones huddled in the roadside ditches. Chill was able to report to General Reinhard that he had cut Highway 69 south of Eerde, while to the north his troops had reached the railway bridge. This was welcome news.

Major Hans Jungwirth's battle group had swung southeast of Schijndel and successfully attacked the road at Koevering around 1800 hours. In the fighting that followed, the Germans destroyed 50 enemy vehicles and took 50 prisoners. This caused a panic in St Oedenrode, but Battle Group Jungwirth was too weak to push farther south. During the evening Jungwirth's men, under artillery fire, dug in amongst the woods either side of the highway. Jungwirth knew that the British and Americans would counter-attack from the south and the north. However, his actions had helped seal the fate of the British 1st Airborne Division at Arnhem.

German units found themselves under attack by elements of the US 101st Airborne striking south from Veghel at 0830 hours on 25 September. Their defences around the road consisted of new King Tigers or Tiger IIs and 88mm guns, backed by men from Hedyte's 6th Parachute Regiment. By noon, shell and mortar fire had brought the Americans to a halt. A Tiger tank commander was alarmed by falling trees, which indicated the approach of British tanks. In a panic, he fired blind and caught a Sherman with a glancing blow. It tried to reverse, but a second round went clean through the turret, killing all the crew. A second Sherman was knocked out with a single shot.

On 26 September, the German troops holding Koevering prepared to meet British tanks. They were supported by 88mm guns, plus a few assault guns and self-propelled guns. At 0730 hours, as anticipated, British tanks and American paratroopers pushed up from St Oedenrode. The German anti-tank gunners swiftly claimed eight Shermans and the battle lasted all day until 1800 hours. To the north of Koevering, the Germans held the road in battalion strength, with about four tanks and self-propelled guns. Despite their best efforts, by 1940 hours the two Allied attacks had linked up and the Germans were forced to withdraw west.

Model, Student and their commanders had every reason to be pleased with the men's efforts. Despite the largely poor quality of their troops, they had repeatedly cut Highway 69, severely disrupting the Allied advance. One of the greatest disappointments had been Major Maltzahn's Panzer brigade, but in light of its strength and lack of heavy weapons support this was hardly surprising. Maltzahn's men were inexperienced, their attacks poorly planned and co-ordinated.

14

Arnhem Retaken

During the night of 17 September, SS-Lieutenant-Colonel Ludwig Spindler's battle group set about creating a defensive line between the Ede–Arnhem road and the rail junction on the Utrechtseweg. This was intended to cut off the British forces, holding a defensive perimeter around the northern end of Arnhem bridge, from the rest of their division gathering at Oosterbeek. It was in place by the early hours of 18 September. Spindler also took charge of Krafft's battalion.

Spindler's forces epitomized the German battle group ethos. During the course of the battle he was to find himself commanding men from 16 different units, most of whom fought as infantry. They included gunners, surplus tank crews and pioneers who were given rifles. They had one common goal: to stop the scattered British units from linking up.

At the same time, SS-Lieutenant-Colonel Harzer was reinforced by Battle Group von Tettau. The latter moved in from the west, from the direction of Heelsum, and on 18 September began attacking the British landing zones in the Wolfheze area. Creating a pincer movement, Battle Group Harzer came in from the east. The fighting became very confused, as there were no discernible front lines. SS-Captain Hans Möller recalled it was 'like a wild west shootout. There was no front, sections and half-sections fought scattered actions'.[1]

SS-Major Krafft, still flush from his success the previous day, was now given an equally important task. His training battalion, bolstered with a mixture of marines and military police, was sent back into action. Spindler ordered Krafft to head towards the Ede–Arnhem road and to link up with Tettau's approaching forces. This would form a western perimeter that would help trap the British in Oosterbeek, where they had their backs to the river.

In contrast to Krafft, SS-Captain Helle was having a bad day. At his headquarters in the Zuid-Ginkel restaurant, he had awoken on a tabletop. It was uncomfortable to say the least, and he would have much rather come to in the arms of his mistress. He was contemplating his aching back and the fighting of the previous evening when he became aware of gunfire, heavy gunfire. Had a counter-attack started without him? Helle slid to his feet, buttoned his tunic and grabbed his sidearm. His orderly suddenly dashed in to inform him that another British airborne landing was taking place, with paratroopers coming down around their ears.

Helle had deployed his companies to surround the British landing zone ready for a counter-attack. Instead, the British were coming down everywhere. Outside, a German 20mm anti-aircraft gun, mounted on a half-track, was frantically firing up into the billowing parachute canopies. Either side, Helle's machine-gunners were also firing into the air at the enemy parachutists and a fast-approaching wave of gliders.

At first glance it looked like a bloody aerial massacre, but Helle's battalion was swiftly swamped and overwhelmed. SS-lieutenants Bartsch and Hink tried to form a coherent defence, but were overrun. SS-Captain Kuhne panicked and abandoned his company. To the south, SS-Lieutenant Fernau was captured. Helle, on seeing his command rapidly disintegrate, ordered SS-Lieutenant Bronkhorst to hold a farm at Hindekamp and then promptly fled himself. Only veteran SS-Captain Einenkel, the heavy weapons company commander, conducted himself with any distinction by organizing a fighting withdrawal. Helle's Dutch SS-battalion all but ceased to exist. Mussert's fascist Dutchmen had not proved so tough after all.

To the southwest of Wolfheze, things were going much better for Major-General von Tettau's counter-attacks. These were co-ordinated by SS-Colonel Lippert and resulted in Renkum and Heelsum being secured. Lippert also organized an attack to take the British drop zone to the west of Wolfheze. Initially he sent six old French Renault tanks north from Renkum, but these were swiftly destroyed and the supporting infantry driven off.

Lippert decided that the British gunners needed to be distracted long enough for his men to penetrate their defences. Climbing into his staff car, he then drove out onto the drop zone, firing flares as he went. After he had gone about 450 yards, the British, recovering from their surprise, began firing at Lippert's wildly swerving vehicle. At that point, his infantry charged forward. 'The bluff was successful and enabled the landing-zone at this point to be cleared of enemy within an hour', said Lippert, 'but not without heavy losses on both sides.'[2] His attack pressed on to the western outskirts of Oosterbeek, capturing many prisoners and quantities of heavy equipment.

Model, Christiansen and Bittrich were still scrabbling about trying to find more reinforcements. Just before dawn, Major Hans-Peter Knaust's Panzergrenadier Training and Replacement Battalion Bocholt arrived in Arnhem. Its task was to replace the last company from Euling's SS-battalion, so that it could head for Nijmegen. Knaust had lost a leg on the Eastern Front and stomped noisily about on a wooden replacement that pained him constantly. Harmel noted 'he never once complained'. While Harmel respected Knaust as a tough veteran, he was not impressed by the quality of his battalion. Many of the teenage recruits had received just eight weeks' training, while the seriously wounded convalescents in Harmel's view were 'close to being invalids'.[3]

Knaust's Panzergrenadiers were strengthened with eight tanks from another training unit, the 6th Panzer Replacement Regiment Bielfeld, which were due to arrive the following day. These included the Panzer IV, a trusted workhorse, and the much more inadequate Panzer III. They were to be supplemented by much newer Tiger tanks from the 506th Heavy Tank Battalion, also due on 19 September. Knaust's forces were to join Battle Group Brinkmann in reducing the British hold in Arnhem.

Largely out of necessity, it was decided to commit another battalion of Dutch 'volunteers'. SS-Lieutenant-Colonel Hermann Delf at Hoogeveen was ordered to mobilize his 3rd Battalion SS Landstorm Nederland and move it to Arnhem. Delf had about 600 men organized into four companies, but few weapons. Furthermore, his battalion was still undergoing training and had no transport. Using bicycles, they reached Arnhem by close of play on 18 September. They did not remain there, but instead were sent south to Elst north of Nijmegen. No one held out much hope for their combat performance.

The British, meanwhile, had managed to get a battalion of paratroops to the northern end of Arnhem bridge.[4] However, they had been unable to secure the southern end. The fighting overnight had been ferocious. Sergeant Petersen discovered that of the 250 men who had tried to reach the bridge, over half were dead or wounded. They had remained trapped and never did get through the British defences. He was bitter about the lack of support they had received. 'For us,' he said sadly, 'it was nothing less than a massacre.'[5]

SS-Captain Gräbner found no sign of the enemy along the 11-mile stretch of road between Arnhem and Nijmegen. American forces had got into Nijmegen, though not in any great strength. When his vehicles crossed the Waal, there had been some desultory firing. He decided, wrongly as it happened, that Battle Group Henke was more than adequate to defend the city. Leaving some of his self-propelled guns to guard the southern approaches of Nijmegen road bridge, Gräbner headed back north.

From radio messages, he understood that British advance units were on Arnhem bridge. He doubted they would have much heavy weaponry, but they would nonetheless need to be cleared off. Stopping at Elst, he split his force, leaving half poised to race back to Nijmegen. Commanding the other half, comprising about 22 vehicles, Gräbner drove towards Arnhem like some dashing cavalry officer.

On reaching the Lower Rhine, he decided to force his way across the bridge at 0930 hours. After all, he thought, what possible harm could lightly equipped paratroopers do against his armoured vehicles? He grossly underestimated the strength and firepower of his enemy. German intelligence indicated the British had about 120 men in the vicinity. If this information reached Gräbner, it may have given him a false sense of security. In reality, the number was nearer 700.

Regardless of enemy numbers, Gräbner seemed blind to the danger that the British might have anti-tank guns, bazookas and mines with which to fend him off. These would be more than capable of stopping his convoy dead in its tracks. Nonetheless, he prudently decided to probe British defences and sent five armoured cars across first, while the rest of the column gathered on the southern ramp with their engines revving noisily. At the same time, German infantry prepared to attack the British from the landward side, forming a pincer attack.

Gräbner's armoured car drivers, going at full throttle, zigzagged round the burning wreckage on the bridge, and miraculously through a British minefield. One vehicle struck a mine, was only slightly damaged and kept going. The armoured-car machine-gunners raked the surrounding buildings with fire to force the British to keep their heads down. In this way, the advance guard successfully drove off into Arnhem. Gräbner was greatly encouraged as it seemed to confirm his belief that the bridge was only very lightly defended.

Now the rest of his force, riding in nine armoured half-tracks and eight lorries, roared over Arnhem bridge. Gräbner, travelling in a captured British armoured car, sent the half-tracks first. While these offered some protection from small-arms fire, the troop compartment had no roof and was therefore vulnerable. To try to protect the men in the lorries, they had packed the sides with sandbags.

The alert British appreciated that the departing armoured cars were just the advance guard and raised their weapons in anticipation. The head of the column was descending the northern ramp when it was caught in a deadly and sustained crossfire from the buildings either side. 'Suddenly all hell broke loose ahead of us', said SS-Corporal Mauga, crouching in one of the half-tracks.[6] The driver and his companion in the lead half-track were hit, as were the crew of the second one. The vehicles lurched to a halt and the British gunners fired relentlessly into them. When their surviving passengers emerged, they were cut down by rifle and machine-gun fire. Red-stained dead bodies flopped back into the vehicles or onto the roadside.

When a third half-track approached, its driver threw his vehicle into reverse on being wounded. In doing so, he collided with the vehicle behind him. As vehicles were hit, a traffic jam blocked the entire northern ramp, and the supporting infantry were shot as they desperately sought cover. British artillery in Oosterbeek added to the mayhem by dropping shells neatly onto the road. All the stalled vehicles were shot to pieces with dead and seriously wounded strewn everywhere. 'All around my vehicle there were explosions and noise', said Mauga, 'and I was right in the middle of this chaos.'[7] In a bid to escape, some vehicles crashed off the ramp and into the streets below. At least six came off the embankment. The whole area was covered in foul-smelling smoke rising from the burning vehicles and blood-splattered corpses. At best, it was little more than a turkey shoot.

Remarkably, Gräbner's men did not give up. They regrouped on the southern end of the bridge and prepared for another attempt. No one knew where their captain was and it could only be assumed that his armoured car was amongst the wreckage on the northern ramp. The infantry tried pushing down the bridge's walkways, which were continually raked by enemy fire. Wounded men plummeted into the water below, or, worse, on to the road beneath the ramp. One group of half a dozen men ran afoul of a British observation post, which poured fire into them to deadly effect. By noon, the survivors had prudently decided to give up. They turned tail and withdrew to the south bank. From there they drove back to Elst, with the bad news that Arnhem bridge was very firmly in British hands. At least a dozen German vehicles were destroyed and around 70 troops killed, including Gräbner.

For two hours the battle raged, as the Germans inside Arnhem pounded British strongpoints with mortar bombs, shells, machine-gun fire and sniper fire. In the process they lost four more armoured vehicles and more men were killed, wounded and captured. Amongst those involved in the street fighting was SS-Squad Leader Alfred Ringsdorf, who had only just arrived at the train station. A veteran of Russia, his company was attached to the 21st SS-Panzergrenadier Regiment. 'I had no idea where we were going to fight', recalled Ringsdorf, 'and I had never been in Arnhem before.'[8]

He and his men took part in the attacks on the British defensive perimeter and fought house to house. The gunfire was such that they could get only about 600 yards from the approaches to the bridge. 'We fought to gain inches', said Ringsdorf, 'cleaning out one room after the other.'[9] To force the British from their buildings, the Germans resorted to using demolition charges, grenades and Panzerfausts. 'The fighting was cruel', he observed. 'This was a harder battle than any I had fought in Russia.'[10] Nonetheless, slowly but surely, the British were driven from their strongpoints.

News of Gräbner's defeat came as a shock to Bittrich, Harzer and Harmel. For the British paratroopers, it was a welcome boost to their morale. Harzer's chief of staff, SS-Captain Wilfried Schwarz, noted, 'we had lost an important part of our combat strength'.[11] Harmel held Harzer responsible for this sorry state of affairs, which left the British firmly blocking the bridge. He also considered Gräbner's actions 'utterly inexplicable'.[12] In the afternoon, Battle Group Brinkmann attacked the northern edge of the British Arnhem perimeter. By dusk the whole area was in flames, including two churches, St Eusibius and St Walburgis.

Bittrich had been surprised by the size of the second British airlift at Wolfheze. The Americans had also been considerably reinforced. Intelligence suggested, quite erroneously, that the Allies had brought in another entire division. As far as Bittrich was concerned, they were now locked in a deadly race against time. He felt they were losing because German reinforcements were not reaching them quickly enough. Amongst those sent to Student's

1st Parachute Army were the remnants of Zangen's battered 15th Army, but they lacked everything.

Bittrich was increasingly alarmed by reports on the British 30th Corps' progress. While Student was continually hampering the enemy advance, he had insufficient strength to stop it completely. When Model was visited by Bittrich in the afternoon on 18 September, the general did his best to convince the field marshal of the merit of severing the Waal crossings. 'No!' ranted Model. 'The answer is no!' Bittrich reasoned if they did this, the British ground forces would have nowhere to go. 'The Nijmegen bridge is not to be destroyed', replied Model angrily, 'and I want the Arnhem bridge captured within twenty-four hours.'[13] Model was adamant that Student's army and the 10th SS must stop the British and Americans before they ever got to Nijmegen. Stop them with what, asked Bittrich, not unreasonably. Student had no armour and the 10th SS were struggling to get their tanks over the canal at Pannerden.

As darkness fell, German guns blasted British positions around Arnhem bridge. Buildings were shattered into rubble, while others caught fire. The air was thick with choking dust and smoke. A northeast breeze served to fan the flames, forcing some of the defenders from their strongpoints. The badly wounded had to be moved regularly for fear they might be burned to death.

During the morning of 19 September, Knaust's forces attacked British positions northeast of the ramp, supported by three elderly Panzer IIIs, losing one in the process. Frightened by the prospect of British tank hunters, the others withdrew, their drivers ramming the gears hard into reverse. Harmel made several requests to the British to surrender, but they took no heed. 'Since the British won't come out of their holes, we'll blast them out', he ordered. Harmel then instructed his gunners to leave nothing 'but a pile of bricks'. Arnhem shuddered under the relentless impact of shells and mortar bombs.

Driving the British from Arnhem bridge became a priority once the British 30th Corps had reached Nijmegen on 19 September. Despite the loss of Gräbner's armoured column, the British were completely hemmed in around the northern end of the bridge by elements of the 9th and 10th SS. German artillery and tanks were used to slowly destroy the buildings held by the British paratroopers one by one. German forces on the south bank of the Rhine also set about British defences around Arnhem bridge. Two 88mm guns were deployed either side of the southern end of the bridge. These then shelled the British at almost point-blank range. Their rounds tore through the brickwork with ease.

Although the 506th Heavy Tank Battalion had been delayed owing to mechanical problems, two Tiger tanks joined Battle Group Knaust. SS-Private Horst Weber watched the Tigers systematically pulverize the houses in front of them. 'The din was awful', he said, 'but even so above it all we could hear the wounded screaming.'[14] The buildings just crumpled, spilling the defenders out on to the street, where they were mown down. Panzer IVs also joined in the demolition mayhem.

Meanwhile, in western Arnhem, SS-Captain Hans Möller's men and Battle Group Gropp, which formed part of SS-Lieutenant-Colonel Spindler's command, fought to stop British reinforcements getting to the bridge. Elements of four British battalions had reached the Den Brink area and the nearby St Elizabeth Hospital. At the same time, the rest of Battle Group Spindler was coralling the remainder of 1st Airborne towards Oosterbeek. From 0430 hours onwards on 19 September, German tanks and SS-Panzergrenadiers repeatedly thwarted British attempts to fight their way eastward from the hospital area along the Utrechtseweg and Onderlangs roads and past the city museum. At first Möller feared the enemy were going to break through, such was their determination, but they had actually walked into a deadly trap set by Spindler.

Krafft's battle group, as instructed, was protecting the Ede–Arnhem road. SS-Lieutenant Gropp's anti-aircraft guns were positioned just north of the railway, in the upper storeys of some houses, while to the south facing westward were Möller's men. They were armed with flamethrowers and Panzerfausts. The area down to the river was held by other elements of Spindler's battle group. On the south side of the river, part of Gräbner's reconnaissance battalion had deployed some self-propelled flak guns on the bank in front of the brickworks.

When the British tried to press forward, they came under sustained fire from three sides and then ran into the assault guns of the 280th Assault Gun Brigade. The south bank flak gunners watched at 0600 hours as the British paratroopers hastened along the river road. Then their 20mm and 37mm cannon rounds tore apart human bodies, cutting the British advance to pieces. The bright tracer, marking the German line of fire, bounced off the road and neighbouring buildings like some obscene firework display. The road was left blood splattered.

Elsewhere, the British pressed forward and got to within almost a mile of the bridge. By the museum, an assault gun and two of Möller's armoured half-tracks confronted the British head on. The Germans counter-attacked and the British were thrown back. As the morning wore on, Möller reported that the enemy 'were completely exhausted... their confidence shaken by excessively high losses'.[15]

German troops on the high ground known as Heijenoord Diependal, north of the railway and opposite Den Brink, were also anticipating an attack. At 1430 hours they began plastering the British on Den Brink with mortar fire and shortly after drove them off this neighbouring high ground. Subsequently, they cleared the British from St Elizabeth Hospital. The remaining British in Arnhem's suburbs were killed, captured, or forced to retreat towards Oosterbeek.

To the north of Arnhem, Spindler's men found themselves fending off a British battalion trying to take the high ground at Koepel, east of the Dreijenseweg. The latter road ran north from Oosterbeek over the railway line to meet the Ede–Arnhem road, called the Amsterdamseweg. They countered with armoured cars, self-propelled guns and infantry, as well as the Luftwaffe. German pressure was such that the British, alarmed at being trapped against the railway embankment, withdrew. Along with the remains of two other battalions, they were driven back to Oosterbeek.

SS-Captain Krafft's training battalion had been strengthened by two marine regiments and a company of police. At 1600 hours his men witnessed a glider landing northwest of Oosterbeek, between the railway and the Ede–Arnhem road. This was bringing in the advance elements of a Polish airborne brigade. It proved to be one of the rare occasions that the Luftwaffe's fighters made an appearance. They shot up the gliders and their tug aircraft. Unfortunately for the Germans, they also attacked an SS-battalion at Wolfheze. Krafft ordered forward two companies, which also opened fire. 'The gliders were holed by countless hits', reported Krafft, 'and the bloodstains inside show that the enemy has suffered quite appreciable casualties in the air.'[16]

Battle Group von Tettau conducted some light probing attacks, as they advanced eastward towards Oosterbeek at 1900 hours. These were driven off. However, by dark Bittrich was very pleased with his men's efforts. Following the first airborne landings, the British had pushed five battalions into Arnhem, numbering about 3,000 men. Since then the Germans had captured over 1,700, most of whom were wounded, and killed about 120. The British had lost almost two entire brigades in a single day.

The Germans continued to strangle the British at Arnhem. 'Our flak shot down 10 supply planes', noted Erwin Kirchhof, a reporter with the army newspaper *Der Westkurier*, on 20 September. 'The major part of the weapons and food containers fell into our hands.' The Luftwaffe also flew some sorties. 'Fierce dogfights took place over the battle area', added Kirchhof. 'Our own fighters attacked the enemy on the ground.'[17]

Major Behr at Model's headquarters reported the confused fighting that day:

At dawn the heavy SS *Frundsberg* Mortar Section moved into position and blasted the Arnhem bridgehead. This was followed by a frontal attack by ten somewhat elderly tanks firing wildly but continuously, and supported by infantry keeping up a steady pounding of heavy machine-gun fire. The tanks were met by the very accurate fire of the British 6-pounder anti-tank guns;

they slowed, came to a stop and then began to back away. The barrage quietened and the machine-gunnners slipped back with the tanks. But, from a safer distance, the SS mortars kept up a continuous fire.[18]

Knaust and the others knew on 20 September that the British could not hold out much longer around the Arnhem bridge. Their positions were smouldering ruins, they had suffered heavy casualties and they were almost out of ammunition. At its peak the British garrison amounted to about 700 men; now after three days of intensive fighting only about 150 were still capable of bearing arms, and most of these men were trapped in and around their headquarters. By the evening, they were finally overrun. The following day around 0500 hours organized resistance at Arnhem bridge ceased and the remaining survivors were rounded up. All eyes were now on Oosterbeek and Elst.

15

SS in the Betuwe

On the night of 20 September, the German defenders in Lent had little time to brace themselves as four British Sherman tanks came charging over the Nijmegen road bridge. Nonetheless, as the Shermans drove down the northern ramp they were greeted by armour-piercing and Panzerfaust rounds. Two tanks were hit and one caught fire. The crew of the latter jumped out and were promptly captured, but the tank commander hurriedly clambered back in and drove off after the others. Just outside Lent a German assault gun waited in ambush. Its nervous gunner, in the failing light, missed and paid the price.

Inside Lent, with two British tanks in their midst, the Germans panicked. They had been expecting an attack from the southwest after the enemy had crossed the Waal. This had been delayed while the Americans fought their way towards the railway bridge. No one had told the Germans to withdraw and they had assumed that Nijmegen's bridges would be destroyed, so were certainly not expecting enemy tanks to turn up.

Soldiers fleeing from their foxholes ran to the church, but found no safe sanctuary. The Shermans opened fire with their machine guns and 75mm guns and the shattered building was soon in flames. Surviving personnel fled up the street, with machine-gun bullets licking at their heels. Dead bodies lay everywhere. Lent had been lost.

The two Shermans pushed on through Lent and reached the railway bridge at the northern end of the village. The road swung under it and just round the bend were two more German anti-tank guns. Both weapons fired and missed. Their presence, though, was enough to cause the enemy tanks to withdraw under the bridge and back towards the river. The gunners were relieved that no further attempts were made on their positions that night. Model was also thankful that the Guards Armoured Division did not press on northwards. His attacks to the east of Nijmegen, at Huemen and Son, had successfully forced the Allies to divert forces away from the Waal. In addition, after the extensive Waal barrage the British were critically short of ammunition.

Harmel, having failed to bring down the Waal bridges, knew their only hope was to stop the British in the Betuwe, the flood plain sandwiched between the Waal, the Rhine and the Pannerden Canal. Over the centuries, to try to protect this region, the Dutch had criss-crossed it with deep irrigation ditches, dykes and high road embankments. Harmel noted, 'the terrain between Nijmegen and Arnhem was the worst possible for tanks – for both sides'.[1] This meant that the British would have to rely on their infantry, but first they had to get them up 'Hell's Highway'. The British 43rd Infantry Division was on its way, but was constantly being held up.

If there was one thing the Germans were good at, after their experiences in Normandy, Italy and on the Eastern Front, it was creating defence in depth or layered defences. Model and Bittrich appreciated that Elst, midway between Nijmegen and Arnhem, provided the best blocking position. It dominated the local roads and the railway line north to Arnhem. A defensive screen could be established to the south of Elst at Bessen Station and Reet. The road to the west of the railway line was built on an embankment six feet high, meaning anything using it would be horribly exposed. To the southwest and southeast they also had forward defences at Oosterhout and Bemmel. These would help slow any Allied attempts to outflank Elst. German defences then swung south across the Waal through the Reichswald to Riethorst.

By the end of 20 September, Harmel had been slightly heartened by news that tanks had finally been ferried over the canal at Pannerden. Reinforcements were finally on their way. These included 16 Panzers and a battalion of men from the 21st SS-Panzergrenadier Regiment. There was also Battle Group Hartung, consisting of a weak battalion of reservists. Additional artillery units had moved to Flieren, to the east of Bemmel. There were also the flak guns at Pannerden that could be redeployed for front-line use.

Bittrich wanted Harmel to immediately counter-attack westward in order to safeguard Elst. Rather optimistically, he instructed 'overwhelm them, and throw the enemy back over the Waal river'. As they arrived, Hartung's reservists were deployed between Elst and Bemmel. The SS-Panzergrenadiers were sent to hold the line on down to the Waal. Harmel instructed Major Hans-Peter Knaust's battle group south once Arnhem bridge had been secured. This included about eight tanks and assault guns. Some of the armour belonged to the Mielke Panzer Training Company, equipped with the obsolete Panzer IIIs. However, they were better than nothing.

Knaust decided to reconnoitre the defences in the Betuwe personally, and arrived at Oosterhout on the morning of 21 September. The garrison there largely comprised the remains of Schwappacher's artillery training regiment, who were now acting as infantry. Looking at their maps, it was agreed that Valburg, to the northwest of Oosterhout and southwest of Elst, would provide the next defensive point. Knaust's advance guard had arrived at Elst by 1600 hours, where he set up his headquarters. As his wooden leg greatly pained him when walking, he directed operations from his half-track.

At Bessen the defences, consisting of guns and infantry, came under British artillery bombardment just after 1300 hours. The shelling was quite accurate, as if the British gunners knew where the German positions were. Unbeknown to them, the British had indeed captured a detailed map of the area. Then some 30 minutes later, just under 50 British tanks carrying infantry came rolling up the Lent road.

Two miles out, the Germans had entrenched some anti-tank guns in a farm surrounded by trees. Before the British tanks reached this gun line they ran into an assault gun, which knocked out three Shermans. Machine-gun nests opened fire, forcing the British infantry to dive for cover. The Germans in turn soon found themselves under mortar fire, though the enemy's fighter-bombers thankfully failed to materialize. On the German right, just after 1700 hours, they found their Oosterhout defences also under attack. British tanks came up the dyke road to the west of Fort Hof van Holland. The Germans were prepared for this and launched a counter-attack. In the process they lost three tanks.

Model was informed of a new complication late on 21 September. A force of Polish paratroopers had come down near Driel, south of the Lower Rhine. This put them well behind his defences in the Betuwe and posed a threat to Knaust at Elst. Intelligence suggested that the drop was of brigade strength. Although this was a very unwelcome development, with Bittrich controlling Arnhem bridge it would be easy for the 2nd SS-Panzer Corps to send help. This, though, would be an unwanted diversion of scarce resources from the ongoing battle for Oosterbeek.

Although it was self-evident that the Poles had come to assist the British 1st Airborne, oddly they were on the wrong side of the river. Their arrival also suggested that the British 30th Corps would probably attempt to break through at Oosterhout and on north to Driel. From there they would be able to support the trapped paratroopers at Oosterbeek and swing east to threaten the Arnhem road bridge. German artillery at Elst and in the Oosterbeek area soon began to shell the Poles. Critically, German control of the high ground at Westerbouwing, on the northern bank of the Rhine, meant that Model could dominate the Poles' drop zone and the exposed Driel–Heveadorp ferry.

By early morning on 22 September, the last of Knaust's forces had arrived at Elst. They were to prevent the British and the Poles from getting to Arnhem. At the same time, to contain the Poles and protect communications with Arnhem, Harzer deployed

BATTLE FOR THE BETUWE, 21–26 SEPTEMBER 1944

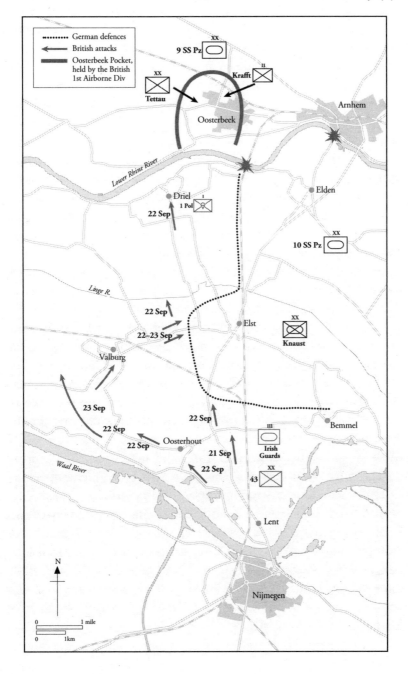

German defences

British attacks

Oosterbeek Pocket,
held by the British
1st Airborne Div

9 SS Pz

Krafft

Tettau

Oosterbeek

Arnhem

Lower Rhine River

Driel
1 Pol

Elden

22 Sep

10 SS Pz

Linge R.

22 Sep

22–23 Sep

Elst

Valburg

Knaust

23 Sep

22 Sep

Bemmel

22 Sep

22 Sep

Oosterhout

22 Sep

Irish
Guards

21 Sep

Waal River

22 Sep

43

Lent

N

Nijmegen

0   1 mile

0   1 km

some 2,500 troops along the railway embankment, south of the Rhine. These were organized into five battalions and were composed of the usual miscellaneous personnel from the army, navy and Luftwaffe. They included some of the Dutch SS. Harzer had been relieved that the Poles made no attempt to seize the railway and his forces were able to deploy without meeting any resistance.

Knaust's defences south of Elst in the Reet area first came under attack mid-morning when they were briefly shelled. Then at 1130 hours, the British pushed up the Arnhem road. German gunners did not wait long before they opened up with their 75mm guns firing high explosives, 20mm quad guns and MG42s. Their anti-tank guns targeted the exposed Shermans and the lead tank was soon a blazing wreck. Dug-in troops waited for the British infantry, working their way along the ditches and through the orchards, to reach point-blank range before they fired.

To the east of Oosterhout, Knaust deployed two Panzer IVs, which knocked out two Shermans and then started shelling the British infantry. The crews were amazed to see a Dutch cyclist coming down the road cheerfully waving at the British sheltering in a nearby ditch. The Panzers' machine-gunners soon ended his revelries. The fighting continued on into the afternoon.

During the morning, to the southeast of Oosterhout, the Germans' vigilance almost failed them. Despite the presence of three German tanks, two troops of British armoured cars slipped by. The crew of a German tank, hidden in an orchard, suddenly woke up and, firing three rounds in rapid succession, knocked out the last three armoured cars. The rest reached the Poles and helped repel Harzer's attacks, which went on until nightfall.

Also that morning, the anticipated attack commenced on Knaust's defences at Oosterhout. It was held by a battalion of infantry, supported by tanks and self-propelled guns. His anti-tank guns were deployed on the northern edge of the village, while some of the tanks were positioned near the Nijmegen–Arnhem road. The southeastern edge of the village was protected by three of Mielke's elderly Panzer IIIs.

Knaust's men spotted British tanks and infantry emerging from some woods, at 0800 hours, coming along the elevated dyke road on their left flank. An hour and a half later they had reached the outskirts of Oosterhout, where they were held up by a tank, backed by infantry. German fire was such that the British infantry were forced to withdraw under the cover of smoke. At about 1100 hours there were reports of British infantry trying to turn their right flank. They were also stopped after they reached north of the village, this time by heavy mortar fire. These probing attacks, though, were just a taste of things to come.

At 1505 hours, German positions around Oosterhout came under sustained artillery and mortar bombardment. This involved over a hundred guns, including a battery of self-propelled 25-pounders and a field artillery regiment. The village and surrounding woods were plastered in hot metal for 15 minutes and became shrouded in a cloud of choking dust. When the storm ended the stunned defenders, their ears ringing from the concussion, were left with little stomach for the fight.

Fifteen minutes later the British attacked again, at battalion strength, and stormed through the village. The Panzer III's 50mm gun was woefully inadequate against the Sherman's 75mm gun. The Germans did not put up much of a fight and were swiftly overcome. Those who could fled, while 139 threw down their weapons and were taken prisoner. The British also captured three tanks, a self-propelled gun and five light flak guns. By 1630 hours, Knaust had been informed that Oosterhout was lost. Resistance in the area spluttered on for another 30 minutes. An 88mm gun, to the north of the village, persisted in shelling the Arnhem road until it was finally silenced.

There was no respite for Knaust. After Oosterhout had fallen, his defences south of Elst came under attack again. They did not give ground and four Shermans were successfully knocked out on the road just as the light was failing. The burning tanks improved visibility for the German gunners. However, this was a distraction, because meanwhile the British swung west from Oosterhout and north through Valburg, turning Knaust's right flank. A British armoured column took just 30 minutes to get to Driel, with a second comprising motorized infantry approaching by a parallel route.

Knaust reacted to this breakthrough by sending five Tiger tanks to get between the two British columns. These lumbering monsters, because of their weight, were confined to the road. They were soon spotted when a British tracked carrier accidently ran into the first Tiger. The occupants of the tracked carrier fled on foot, but not before killing the tank commander, whose head was poking from the turret.

The British ambushed the Tigers at the De Hoop Cross, using a combination of anti-tank mines and PIATs (Projector, Infantry, Anti Tank weapons). The inexperienced tank crews easily fell victim to the British tank hunter teams, who successfully knocked out three Tigers. One of them was disabled by a mine and the crew watched helplessly as a young British soldier ran to within a few yards and fired his PIAT. The rest tried to withdraw only to slip into ditches, and these were then destroyed by hand grenades.

Reports on the progress of the fighting filtered into Model's headquarters. He was insistent that the forces in the Betuwe hold the Allies until 1st Airborne at Oosterbeek was liquidated. At Doetinchem he demanded that Bittrich conduct 'a quick finish'. To press the point, Bittrich visited Knaust. 'Can you hold for another twenty-four hours, while we clean up Oosterbeek?' he asked.[2] Knaust's response was yes. Horst Weber, serving with the 21st SS-Panzergrenadiers at Elst, was likewise confident: 'We were convinced that we would gain another victory here, that we would smash the enemy forces.'[3]

Knaust's battle group comprised about 350 men from both the army and SS, supported by ten remaining Tigers from the 506th Heavy Panzer Battalion and ten assault guns from the 280th Assault Gun Brigade. While the Tigers were powerful weapons, they were completely unsuited to the local countryside and had a habit of getting bogged down. His group also had a number of Panther tanks on call. Further support was provided by 16 88mm guns and two batteries of rocket launchers belonging to the 102nd SS Werfer Detachment.

His second armoured counter-attack westward from Elst to cut the route to Driel proved ill fated. A Tiger was knocked out and enemy infantry captured a Panther. Three other Panthers became stuck and were abandoned by their frightened crews. Knaust knew that it would be only a matter of time before the British tried to take Elst from him. This was especially the case once the British were in the village of Lienden immediately to the west.

The British attack was heralded by an artillery bombardment at 1600 hours on 23 September. A German observation post in Elst's large church tower provided a grandstand view, from where they could see for miles in all directions across the Betuwe. They were soon targeting shells and mortar rounds onto the British approaching from the west and the south. Knaust's gunners used airburst shells, which inflicted terrible multiple shrapnel wounds on those caught in the open. Elst would not be taken easily.

The British were initially greeted by machine guns, 88mm guns and two Panther tanks. The latter were soon lost. Knaust, like his colleagues, cursed the Luftwaffe for their lack of help. Clear skies meant that circling Allied fighter-bombers made short work of his remaining tanks. 'We had four Tiger tanks and three Panther tanks', recalled SS-Panzergrenadier Weber. 'But then Typhoons dropped these rockets on our tanks and shot all seven to bits.'[4]

Weber and his comrades were appalled as they watched burning tank crews falling from their vehicles, screaming in agony. Their morale broke and they began to abandon their positions, but at that moment Major Knaust appeared and rallied them. Such was his example that although he was not an SS officer, they heeded his orders. He also reinforced their position with two remaining Tiger tanks. SS-Corporal Rudolf Trapp from the 21st Panzergrenadiers, who had survived Arnhem, was hit during this fighting. 'In Elst I was wounded by small arms fire in the knee', said Trapp, who was now not hopeful about his chances of survival.[5]

The British fought their way into the outskirts of the village, but as night fell Knaust held on and the fighting died down. Neither side was prepared to conduct house-to-house fighting in the dark. The British tanks, fearing German 'Bazooka boys', withdrew, leaving their infantry to maintain a foothold. Although Knaust's defences had held to the south at Reet, his men were now in danger of being cut off. Sometime after 0300 hours, he ordered them to withdraw on Elst. They were halfway there when British artillery began to fire on them, causing some casualties. Most, though, made it safely to the village.

The following day the battle for Elst was resumed, with fierce fighting taking place around the brick church. By this stage, Knaust had hardly any tanks left. A solitary Panther, fresh from the factory, was manoeuvred by its young crew into the middle of Elst. Owing either to a mechanical problem or simply inexperience, the tank's turret was facing to the rear. The noise of the engine alerted a Sherman tank, which promptly shot the Panther's tracks off. The muzzle brake on the barrel was also torn off. The startled crew clambered out and fled. Their brand-new tank had just 45 kilometres on the clock.

Knaust's spotters in the church tower now came under fire from British anti-tank guns intent on knocking it down. Round after round thudded into the brickwork, though the resilient structure refused to collapse. The tenacious artillery observers, showered in dust and flying rubble, finally abandoned their post. The British stormed in and overwhelmed the defenders. A few resisted to the last and the interior was riddled with bullet holes. To stop the British from using it, German artillery shelled the building, setting it alight. The spire and roof were lost in the blaze and the wooden interior incinerated. Many other buildings in Elst likewise burned down.

Knaust's exhausted men finally withdrew from Elst at about 1330 hours on 25 September, to Elden just southeast of the Arnhem road bridge. Their column of just ten armoured vehicles was sped on its way by artillery and fighter-bomber attack. SS-Corporal Trapp was evacuated in Knaust's armoured half-track and ended up in hospital in Rees. Trapp recalled Knaust being 'a very good officer', adding, 'When I moaned he showed me his wooden leg and told me to cheer up.'[6] Model and Bittrich were highly pleased with Knaust's efforts, as he had bought them the time they needed to finish the British at Oosterbeek. Driel and Elst had proved the high water mark of the Allies' Operation *Market Garden*. British 30th Corps had been prevented from getting to 1st Airborne in time.

16

Model Triumphs

Once Arnhem bridge had been secured, Model's next priority was to crush the remains of 1st Airborne at Oosterbeek. Although he had half a dozen battle groups converging on the British thumb-shaped defensive perimeter, this was much easier said than done. Many of these units were not trained to operate at brigade level, let alone divisional or corps level. Co-ordinating them with a coherent chain of command was an ongoing struggle. Furthermore, friction between the army and the Waffen-SS was never far from the surface. The allocation of ammunition, rations and reinforcements was a constant problem. The British were well dug in and determined to hold out. Model's shortage of tanks meant that he was forced to fight a battle that was more akin to siege warfare. Besides, Oosterbeek and the surrounding wooded parkland was not good tank country. His armour was being ambushed at every turn. These attacks were also hampered by 1st Airborne getting artillery support from 30th Corps just across the river.

Model knew he needed to act quickly before 30th Corps battered their way through his defences in the Betuwe and tried to make for Arnhem bridge. News of the arrival of a Polish parachute brigade at Driel hampered matters. The need to hold the railway line south of the Rhine, as well as Elst, was a drain on already-stretched resources. Model and Bittrich had assumed that the wide and fast-flowing Rhine was too difficult to cross without specialized equipment.

The Americans' audacious crossing of the Waal showed that the Allies were prepared to improvise in spectacular fashion.

To the west of the British defences at Oosterbeek, General von Tettau moved forward a miscellaneous collection of units through the Bilderberg woods. These comprised the Worrowski Battalion from the Hermann Göring Training Regiment, plus the Arnheim, Eberwein, Helle and Schulz SS-battalions. The north was covered by Krafft's battle group and Battle Group Bruhns, while to the east forces included the Allworden, Spindler and Möller battle groups.

Operations commenced all along the British perimeter at 0800 hours on 21 September. The morning started off well when Colonel Schramm's Worrowski Battalion drove the British from the Westerbouwing Heights overlooking the Heveadorp ferry. Although this was achieved at great cost, it meant German fire dominated the Rhine. It also reduced the base of the British perimeter at Oosterbeek to less than 700 yards along the river.

Ironically, General von Tettau captured Westerbouwing more by accident than design. SS-Colonel Lippert and Lieutenant-Colonel Fritz Fullriede, commander of the Hermann Göring Regiment, had little faith in the abilities of Tettau or that of his staff. Tettau's instructions were simply to press eastward; there was no explicit plan to take Westerbouwing. Nor had he considered its tactical importance.

Herbert Kessler and his comrades in the Worrowski Battalion had no idea where they were going or what their objectives were. They had been redeployed from the Rotterdam area on bicycles and were strafed on 20 September. The following day Kessler's company made no effort to patrol ahead and exposed themselves to the British observation post in the Westerbouwing Inn. Three British platoons were holding the hill, with another one in reserve. When they opened fire, Colonel Schramm ordered the entire battalion to attack, supported by four old French Renault tanks. Schramm, worried about friendly fire, refused to commit his heavy weapons. This said much about the inadequate training his battalion had received.

Therefore, largely unsupported, Schramm's men attempted to storm the high ground. Kessler's company was initially pinned down and he was thankful their machine gun platoon made some effort to provide suppressive fire. He watched as the machine-gunners opened up from the sanctuary of some bushes. Kessler suspected they had done so just to hear the sound of their own weapons rather than with any targets in mind. However, this fire enabled them to work their way through the woods.

The tanks, with another company, came out of the trees and into the grounds of the inn. They hit a British anti-tank gun, but the infantry suffered heavy casualties. However, the British were forced to retire when their only light machine gun jammed. The tanks pressed on after them and three were subsequently knocked out by a PIAT. The British then counter-attacked, but were unsuccessful.

When the dust settled after several hours of fighting, it was discovered that every officer except one and half the Worrowski Battalion were casualties. Fullriede was absolutely furious and demanded that Schramm be sacked on the spot for incompetence. He also defied orders and sent 1,600 poorly trained recruits back to Germany rather than see them become cannon fodder for the British. Lacking manpower, Tettau now missed a golden opportunity and failed to strike farther along the river. Such a move would have completely cut 1st Airborne off from the outside world.

The only compensation was that from the hill the Germans could see all of the northern bank of the Rhine, which formed the southern edge of the British perimeter. Sailors, fighting as infantry from the 10th Naval Manning Division, were sent to occupy Westerbouwing. Other attacks conducted by Battle Group von Tettau that day made little or no progress. In the face of strong resistance, the 9th SS gained even less ground attacking the eastern Oosterbeek perimeter.

By now the British had withdrawn all their surviving units behind their defences looped around the Hartenstein Hotel. This had been achieved at some cost by the remnants of the battalions who had tried to fight their way back from Arnhem. Now just 3,500 survivors of 1st Airborne were gathered in the western half of Oosterbeek, along with some 8,000 terrified Dutch civilians. This once-quiet market town was in ruins and its hotels turned into bloody field hospitals. The Germans, with good reason, were calling this pocket 'the witches' cauldron'.[1]

An impatient Model pressed Bittrich daily for results and he in turn pressured his officers. 'It is particularly important that the remaining British forces north of the river Rhine are quickly destroyed', noted SS-Lieutenant-Colonel Harzer, as the 9th SS battle groups closed in for the kill.[2] However, the attack launched from the north on 22 September under the command of SS-Colonel Lippert did not go well. Once again, Helle's Dutch SS performed badly. 'The commander Helle was not a field officer of any experience', grumbled Lippert. 'I had therefore to relieve him of his command.'[3] Ultimately the Germans had only themselves to blame for deploying such an unreliable unit.

The following day, the Germans brought up 15 heavy Tiger IIs. In theory these should have crashed through the British defences with impunity, but the inexperienced crews were afraid of British tank hunters. Their lack of infantry support was also symptomatic of the very poor co-ordination between the different units. After one of the Tigers was lost, the rest resorted to acting as mobile artillery. By 23 September, Model had lost 13 tanks and three assault guns attacking Oosterbeek. Another six were destroyed recapturing Arnhem bridge. 'The more the perimeter shrank', remarked Harzer, 'the more stubbornly the British troops defended every heap of ruins and every inch of ground.'[4]

Lippert, thoroughly fed up with Tettau's uninspired methods, fell out with him. He claimed that the army was not adequately supplying his men, meaning constant recourse to SS-General Rauter's SS-police commissariat. The final straw came when Tettau's intelligence reported that Lippert's headquarters in Kasteel Doorwerth west of Heveadorp had been captured. This was not true and when Lippert angrily confronted the general he was promptly sacked on the spot.

Battle for the 'Witches' Cauldron',
21–26 September 1944

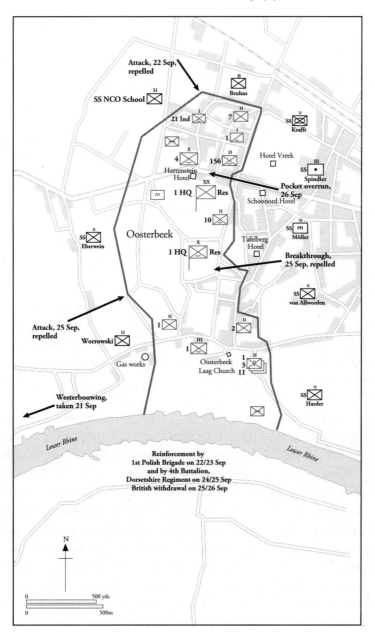

While the battle for Oosterbeek was developing into a very messy affair, Model and Bittrich were heartened by the news that their forces had prevented the British from getting reinforcements and supplies over the Rhine. The arrival of elements of the British 43rd Infantry Division at Driel had been a very worrying development. On 22 and 23 September, at 2100 hours and 0200 hours respectively, two attempts were made by the Poles to reinforce 1st Airborne. The first crossing, made in rubber dinghies, was revealed by a German parachute flare and met by punishing machine-gun and mortar fire. The second attempt using amphibious trucks was largely stillborn, thanks to the muddy conditions and poor visibility caused by a ground mist. By dawn only a few hundred Poles had got across.

For the besieged British, the conditions in the 'witches' cauldron' were almost intolerable. Harzer observed their 'morale was sagging rapidly!'[5] On the morning of Sunday 24 September, Bittrich and Harzer were visited by a British medical officer at the Villa Heselbergh north of Arnhem. Colonel Graeme Warrack was accompanied by SS-Major Dr Egon Skalka, his opposite number from the 9th SS. Under a Red Cross flag Warrack had first presented himself to Skalka at the Schoonoord Hotel, which was now behind German lines. 'I want to make arrangements for the evacuation of our wounded', said the colonel, after being escorted into the hotel. 'I would like to see your divisional doctor.'[6] Skalka responded that he had come to the right man.

Warrack explained that within the British perimeter there were at least 600 British, Dutch, German and Polish wounded gathered at seven locations. In reality there were over double this number, but Warrack did not want the Germans to know just how weak the division was. Earlier a dressing station had been hit six times, caught fire and 150 wounded were now lying outside. Major-General Robert Urquhart, 1st Airborne's commander, wished to evacuate as many as possible into the care of the Germans. Skalka was sympathetic because he had come to exactly the same conclusion.

Skalka's actions suggest he was a doctor first and a soldier second. When he drove Warrack and his interpreter, Dutch liaison officer Lieutenant Commander Arnoldus Wolters – who was introduced as 'Johnson' – to headquarters he did not blindfold them. He may have had psychological reasons for this decision, because it meant both emissaries were witness to the terrible carnage in Arnhem. All about them were burnt-out buildings, bodies in the streets and smashed military vehicles. It was grim testimony to the fate of those British forces who had tried to battle their way to the bridge.

The group met with Harzer and acting chief of staff SS-Captain Wilfried Schwarz. Both officers agreed in principle and said the matter would have to be referred to the commander of the 2nd SS-Panzer Corps. Schwarz laid out a map and asked Warrack to highlight where their dressing stations were located. Bittrich then appeared and Skalka, after saluting, said he supported the proposal, as the medical facilities on both sides were under constant fire. A logical solution would be to move the British casualties to St Elizabeth Hospital in Arnhem, where British and German medics were already caring for wounded prisoners.

Bittrich eyed Skalka, who was smartly turned out. The tall, dark-haired English colonel in contrast looked grimy and terribly tired. Being a combat medic was a respected military profession; everyone was grateful for their desire to save lives, even in the heat of battle and no matter the nationality of the injured. The general agreed that the wounded could be moved under a two-hour ceasefire. He said he regretted they were at war and added, 'a man cannot… lose all humanity, even during the most bitter fight'.[7] Bittrich then presented Warrack with a bottle of brandy, saying, 'for your general.'[8] On the way back to Oosterbeek his escort gallantly stopped off at St Elizabeth Hospital so that Warrack could check on the British wounded.

Privately Bittrich and the others were very disappointed that the colonel had not come to negotiate terms for a surrender. Continued resistance by this stage seemed futile and they were amazed by the British airborne forces' continuing resilience. However, fighting to the last was not a new notion to the Germans. On the Eastern Front they had developed a mantra – never give up, regardless of the situation.

When the ceasefire ended at 1700 hours about 450 wounded had been taken into German custody. They also took control of the Tafelberg Hotel, which was full of wounded. Skalka reported that inside Oosterbeek 'it was nothing but death and wreckage'.[9] During the transfer an SS doctor suggested that given their losses and that they were surrounded, they should surrender. Colonel Warrack responded, 'We have not come to surrender'.[10]

The moment the truce finished, German shelling recommenced, while tanks and infantry once more infiltrated British positions. The tanks were met by the last of the British anti-tank guns. One was caught in a cabbage patch by a 6-pounder, which knocked out the tank and sent cabbages showering in all directions. For the first time in eight days the 1st Airborne received air support when RAF Typhoons appeared. They pounded German positions and troop movements. As far as Bittrich and Urquhart were concerned, it was too little too late.

On the night of 24 September, the Germans were put on alert by a British artillery bombardment. The British then tried to get more reinforcements over the river and were met by sustained German fire. They also struggled with the fast current, which contributed to a chaotic landing. Just over 300 infantry reached the far bank, where they struggled to get past the Westerbouwing escarpment. It was a brave act, but very few ever got to the airborne perimeter, with the rest scattering amongst the German-infested woods. That day the Germans attacked the base of the British perimeter from both the west and the east, but on each occasion were repulsed.

British guns once more opened up on German positions surrounding the pocket at 2100 hours on 25 September. Their fire was indiscriminate, hitting Germans and Dutch alike. The Germans responded with their own mortar and shellfire. 'The earth was trembling', recalled SS-Captain Möller, 'and a curtain of fire and dirt of hitherto unknown dimensions rose over and between our positions.' He and his men sought cover, but the 'impacts dealt death and destruction'.[11]

In the failing light, the sailors on the Westerbouwing struggled to see what was going on along the river. On the south bank there were two points, roughly a mile apart, where British and Canadian engineers had gathered a fleet of small boats. These started crossing at 2130 hours and the current rapidly forced some of them downstream. The observation posts up on the Westerbouwing assumed that this was yet another attempt by the British to get reinforcements to 1st Airborne. Meanwhile, German patrols ambushed British paratroopers with blackened faces and their equipment and boots wrapped in cloth. This indicated they were making a break for the river. The reports reaching the various German headquarters gave a confused picture. Although the Germans were not sure what was going on, their flares soon showed that some sort of sustained ferrying operation was under way.

Field telephones started ringing and German artillery and mortars began to drop shells and bombs into the water. The German machine-gunners on the Westerbouwing went to work and the night sky was lit up by deadly tracer fire. The mortars began to range in on the British embarkation points. 'Suddenly German mortars caught them', said war reporter Erwin Kirchhof. 'Three, perhaps four assault boats succeeded in reaching the opposite bank.'[12] Some 95 men were hit on the north bank or while trying to cross. Many others were wounded. In the space of about 60 minutes, half the British boats had been sunk. Some men bravely swam the Rhine; others were rescued mid-river by returning boats.

Captain Derek Bogaerde, who later became a highly respected actor and author, remembered:

Helplessly staring across the wide flowing river to the burning city, the chatter and crump of machine guns and mortars, crimson tracer-bullets ripping through the night, the little huddle of Dutch civilians weeping, not for themselves, but for the few returning guests departing from what someone on the Staff had chosen to call a 'party'.[13]

In places it was hard to tell if it was an organized evacuation or a chaotic flight. Bogaerde witnessed the ashen-faced survivors 'straggling back desperately across the strong current hanging on to rubber dinghies or anything which would float; the mouth sour with the bitter knowledge that we had lost'.[14]

Despite the losses, the ferry service pressed on. The Germans remained confused as to its purpose until well after 2400 hours.

'In the sector of Battle Group Knoche on the Lower Rhine front the enemy made renewed crossing attempts from opposite the 10th SS', noted General von Tettau, 'which were mostly repelled by concentrated fire.'[15] Tettau had little faith in Battle Group Knoche, as it had been formed from various Luftwaffe ground personnel units. Nonetheless, it had been moved into a blocking position on the Rhine. Previously it had been assigned to rear area security duties.

There was an almighty explosion from within the British Oosterbeek perimeter at 0200 hours, as 1st Airborne blew up the last of its remaining ammunition. Guns covering the withdrawal fired off their few shells before being disabled. The western crossings stopped at 0330 hours, but to the east they continued until 0720 hours, by which time 2,398 men from an original force of 10,000 had been evacuated. Tettau still had no real idea what had happened. 'Only individual boats managed to cross and infiltrate', he claimed. 'The crews were eliminated or captured during the course of the morning.'[16]

'Uselessly one wept, or dragged muddied, soaking bodies up the slithering river banks', Bogaerde recalled, 'and watched as our youth (I was twenty-three) drained away into the swirling waters of the Rhine.'[17] He felt there was nothing they could do except 'help any stray escapee who managed to get across the river, and file useless intelligence reports'.[18] His only solace from the misery of it all was attending a production of *The Merry Widow* at Eindhoven theatre. Later he was to write with some bitterness, 'We'd lost this part of the war'.[19]

SS-Captain Möller was much better informed than Tettau. He knew that the enemy 'had withdrawn and disappeared during the night behind the curtain of dirt and destruction'.[20] All that remained behind were the badly wounded, their medics and brave rearguard units, who had missed the boats. The Germans launched three attacks at dawn on 26 September, with the Hartenstein Hotel as their goal. Although they encountered some resistance, by 1400 hours it was all over. About 315 prisoners were rounded up in Oosterbeek and another 300 were found huddled along the north bank. Many of them were wounded and filthy. Another 250 men were on the run, some of whom would make it back.

When German casualties were reported to Model, he discovered the battle for Arnhem had cost him 1,100 dead and 2,200 wounded.[21] The British suffered around 1,200 dead and 6,642 captured, around a third of whom were wounded. Total German losses incurred stopping *Market Garden* amounted to about 6,400 men. Model had finally won the battle for Arnhem, the airborne spearhead had been sheared off and the Allies denied Arnhem bridge. After the loss of Eindhoven and Nijmegen, this was a victory he was happy to report to Hitler.

17

Unrepentant Advocate

After the British evacuation of Oosterbeek, Model continued to make his presence felt in the Betuwe and east of Nijmegen. Despite the liberation of Eindhoven and Nijmegen, Lieutenant-Colonel David Niven found the Germans still very active. He was running an errand to Nijmegen when he bumped into an old acquaintance, Captain Tony Bushell, serving with the Welsh Guards. They were chatting in the tank park when an enormous explosion caused Niven to dive for cover. The captain did not move and stood laughing at Niven's response. 'Oh, that's an old friend', explained Bushell. 'They've got a bloody great gun in a railway tunnel across the river. About once an hour they wheel it out and let off a big one – then they pop back in again. We're used to it.'[1] It was a constant reminder that the Allies had been stopped.

Model, Student and Bittrich, or more precisely their men, had performed miracles during the hard-fought battle for Arnhem. Deserters, stragglers, teenagers, trainees, old men and Luftwaffe staff somehow stopped three airborne, three infantry and one armoured division. Forming *ad hoc* battle groups, they literally fought Operation *Market Garden* to a standstill. This was a quite remarkable achievement and represented a major blot on Field Marshal Montgomery's reputation that he could never quite escape.

German war correspondent Erwin Kirchhof was amazed at the performance of these battle groups:

Only 24 hours before they had not known each other: the
aeroplane technicians still worked on their planes; the soldiers
of the Waffen SS were refitting... the reserve units were still
employed as guards... the naval coast artillery men had just
returned... the boys of the Reich labour organization were still
constructing field positions. Only a few of them were familiar
with the principles of fighting... But they fought.[2]

In his view, they had done so with 'miraculous strength'.[3]

Whatever way you look at it, Arnhem was a victory for Model
and his generals. They had thwarted the Allies by denying them their
ultimate objective – a bridge over the Rhine. The British, as they
had done with Dunkirk, tried to paint Arnhem as a partial victory.
There is certainly no denying the bravery and professionalism
of the British 1st Airborne Division, but they were betrayed by
appallingly inadequate planning and intelligence.

The quick thinking of Bittrich, and his highly competent
subordinates Harmel and Harzer, saved the day for Hitler. It was,
though, the eight-mile gap between the British landing zones and
Arnhem that truly sealed 1st Airborne's fate. If the British had got
three battalions to Arnhem bridge, instead of just one, they could
have held out much longer. Once the bulk of the division became
trapped at Oosterbeek, their mission was dead in its tracks. 'I take
the blame for this mistake', Montgomery later ruefully conceded.[4]

Model and Student were very lucky from the outset. If they had
been killed or captured at their headquarters by Allied paratroopers,
the battle would have gone very differently. The death of General
Kussin clearly illustrated the type of problems created by the loss of
a senior commander. Bittrich was much safer at Doetinchem thanks
to the close proximity of the remains of his two Panzer divisions.
Nonetheless, had he been killed the response of the 2nd SS-Panzer
Corps would inevitably have been much slower. After the dark days
of Normandy, the German reaction was simply exemplary.

A poor intelligence assessment of the German armed forces, and
in one instance a wilful ignoring of intelligence to hand, meant
the British underestimated Bittrich, Student and Zangen's ability

to fight with any determination. Montgomery refused to conceive that the Germans would stand their ground. He seems to have assumed they would not do this until their forces were safely back on German soil. Instead, as General Brian Horrocks, commander of 30th Corps, noted, the Germans 'made one of the most remarkable military recoveries in history'.[5]

Respected historian Basil Liddell Hart was firmly of the view that it was the Allied delay just before *Market Garden* that helped Model. He observed, 'Most fatal of all to the prospect of reaching the Rhine was the pause from September 4 to 7 after reaching Brussels and Antwerp'.[6] Montgomery had hoped to drive from the Seine straight to the Rhine and get over the river 'before the enemy succeeded in reforming a front to oppose us'.[7] He was too slow.

One of Montgomery's biographers, Alun Chalfont, agreed with this damming assessment, concluding:

> The failure to exploit the German collapse in early September (with the final failure at Arnhem) was due partly to a lack of supplies, and partly to grave mistakes in the execution of the pursuit in the first week of September; mistakes which culminated in the failure to capture the Scheldt approaches to Antwerp.[8]

This criticism was made with the benefit of hindsight. 'How could we know that the 4th of September', reasoned Horrocks, 'was the fateful day when victory in 1944 slipped through our fingers?'[9]

Model and Student were very fortunate that Allied logistical problems caused the British 2nd Army to halt on the Meuse–Escaut Canal for a week. This was because General Patton's US 3rd Army was busy attacking in Lorraine. Likewise, this had delayed the US 1st Army's attack on the Siegfried Line. Model and Student were granted vital time during which they strengthened their defences in the Netherlands. Crucially, 2nd SS-Panzer Corps deployed to the Arnhem area, and the two divisions of Corps Feldt moved to Roermond from the Reichswald. Göring's paratroops were organized into divisions and Zangen was able to get three divisions across the Scheldt Estuary. This meant that Model was able to double the strength of his forces in the *Market Garden* area.[10] The British achieved their breakthrough only because Student's newly created 1st Parachute Army was still in the process of deploying from Germany.

The failure to trap Zangen's 15th Army in the Breskens pocket sowed the seeds for the German victory at Arnhem. It enabled Zangen to feed desperately needed reinforcements to Student's army, which started life as little more than a weak division. As a result, they were able to slow the British attack up Highway 69, thereby delaying the capture of Nijmegen. This in turn gave the Germans time to recapture Arnhem and strengthen their meagre defences in the Betuwe.

By 22 September, Student had been reinforced by the 6th Parachute Division, two depot divisions and the 107th Panzer Brigade. At that point 15th Army assumed control of the western flank, which was reinforced by two more divisions ferried over the Scheldt Estuary. These troop movements were achieved largely thanks to the weather, which had greatly restricted Allied fighter-bomber operations. The result was that by 24 September the British were being resisted by 14 German divisions, although many of these were terribly under strength, ill-equipped and ill-trained.

Over the intervening years, Montgomery has been blamed for seriously underestimating the German defences and combat effectiveness of their battle groups. There is no excuse for this, as in all armies every soldier is trained to fight as an infantryman, regardless of his assigned military trade. Regarding the 2nd SS-Panzer Corps, Montgomery confessed, 'we were wrong in supposing that it could not fight effectively; its battle state was far beyond our expectation'.[11]

Horrocks' 30th Corps was accused of being much too slow. 'If this is so', he said with regret, 'it was my fault, because all the troops were imbued with a sense of desperate urgency.'[12] Montgomery should share the blame. Not once did he visit Horrocks during the operation and urge him on. He was preoccupied by his ongoing struggles with Eisenhower over resources and strategy. Also,

Student's swift actions ensured that it was not safe for Montgomery to visit the forward areas of the battlefield.

To many German commanders, the British threw away their chance of getting to Arnhem by stopping at Valkenswaard on the very first night. 'Their attack could have worked', said SS-Captain Karl Godau of the 10th SS.[13] There were very sound tactical and logistical reasons for Horrocks stopping overnight. However, if he had pressed on he could have capitalized on the confusion and poor communication amongst the disparate German units. Instead Chill, Heydte and Kerutt were given a much-needed breathing space before Aalst. This meant another fight before Horrocks could get to Eindhoven.

At Nijmegen the weak German defence was greatly aided by the American decision to secure a 25-mile perimeter to the south, before taking the key bridges. The seizure of the Groesbeek Heights, to the south east, was a wholly nugatory operation prompted by faulty intelligence. This stated the heights overlooked the road bridge, which they did not, owing to a bend in the river, and that there were Panzer units in the nearby Reichswald Forest. The German defence was also greatly assisted by the Americans not landing a *coup de main* on the northern end of Nijmegen road bridge. The British committed the same error at Arnhem by not dropping forces at the southern end of the road bridge.

Euling and Henke, in light of their poor resources, did a very good job at Nijmegen. Once the Americans had paddled over the Waal, the German flank was turned and they lacked the manpower to counter-attack. A major failing was not blowing either of the bridges before they were captured. Had they done so, this would have speeded up the British defeat at Oosterbeek and safeguarded the Betuwe. After Nijmegen was taken, the Allies hoped the German defence in the Betuwe would collapse. It was not to be.

Once again, Horrocks was delayed by determined German battle groups, giving Bittrich time to overwhelm the Oosterbeek Pocket. Only British tenacity ensured they held out as long as they did. This in part was due to the poor co-ordination of the German attacks.

It was only at this stage of the operations that their battle group tactics began to let them down. By now it did not matter, however, as Student and Bittrich had sufficiently delayed the British ground attack, and Bittrich had retaken Arnhem road bridge.

Notably, SS-Major Krafft was instrumental in helping derail British plans on the opening day of Operation *Market Garden*. His delaying tactics bought valuable time, which enabled Harzer's 9th SS to reach Arnhem and cut off the British at the northern end of the road bridge. Likewise, it won time allowing units to move in from the west and east to cut off the main British force at Oosterbeek. His actions helped Model ensure that just 700 of the 10,000 paratroopers and airborne infantry dropped around Wolfheze ever reached Arnhem bridge.

Krafft was personally very impressed by 1st Airborne's performance. 'They all had some five or six years' service and most of them were veterans of North Africa, Sicily, Italy and Normandy', he observed. 'They were well trained, particularly for independent fighting, and of good combat value.'[14] General Student, who had his hands full countering Horrocks' ground attack, understood how the British 1st Airborne Division misjudged the race for Arnhem. He noted 'the foremost British Parachute Brigade… lost too much time whilst overcoming the resistance by [the] weak German garrison and units of the Luftwaffe'.[15]

Despite getting hold of the Allies' plans, Model did not share them with anyone. 'I never realized until after the war that the *Market-Garden* plans had fallen into our hands', said Bittrich. 'I have no idea why Model did not tell me. In any case, the plans would simply have confirmed my opinion that the important thing to do was prevent the link-up between the airborne forces and the British 2nd Army.'[16]

Bittrich held 1st Airborne's sacrifice at Arnhem responsible for the loss of Nijmegen. 'The heroic fighting of this group of British parachutists at Arnhem bridge made it impossible for the 10th SS-Panzer Division to advance quickly along the main Arnhem–Nijmegen road', he noted. 'These forces consequently arrived at Nijmegen too late to reinforce the bridge-head effectively.'[17]

Arnhem proved to be a sobering wake-up call for the Allies after the unparalleled triumph of the D-Day landings. 'This time we failed disastrously', said Captain Bogaerde. 'There was to be no liberation for Arnhem.'[18] While Hitler considered Model and Bittrich the heroes of the moment, on the British side Bogaerde knew who the villain was. Montgomery blamed Eisenhower for not committing sufficient resources to the enterprise. He reckoned if these had been provided 'it would have succeeded in spite of my mistakes, or the adverse weather, or the presence of the 2nd SS Panzer Corps... I remain Market Garden's unrepentant advocate.'[19] Montgomery's brother optimistically called it 'an administrative victory' by virtue of taking and holding the Nijmegen bridges.[20]

Two days after the evacuation of Oosterbeek, Montgomery's chief of staff, Major-General Freddie de Guingand, was obliged to face hostile reporters. 'I was pressed', he recalled, 'to admit that the whole operation had been a failure.'[21] He was given a tough time because of a previous news blackout. 'There were one or two particularly critical correspondents who made frequent interruptions.'[22]

Eisenhower was more generous when he held a press conference in Paris on 12 October, saying, 'They did beautiful work and I am proud of them all'. He not only praised the gallantry of 1st Airborne, but he also pointed out that 'by drawing upon themselves the bulk of the German counterattack, they enabled us to hold important bridges'.[23] Later, writing with the benefit of hindsight, he claimed the Allies had been simply testing Hitler. 'We felt it would prove whether or not the Germans could succeed in establishing renewed and effective resistance', he said; 'on the battle's outcome we would form an estimate of the severity of the fighting still ahead of us.'[24] This was rather disingenuous, as Hitler was husbanding his re-formed and new divisions ready for a massive counter-offensive in the winter.

Eisenhower, like Montgomery, preferred to ignore the ignominy of being outfought by what was thought to be a defeated enemy. He preferred to blame the weather. Eisenhower believed that *Market Garden* 'unquestionably would have been successful except for the intervention of bad weather. This prevented the adequate reinforcement of the northern spearhead...'.[25] It was many years before he was prepared to concede that the thrust on Arnhem had 'miserably failed'.[26]

At senior levels in London there seemed to be some confusion about what had transpired. According to intelligence available to Field Marshal Alan Brooke, the 1st Airborne Division had 'dropped by ill-luck in the middle of a German parachute corps'.[27] This was incorrect, as it was the Americans who had landed amongst Student's forces. Brooke blamed Montgomery, stating, 'Instead of carrying out the advance on Arnhem he ought to have made certain of Antwerp in the first place'.[28]

Prime Minister Winston Churchill, while addressing the House of Commons on 28 September 1944, briefly paid fulsome tribute to 1st Airborne's 'sacrifice'. He tried to portray the operation as a victory by saying as a result the Allies had been able 'to form a strong bridgehead over the main stream of Rhine at Nijmegen'. He then added, 'The cost has been heavy... "Not in vain" may be the pride of those who survived.'[29] Churchill then reverted to describing the Allied victories in France. To some, this might be construed as deliberate spin. However, to be fair to Churchill, he had been in America with Brooke while *Market Garden* was under way and had returned only on 26 September. The full implications of what happened had yet to sink in.

On the British side, those involved knew that however you dressed up the failure of Operation *Market Garden*, it was still a humiliating defeat and a remarkable recovery by the Germans. As far as Captain Bogaerde was concerned, Arnhem had been a 'catastrophe'.[30] 'Ninety per cent successful they had said at Headquarters; what could a ninety per cent failure conceivably look like?'[31] He knew, as did many others, that there would be excuses aplenty. 'We had no need of the books the generals might later write to explain things. We saw it happen before our eyes, unwilling witnesses to a shattering disaster.'[32] Bogaerde aptly summed up the experience of all involved when he said, 'The agony of Arnhem burned deeply into each and every one of us who had survived'.[33]

Despite all the recriminations, the Allied generals knew what their greatest crime was. 'I think we had perhaps underestimated the enemy's powers of recuperation', wrote de Guingand. 'We were, no doubt, influenced too much by the devastating defeat we had witnessed [in Normandy].'[34] General Horrocks was in agreement that the credit should go to Model. 'The failure at Arnhem was primarily due to the astonishing recovery made by the German armed forces after their crippling defeat.'[35]

The Germans were impressed and surprised by Montgomery's audacity. 'The operation hit my army nearly in the centre and split it in two parts', said Student with admiration. 'In spite of all the precautions, all the bridges fell intact into the hands of the Allied airborne forces.'[36] In his opinion, *Market Garden* in terms of the airborne element 'proved to be a great success… The conquest of the Nijmegen area meant the creation of a good jumping board for the offensive which contributed to the end of the war.'[37]

General Blumentritt, the German chief of staff on the Western Front, recognized the threat posed by Operation *Market Garden*:

> He who holds northern Germany holds Germany. Such a break-through, coupled with air domination, would have torn in pieces the weak German front and ended the war. Berlin and Prague would have been occupied ahead of the Russians. There were no German forces behind the Rhine, and at the end of August our front was wide open.[38]

However, he was critical of Allied strategy elsewhere:

> There was an operational break-through in the Aachen area, in September. This facilitated a rapid conquest of the Ruhr and a quicker advance on Berlin. By turning forces from the Aachen area sharply northwards the German 15th and 1st Parachute Armies could have been pinned against the estuaries of the Maas and the Rhine. They could not have escaped eastwards into Germany.[39]

For Model, the battle for Arnhem had been a close-run thing. By the end of September, from a total force of some 52 'divisions' forming Army Group B, he had been obliged to deploy 33 of them to contain the British. By the time of 1st Airborne's evacuation, he was holding a front that stretched from the Scheldt to Arnhem on to Aachen and Trier. In all this was some 300 miles. Through September, his forces suffered 75,000 casualties and his armour was reduced to two weak Panzer divisions. The Allies had the equivalent of a dozen armoured divisions. His forces were at breaking point, especially as Hitler was holding back the better-quality reinforcements.

There were no accolades for Model and the others. The battle had only lasted just over a week and was part of a much wider war, a war that Hitler was losing. Hitler, preoccupied with plans to launch two whole Panzer armies towards Antwerp, had left Model to get on with it. As far as he was concerned, Arnhem was just a holding action. Nonetheless, for the Germans their victory was a much-needed morale booster. It showed that even after their defeat in France they still had fight left in them. 'We felt proud of ourselves', recalled SS-Sergeant Erwin Heck, 'especially when we had achieved victory with so few resources.'[40] 'Morale was particularly good at the end', said SS-Captain Schwarz. 'We had actually succeeded in forcing this elite British division to stop, and pushed the remnants back over the Rhine!'[41]

Members of the 1st Airborne division were impressed by the performance of the Germans. 'They fought like tigers', said Godfrey Freeman, a British glider pilot captured at Arnhem, 'and eventually, against a force gradually running out of ammunition and suffering casualties at an ever increasing rate, they overcame.'[42] Freeman, like so many others, held Montgomery to blame.

18

Panzer Corps Controversy

What really puzzled Model and Bittrich was why the British had chosen to land almost on top of their two Panzer divisions belonging to the 2nd SS-Panzer Corps. The Luftwaffe, which had flown regular missions in support of the SS, army and its own ground units, was equally baffled. An intelligence report for the Luftwaffe high command assessed one of the reasons for their victory was that 'Allied intelligence was not aware of the location of the SS Panzer Corps which was refitting north of Arnhem. Or, if the Allies were aware of this force, they did not make proper dispositions to meet it.' The Luftwaffe concluded that 'the former view is more likely'.[1] In reality, it was the latter. Model and Bittrich could only assume that Montgomery foolishly dismissed them. He actually had good reason to do so. 'It had been thought that the well-known 9th and 10th SS Panzer Divisions had been written off in the Falaise battle on the far bank of the Seine', said Lieutenant-Colonel John Frost, tasked with capturing Arnhem bridge.[2]

By the end of the first week of September, Model's Army Group B was reporting that it had only 100 tanks combat ready. This figure fluctuated day to day, as the workshops made combat repairs in a desperate effort to return damaged tanks to their units. Nonetheless, it was terrible news. Hitler was so alarmed that he had ordered 'all 88mm anti-tank guns, all Tiger II and all Jagdpanthers'[3] to be sent to the Western Front. The Jagdpanther was a turretless version of the Panther armed with an 88mm gun. Fortunately for

the Allies not many were built, and those that were Hitler ended up
keeping back for his winter offensive in the Ardennes.[4] Rundstedt
had been promised over half of the Panthers built in August, which
amounted to some 200 tanks. All the Panzer IVs and assault guns
were allocated to the Eastern Front. Such numbers were a drop in
the ocean, as Rundstedt needed some 2,000 tanks, and losses were
constantly outstripping production.

The 1st Airborne Division's intelligence summary on 7
September 1944 reported, 'one of the broken panzer divisions has
been sent back to the area north of Arnhem to rest and refit; this
might produce some 50 tanks.'[5] This was the very day that the
2nd SS-Panzer Corps had started to congregate around Arnhem.
British intelligence was also aware that the Corps had lost 120 tanks
during its failed counter-attack at Falaise in late August. During
the battle for Normandy both divisions had lost about a third of
their manpower.

Far more worrying was intelligence claiming 'One thousand
tanks reported in Forest of Reichswald in Holland on 8 September,
presumably a pool for refitting panzer divisions'.[6] This was risible,
as there was no way Model could have conjured up so many tanks.
If their presence had been confirmed, it would have made *Market
Garden* impossible. What it did signal, though, was that German
tanks, even limited numbers, might pose a threat to the American
drops at Nijmegen. This did not deter the landings, but it forced
the Americans to expand their defensive perimeter.

Model could not understand why the British ignored what
was going on in the Netherlands and specifically in the Arnhem
area. Major 'Teddy' Behr, on General Krebs' staff, stationed in
Oosterbeek, was witness to this. He recalled:

There was an enormous concentration of heavy armour in
all stages of preparation, from cannibalized wrecks to fully
battle-ready Tigers. Some of these were the updated Royal
Tigers, with much thicker armour-plating and larger guns,
which had proved a match for the Russian T-34s. Among

its armament was the 8.8cm gun (originally an anti-aircraft weapon) that had wrought such havoc among the British tanks in North Africa.[7]

'To Model and his staff it seemed impossible that the British should not have known what was going on behind German lines', said British glider pilot Sergeant Louis Hagen.[8] According to Bittrich, 'there was no particular significance in Model choosing the Arnhem vicinity – except that it was a peaceful sector where nothing was happening'.[9] For some reason, it had taken three days to arrange the move of 2nd SS-Panzer Corps. Model's headquarters first issued orders on the evening of 3 September, but Bittrich seems not to have received them. The following day, Model instructed him verbally. Bittrich recalled, 'Pending official orders which would follow, I was told to move my Corps Headquarters north into Holland'.[10] The 9th SS and 10th SS then started redeploying on 5 and 6 September. Bittrich was also told to oversee the refitting of the 2nd and 116th Panzer Divisions, but both these units were tied up in the Aachen area.

Arnhem soon became a hive of activity, as Behr noted:

Every day specialized freight trains brought back the battered tanks and mobile guns which had stubbornly held back the Allied advance, allowing the infantry and other troops to fall back towards Germany. Here in relative peace the fitters and engineers worked on urgent repairs and refitting: the weapons were repaired or replaced and crews re-equipped and retrained. Then as soon as the tanks, self-propelled guns and fighting vehicles were ready for action, they were sent eastwards without delay to help in the defence of Germany.[11]

The 9th SS-Panzer Division commenced heading home on 12 September, but this was rear echelon personnel, not tanks and artillery. 'As the critical weekend approached', noted General Urquhart, commander of 1st Airborne, 'few of them had started to roll into Germany.'[12]

The Allies' Top Secret Ultra signal intercepts, decoded by Bletchley Park, revealed the deployment of Bittrich's armoured divisions to the Nijmegen and Arnhem area. 'Elements retreating from the [Falaise] pocket in August and September', said Ralph Bennett, serving at Bletchley, 'filled the air with reports of their movements and strength.'[13] Aerial reconnaissance by the RAF and the Dutch Resistance also confirmed their presence. However, RAF photo reconnaissance was not as thorough as it could have been in the week leading up to *Market Garden*. The RAF was distracted by the urgent hunt for the V-2 launch sites and other operational requirements. It was also hampered by the poor weather, which helped conceal German troop traffic.[14]

Major Tony Hibbert, 1st Parachute Brigade, recalled a meeting with Major Brian Urquhart, chief intelligence officer, 1st Airborne. 'He showed me photographs of German Panzer IVs; mainly I think they were tucked in underneath woods. He went to General 'Boy' Browning, commander of the British Airborne Corps, and said that in his view the operation could not succeed, because of the presence of these two divisions.'[15] Senior British commanders would not be distracted by this inconvenient news.

When Major Urquhart presented his findings to his boss, he found himself placed on sick leave. Browning, with just a week to prepare, decided that the operation would go ahead. 'I thought that 1st Airborne was too light on anti-tank weapons', said Major Urquhart, 'and that troops should land on the south side near the bridge.' He knew it was too late to cancel and that any changes would be difficult. 'What distressed me was that the intelligence was dismissed without considering possible options'.[16]

The photos were of both Panzer IVs and obsolete Panzer IIIs. They did not belong to the 2nd SS-Panzer Corps, as first suspected, so were not the smoking gun that many have since claimed them to have been. They were being used by a training and replacement battalion of the Hermann Göring Panzer Division for driver instruction.[17] This was a Luftwaffe unit that came under the control of the army and was nothing to do with the SS. The new crews were destined for the Eastern Front. As these vehicles were for driver training, they were probably not in the best condition.[18] Nonetheless, they were still tanks. The reality was that a proportion of the armour faced by the Allies arrived after the battle started.

Montgomery was briefed on 10 September about these developments, but was not unduly concerned. 'So firmly entrenched… was the conviction that German resistance was nearing its end', observed Ralph Bennett, 'that this knowledge was not enough to cast doubt on the wisdom of launching Operation *Market Garden*.'[19] Montgomery was confident that 1st Airborne, with its 6-pounder and 17-pounder anti-tank guns, would be able to fend off Bittrich's weak armoured brigade until help arrived.

This was not the first time that Bennett had experienced Montgomery ignoring Ultra intelligence. Two years earlier after Montgomery's victory at El Alamein, Bennett and his colleagues were surprised by the feeble pace of the British pursuit towards Tripoli. He felt that it was odd 'in light of the mass of Ultra intelligence showing that throughout his retreat Rommel was too weak to withstand serious pressure'.[20] On that occasion Montgomery had erred on the side of caution; this time he threw it to the wind.

Just four days before *Market Garden* kicked off, Browning issued the following reassuring assessment: 'The total armoured strength is probably not more than 50–100 tanks… There is every sign of the enemy strengthening the river and canal lines through Nijmegen and Arnhem… but the troops manning them are not numerous and many are of low category.'[21] General Urquhart was not impressed, noting, 'Corps blithely passed on the information… I had no illusions about the Germans folding up at the first blow'.[22]

This estimate was very accurate. Bittrich had been dismayed by the condition of the 2nd SS-Panzer Corps following its flight from France. After Falaise, the 9th SS had only 20 operational assault guns and tanks. In early September it had been forced to surrender 10 of its tanks to the battered 11th Panzer Division, which had retreated to Alsace after fighting in the south of France.[23] The 10th SS had no armour available. Frustratingly for Harmel, his tank regiment was missing its second battalion, as it was in Germany at Grafenwöhr waiting to be issued with new Panther tanks.

Although both the 9th SS and 10th SS were expecting to be refitted and brought back up to strength, their commanders were well aware that they were not out of the fight. Not long after his arrival in the Arnhem area, Harmel was told that he would have to put together quick-reaction battle groups to help shore up the front and to assist Student's 1st Parachute Army. This was why his men ended up south of Eindhoven and defending Valkenswaard. The Allies seemed oblivious to the implications of Bittrich still being able to deploy effective combat units, even though they were supposedly withdrawing.

The Allies should have known just how resourceful Harmel and Harzer were after their successful escape from France and Belgium. Despite their losses on the road, they had lived off the land. Both divisions had re-equipped themselves as they had gone along by requisitioning abandoned vehicles and weapons. It did not matter if they belonged to the army or the Luftwaffe. Everything was up for grabs. In Belgium they had made use of the army's abandoned supply depots, taking ammunition, food and weapons as they went.

By the time of *Market Garden*, Bittrich had to hand around 50 armoured cars (most of which were in reality half-tracks), 26 tanks, tank destroyers and assault guns, three flak Panzers and two flak half-tracks. This gave him an 'armoured' force of 81 vehicles. However, Model was subsequently able to call on almost double this number with reinforcements, so could field 155 armoured fighting vehicles in the Arnhem area alone. Of these over 100 were tanks.[24] This amounted to a weak Panzer division. What the Allies could not foresee was what units the Germans might redeploy from elsewhere. Most worrying was the availability of 30 heavy Tiger tanks. Nor did this estimate take into account what Panzer forces would be available to attack British 30th Corps and the US airborne divisions. These would inevitably slow the relief of 1st Airborne.

Bittrich fully appreciated that the number of tanks available to his Panzer Corps was not really a true measure of its combat power, as this did not take into account things like artillery, anti-tank guns, mortars and self-propelled guns. These would contribute considerably to its firepower. During the Normandy campaign, both divisions were equipped with towed 105mm and 150mm howitzers as well as Hummel 150mm and Wespe 105mm self-propelled guns. They also had heavy mortars and towed 75mm anti-tank guns. Not all of these were lost.

Both divisions were waiting on their tank destroyer battalions equipped with Jagdpanzer IVs. The 9th SS received 28 of these vehicles on 12 September, some of which may have been handed over to the 10th SS. Certainly SS-Captain Roestel's battalion ended up with 15. Harzer's men, as they were returning to Germany, were supposed to surrender all their heavy equipment to Harmel.

In late August, Spindler was able to report to Harzer that his 9th SS-Panzer Artillery Regiment still had 20 guns from its original strength of 28. Those that survived were moved to Dieren just northeast of Arnhem. Once 1st Airborne Division arrived, it was easy enough to deploy them against Arnhem and Oosterbeek. At least one 150mm gun was used to smash Frost's defences at point-blank range until driven off.[25] Likewise, the 9th SS retained many of its flak guns, which were also used against 1st Airborne. Notably, those on the south bank of the Rhine helped cut Frost off from outside help. Harmel's heavy 120mm mortar section remained intact. He also formed an anti-tank company with 12 guns, again probably from the 9th SS.

These units were reinforced by the guns, mortars and rocket launchers of the 191st Artillery Regiment and Flak Brigade Swoboda. The latter was equipped with 20mm, 37mm and 88mm anti-aircraft guns that could be used in a ground fire role. In the event, most of Spindler's regiment fought as infantry, as did members of the 184th Artillery Regiment, a training unit based at Wageningen. The latter had been issued with 12 new 105mm towed guns, but these along with their crews were sent to Doesburg.

The Allies grossly underestimated how quickly 2nd SS-Panzer Corps could be reinforced. On the eve of the battle, Bittrich had about 9,500 men available, about two-thirds of whom ended up stretched all the way down to Valkenswaard. Once reinforced by other SS, army, Luftwaffe and naval units, this force was probably doubled in strength. A proportion of them came from the SS training schools, which the Allies seem to have simply ignored or dismissed. The SS NCO school provided up to 3,000 men, while Krafft and Helle provided another 1,200. General von Tettau's forces numbered up to 4,000. Granted, the quality of these forces was extremely variable, but they provided much-needed manpower.

The Allies overlooked the 2nd SS-Panzer Corps' other capabilities. It had been conceived of to deal with the occupation of Vichy France in 1943. That same year, in light of the anticipated Allied invasion, its divisions had undergone extensive anti-airborne exercises. 'This training benefited us enormously during the Arnhem operation', recalled Harmel.[26] It had instructed the troops to show initiative and above all be aggressive. The enemy should not be allowed to consolidate, was the message. 'NCOs and officers were taught to react quickly and make their own decisions', added Harmel. 'NCOs were taught not to wait until an order came, but to decide for themselves what to do.'[27]

As a result, on the eve of *Market Garden*, Harzer had organized 19 quick-reaction companies and Harmel had formed an all-arms battle group ready for immediate action. Ironically, Ultra decrypts highlighted on 14–15 September that the Germans were anticipating an airborne assault in the Netherlands.[28] Again, the Allies chose to ignore the fact that 2nd SS-Panzer Corps would know exactly what to do in the face of such an airborne attack.

Before the war, the Dutch had carried out military exercises in the area of *Market Garden*, so knew what could and could not be achieved on the local roads. Crucially, Dutch officers serving with the Allies were excluded from the planning process. 'Had they been there, they would also have reported that two SS Panzer Divisions were refitting near Arnhem', said Sergeant Hagen. 'Perhaps the Dutch were excluded because of fear of possible leakage of information to the Dutch Nazis.'[29]

The Dutch Resistance was fully aware of the German build-up at Arnhem. Henri Knap, their head of intelligence for the area, was suspicious when the Germans started taking over the hotels in Oosterbeek. His interest was heightened when staff officer Major Horst Smöckel visited shops in Arnhem, Oosterbeek and Renkum with a list of luxuries. Smöckel ordered rare foods, and even gin, to be delivered to the Tafelberg Hotel. Intriguingly, German signallers had been seen laying telephone cables between Oosterbeek's main hotels.

The presence of Model at Oosterbeek was then visually confirmed by the Dutch. Wouter van de Kraats achieved this by casually cycling past the Tafelberg. There he spotted the insignia of a German army group commander. Although challenged by the German guards, they had let him past when he convincingly insisted he was on the way to work.

Knap's network was soon reporting the presence of German tanks to the north and northeast of Arnhem. Initially he was frustrated in his efforts, remarking that 'at least one or even two Panzer divisions' were in the area, but he was unable to identify them.[30] On 14 September, Knap received word that there were '20 to 30 Tiger tanks' in the area. Notably, most civilians were unable to tell the different German tank types apart and tended to call every Panzer a Tiger. Nonetheless, the presence of 20 Panzers of any sort was an unwelcome development.

One of Knap's sources subsequently identified the 9th SS-Panzer Division as being in the locale. It was billeted between Arnhem and Apeldoorn and southeast to Zutphen. Knap's intelligence was then passed on to London by the Albrecht Group. He also later contacted the British at Oosterbeek by telephone to warn them that a column of 50 tanks was heading their way, but they dismissed his report.

General Urquhart recalled, 'Dutch Resistance reports had been noted to the effect that "battered panzer remnants have been sent to Holland to refit", and Eindhoven and Nijmegen were mentioned as reception areas.'[31] General Eisenhower's chief of staff, General Bedell Smith, visited Montgomery on 15 September to warn him. He suggested a second division should be dropped on Arnhem or an American one deployed further north. Montgomery was not receptive and there was no time to change his plans. He 'waved airily aside' the new proposals.[32]

Model was fortunate that no one saw fit to tell General Horrocks about the presence of 2nd SS-Panzer Corps. 'Quite unknown to me',[33] he confirmed. 'I had no idea.'[34] He then adds, 'it was this corps which turned the scales against us in the subsequent fighting'. Horrocks was aware of 2nd SS-Panzer Corps' anti-airborne training, noting, 'so the dice were loaded against us from the start'.[35] He appreciated that 'they were too heavily armed for the lightly equipped Airborne Troops'.[36] Once British resistance around Arnhem bridge had been crushed, Bittrich was able to send tanks southwards. By the morning of 21 September, at least 20 had crossed the Rhine and were heading into the Betuwe.[37] They deployed three vital hours before British tanks rumbled over the Waal at Nijmegen.

Only at the last minute did the Allies begin to realize the seriousness of what was going on around Arnhem. On 16 September an intelligence summary warned, '9th SS Panzer Division, and presumably the 10th, has been reported withdrawing to the Arnhem area in Holland; there, they will probably collect new tanks from a depot reported in the area of Cleves'.[38] This indicated that the 9th SS were re-equipping and possibly staying put. The mention of 'new tanks' also suggested that the 50 to 100-tank estimate might be wrong. The British 2nd Army and Allied 1st Airborne Army chose largely to ignore this, as the wheels for Operation *Market Garden* were already in motion.

Browning had promised 1st Airborne Division that 'the latest Intelligence will be sent to you up to the time of take-off'.[39] This did not happen. The men were not warned beforehand about Bittrich's presence, despite Major Urquhart's efforts. He had shown his photos to the divisional brigade chiefs of staff and told them about the intelligence from the Dutch Resistance. They, like Browning, chose to ignore him. 'A tall, dapper-looking officer [Brigadier Johnson]... gave a brief summary of the known troops in northern Holland', recalled glider pilot Captain Alexander Morrison, 'which incidentally made no reference to the two depleted divisions of German armour in the Arnhem area!'[40]

Lieutenant-Colonel Frost had to find out the hard way. After his briefing, he recalled, 'the information about the enemy was such that we were assured there was nothing to worry about'.[41] Intelligence indicated that although there were some new SS recruits in the area they lacked tanks and artillery. This presumably referred to Krafft's training battalion, which on its own hardly constituted a danger to 1st Airborne. Frost was assured that all the German Army's remaining reserves were holding the Albert Canal. The only possible threat was from Luftwaffe personnel stationed at Deelen. They, though, would take time to react. He was also warned not to trust the Dutch Resistance, as it had been penetrated by Nazi sympathizers. Had Frost been alerted to the presence of Bittrich's forces he could have opted to take more anti-tank weapons.

It was not until Frost was holding Arnhem bridge that he was made aware that German prisoners included members of the 9th SS. 'We had been given absolutely no inkling of this possibility', complained Frost.[42] An SS-Captain was brought before him and when questioned replied, 'We have been resting, re-equipping and getting reinforcements between here and Apeldoorn for several days'.[43] Frost quickly surmised that the SS would be able to apply increasing pressure on 1st Airborne and that the wooded countryside would enable them to 'paralyse' the roads leading into Arnhem.

British paratroopers had run into the SS way before they even reached the road bridge. James Sims recalled after passing the pontoon bridge that some of the enemy wounded included SS. 'I was curious to see what these supermen looked like, but apart from their distinctive uniform, they were just like us.'[44] Then as he and his comrades made a final push towards the bridge, he noted, 'We ran past an SS police barracks, which was now on fire'.[45]

Frost knew of the presence of the SS before he reached the bridge. Prior to getting to Oosterbeek, his men had captured over 30 German prisoners. 'I learned that a company of SS had been in Arnhem that morning and were now thought to be covering the entrances to the town from the west.'[46] Within seven hours of landing, his A Company had taken 150 German prisoners, most of whom were SS. What they did not know initially was that some of them were from the SS-Panzer divisions.

Although many of the tanks used to attack the British hold on Arnhem road bridge did not belong to the Panzer Corps, at least one Panzer IV from the 10th SS got close to the bridge before it was knocked out. For Frost and his men, this was one too many. Brigadier Philip Hicks, defending Oosterbeek, also rapidly discovered he was facing the 9th SS and 10th SS after prisoners were taken. 'Enemy pressure and the steadily increasing strength of German armour was building up everywhere', he noted with alarm.[47]

Sergeant Hagen came across the SS at Oosterbeek, when he helped to interrogate two SS-Panzergrenadiers. 'They said they had been in the army for six weeks and this was their first action', he recalled. 'They were both about forty, and obviously had no intention of fighting anyone or for anything.'[48] Subsequently he was grateful that the 9th SS were not up to full strength:

> If there had not been a sprinkling of first-class and fanatical officers and NCOs in this division, no fight would have been possible. But even with the present state of affairs, it was ridiculous that they did not wipe us out within a few hours. This Panzer division, with tanks, mobile guns, flame-throwers, very close Focke-Wulf support and the heaviest and most concentrated ack-ack seen by any of the RAF pilots whom I met later on at the 'drome,' and even mobile loudspeakers with trained German propagandists spouting English, never dared to change over to direct assault or succeeded in penetrating our perimeter. No body of men, with only small arms as we had, could possibly have withstood a German Panzer of the old material.[49]

Major Geoffrey Powell, who served with the 4th Parachute Brigade at Arnhem, concluded:

> Whether or not Browning did suppress some of the information he received from his intelligence staff about the presence of German tanks near Arnhem is hardly material to the issue…

adding as it did little to what those concerned already knew about the size of the enemy forces they were likely to meet.[50]

Ultimately, it was Bittrich's reaction the Allies underestimated, and this proved fatal. Powell supported Montgomery's decision to go. 'After the chaos of the German retreat across France', he said, 'a report of two Panzer divisions in Holland meant little in terms of men and tanks… His reasons for not wavering were sound indeed.'[51] Lieutenant-Colonel Frost was of a different opinion and after the war wrote, 'it was the presence of the much experienced Waffen SS Panzer divisions that spelt doom for our venture'.[52]

19

Last Battles

By the end of September 1944, despite thwarting the Allied advance and retaking Oosterbeek, for Model and his men the fighting was far from over. There was no time to celebrate or rest; it was business as usual. The British remained firmly established between the Rhine and the Waal. Intelligence showed that their forces consisted of four brigades, with artillery and tank support, deployed in the Driel, Elst and Oosterhout areas. They also had ample air cover. Model's only consolation was that they were hemmed in on three sides. His intention was to drive them back over the Waal, or even better into it. He knew he had to do this quickly, because there was every likelihood that the Allies would seek to bring down the vital Arnhem road bridge.

Model had discussed this latest stage of operations with Rundstedt on 25 September. He knew Bittrich, Harmel and Harzer would not be happy as their units and the other *ad hoc* battle groups were exhausted. There could be no avoiding it, though, as instruction had come from the highest authority – Hitler. Rundstedt promised Model reinforcements in the shape of the 9th and 116th Panzer Divisions, redeployed from Aachen, and the newly formed 363rd Volksgrenadier Division. Bittrich and his 2nd SS-Panzer Corps were to direct the attack at the end of the month. The 10th SS would distract the British at Bemmel, while the other two Panzer divisions struck towards Driel and Elst. His immediate objective was to take Elst. There was a slight snag in that the reinforcements could not be brought up until early October. Also, they were very short of tanks.

The battle for the Betuwe was a battle for the bridges. While Model controlled Arnhem, he could feed reinforcements into the area. However, with the Allies in Nijmegen, they could do the same. Model wanted to cut their supply lines, but the Luftwaffe accurately bombing the Nijmegen bridges was never going to happen. The railway bridge presented a particularly narrow target. Besides, both were bristling with anti-aircraft guns and patrolled by large numbers of Allied fighters.

Nonetheless, the Luftwaffe was ordered to give it a go. Their twin-engine medium bombers were too slow, so it was down to the dive-bombers and fighter-bombers. Sure enough, on 26–27 September, the Luftwaffe launched a series of raids that missed their target. The first was conducted at night by Stuka dive-bombers. A second heavier attack was carried out in the morning by fighter-bombers protected by fighters. They were intercepted by British aircraft and in the ensuing aerial mêlée lost 45 planes.

The only other option was to strike along the Waal. A call was put through to the German Navy; could they deploy a frogman demolition team? To Model's delight the answer was yes, although it would take a few days to get them in place. A dozen men from the 65th Marine Special Command would be assigned the task. When they reached Harmel at Pannerden, he warned them that the British and Americans were 'exceptionally alert' at Nijmegen.[1] The British had also deployed heavy anti-tank guns in anticipation of a ground attack. This was thanks to the Luftwaffe's efforts and attempts to collect intelligence on the bridges.

The frogmen were a tough-looking bunch, who had originally been trained in Italy. Such units had been active in the West since D-Day, particularly on the river Orne. In mid-September a team had managed to get themselves into Antwerp docks despite the defence nets and blown up the main canal lock, putting it out of action for three months. Harmel enquired about their plans. The officer in charge pointed to a map and explained they would go into the water with their torpedoes six miles up river. After they had delivered these, they would travel a further 15 miles downstream until they reached friendly lines. He made it sound so simple. They would target the bridges at first light. At night, visibility would be too poor for them to locate the supporting pillars. Harmel nodded. Whatever way you looked at it, this was a suicide mission.

In the meantime, Model proposed to attack the British in the Betuwe from both the east and the west, with a third diversionary attack from the north. General von Tettau was instructed to get a battalion across the Rhine and land near Randwijk, to the west of Driel, on the night of 26/27 September. This would place his men on the immediate western flank of the British and serve to distract them. His force consisted of a company of SS-Panzergrenadiers and three companies of Volksgrenadiers.

Tettau's soldiers successfully crossed at several points, using the ferry at Renkum to get their heavy weaponry over. They had approached the river cautiously, fearful that they would trigger a British artillery bombardment. In light of the barrage put down to cover 1st Airborne's withdrawal, that was the last thing they wanted. Once across in the early hours of the morning, confident that there were no British forces in the immediate area, the men began to dig in ready for an inevitable counter-attack.

An anti-tank gun crew were manhandling their weapon into position when a light machine gun opened fire from just yards away, killing all of them. When a German patrol of 20 men was sent forward, it also came under fire and was driven back. Tettau's intelligence was faulty because he had not been warned that the British were so far west. His battalion had landed very near to a lightly equipped British armoured car regiment.

Come daylight, the German trenches came under fire from British mortars and three armoured cars. However, these forces were insufficient to prevent Tettau's battalion from pushing into Randwijk. In response, the British counter-attacked with Sherman tanks and infantry from both the south and the east. This region was exposed, flat and marshy. When Tettau tried to get reinforcements over the river they were accurately shelled, suffering considerable casualties. He was unaware that a member of the Dutch Resistance was directing the British fire from a house in Renkum. Although not a trained artillery observer, he was able to describe the fall of the shells. This enabled the British gunners to adjust their gunsights.

The Germans were driven back into Randwijk, but after some heavy street fighting the outnumbered British retreated to the eastern edge of the village. They then contented themselves with establishing a line along the Ligne–Wettering Canal to await reinforcements. The British attack from the south drove towards Rustenberg and Randwijk. In response, the Germans greeted them with 88mm and machine-gun fire. Around 20 German fighter aircraft strafed the exposed British columns. By 2030 hours the Germans were still holding the dyke road.

During this period Model had some not entirely welcome visitors. Armaments Minister Albert Speer and Luftwaffe Field Marshal Erhard Milch had for some reason taken it upon themselves to visit the parachute units in the Netherlands. Bearing in mind that they were responsible for weapon and aircraft production, Model was unclear of the exact purpose of their trip. Speer, by his own admission, knew that such visits to the front were increasingly a waste of time. The only real benefit was that these got him out of Berlin and away from the political infighting that plagued the Nazi party. Touring the Arnhem battlefields, the pair rather assumed they would find their colleagues celebrating their recent victory at Oosterbeek. It transpired that not all the generals were happy.

'At Arnhem, I found General Bittrich of the Waffen-SS in a state of fury', noted Speer in some surprise. '[Nazi] party functionaries had taken it upon themselves to kill British and American pilots, and Bittrich was cast in the role of a liar.'[2] Bittrich had given an undertaking that Allied casualties would be well treated and now he looked like he had reneged on his word. Speer and Milch were not impressed by this turn of events. 'Milch usually declared firmly that the enemy would make short work of the leadership of the Third Reich', observed Speer. 'I shared his view.'[3]

The Luftwaffe, despite its recent losses, decided to have another go at the Nijmegen bridges. This time they employed fighter-bombers carrying 1,400kg bombs. Flying in on 28 September, they were met by Canadian Spitfires. Once more minimal damage was inflicted on their targets. Model's commando raid was carried out on the night of 28/29 September. Three units of frogmen, using torpedo mines, were greatly hampered by the strong current as they came down the Rhine. Nonetheless, they successfully got near both bridges and detonated some of their explosive charges. Around 0600 hours the blast at the railway bridge caused one end of the central span to be blown from its concrete support and drop into the river.

At the road bridge, the team were spotted before they could get their explosives fully into position. The guards opened fire and the frogmen could not complete their mission. Although the road bridge was damaged, it was nothing more than an inconvenience and was quickly repaired. The frogman teams were swiftly rounded up and captured, with just two men managing to get away. Most of them were wounded and three later died of their injuries. When Harmel reported the results to Model, both appreciated this was not the outcome they had hoped for. It was all or nothing; with the road bridge still intact, the Allies would continue to pour men and materiel into the Betuwe. Despite their bravery, the frogmen's raid was a failure.

Tettau knew it would be only a matter of time before the British attempted to crush his exposed Rhine bridgehead. At 0600 hours on 28 September, British mortars began to pound his defences around Randwijk. These scored direct hits on German slit trenches in some nearby woods. To make matters worse, the British reached the ferry, cutting them off. An SS unit ambushed a British ammunition convoy and a gun battle ensued until the Germans withdrew into the village. They made a last stand in the area of the church and 130 men were captured.

That same day, Model ordered an attack on the Allies' eastern flank, stretching from the Betuwe to the Groesbeek Heights. Rundstedt was under remit from Hitler to nip the Allied corridor off as far as Grave, but he did not have the resources to do this. Besides, venturing out of the Reichswald was a pointless exercise when it offered such a good defensive position. Nonetheless,

General Meindl's 2nd Parachute Corps attacked westward towards Groesbeek, once more taking on the US 82nd Airborne. The 15th Army struck eastward towards Grave. Both attacks soon petered out with heavy losses.

Meindl, against his better judgement, renewed his attacks on the American positions on 1 October, but within two days was forced to stop. The quality of his recruits was just not up to the job and they wilted in the face of Allied firepower. 'The attempted attack was unsuccessful', he reported to Model on the night of the 2nd. 'Massive enemy air superiority during the day. Troop training too poor for night attacks.'⁴

Although Model's priority was to drive the Allies away from the German frontier, an attack on the British north of the Waal stood the best chance of success. He instructed Tettau to attack across the Rhine again. This was to be conducted by SS-Captain Oelker's battalion. They crossed in flimsy rubber boats at Castle Doerweth, just over a mile downstream from Driel, at 0600 hours on 1 October. Oelker's men were screened by a thick mist as they paddled out into the water. Reassuring covering fire was provided by artillery and mortars.

The British were waiting for them. The first wave was greeted by mortar bombs, shells and machine guns. They suffered heavy casualties and only a few reached the far bank by swimming the rest of the way. The next wave included the battalion commander's headquarters staff. 'As we neared the bank', recalled Oelker, 'a machine gun burst hit the boat... We lay on the muddy bank the entire day.' When it got dark, Oelker led his men towards the brick factory opposite Castle Doerweth. 'We attacked the objective from the right', he said, 'something the British had not anticipated. But where were the rest of the troops?'⁵ Half his battalion, including his signals detachment, were still on the opposite bank.

A company from the Hermann Göring Training Regiment was brought forward as reinforcements. When they got to the river, they found all the boats were full of bullet holes. 'Then up comes a messenger from the rear', said Herbert Kessler. '"No crossing! The moon is too bright!"'⁶ Kessler and his comrades waited nervously until midday for a crossing to be attempted. To screen them smoke was laid down on the far bank. It did no good. The 200 yards to the river were a killing ground that was hemmed in by flanking machine-gun fire. The first squad leader to try it was severely wounded and his boat shot to pieces.

Kessler and three other men made it to a boat. 'The shots splashed into the water all around us like hailstones', he observed, 'and how we managed to get to the other side, I don't know.'[7] Kessler and 20 men dug in and kept their heads down. They were grateful not to be in the brick factory, because this was regularly shelled. Frustratingly, Oelker's men could hear the 10th SS-Panzer Division fighting to the east and the 363rd Volksgrenadier Division to the west. Neither unit, though, was able to reach his beleaguered bridgehead.

Meanwhile, Harmel assessed that Bemmel, to the northeast of Lent, was the key to cutting the British off in the Betuwe. It was on the most direct route to Nijmegen's bridges. His opening attack on 30 September was conducted across open ground in broad daylight, with predictable results. British artillery and machine guns soon brought proceedings to a halt. The following day, he launched a feint over the Wettering Canal, but the British were not fooled.

At 0500 hours on 1 October, German infantry and tanks, under the cover of a creeping barrage and the morning mist, tried to take Bemmel and Elst. The British infantry were not expecting tanks and in places gave ground. However, the German troops and armour suffered heavy casualties thanks to the enemy's artillery, and after two hours of fighting their advance had been held. British field guns fired 12,500 rounds that day and they inflicted a punishing toll. The 10th SS lost eight of its supporting Tiger tanks to anti-tank guns, artillery fire and mines. Over the next three days, Harmel's men found themselves under counter-attack and were slowly driven back from Bemmel. 'The vitals of the division had been torn out', he noted, 'to such an extent that it was not capable of offensive action.'[8]

A battle group from 116th Panzer got just over a mile north of Elst and a third of a mile west of the railway embankment. 'Extremely difficult terrain', noted General Siegfried von Waldenburg, the divisional commander. 'Tanks barely effective, since they could only move on the few dams and roads!'⁹ To support their advancing Panzergrenadiers, the division's Panther tanks were used to lay down a barrage of 500 high-explosive shells. The choking fumes from this sustained fire inside the Panthers were such that some tank crews had to be withdrawn. A thick ground mist impeded them from targeting British positions accurately. By 4 October, the Panzergrenadiers had made little headway and were only half a mile west of the railway. The 10th SS had been driven from Baal and Haalderen and the 9th Panzer had lost Heuvel. The 116th alone suffered over 800 casualties in the fighting. 'The biggest worry', said Major Fritz Vogelsang, 'was the lack of much needed NCOs.'[10]

Before returning to Germany, Milch and Speer could not help themselves and decided to witness one of the pre-dawn counter-attacks on 1 October. Afterwards their driver, trying to make up lost time, skidded into a tree at high speed and ended up in the ditch. Milch was knocked unconscious and injured his ribs.[11] He was revived only in hospital and was bedridden for the rest of the year. Back in Berlin, Speer wrote of his encounter with Bittrich that 'his violent denunciation of the party was all the more striking since it came from an SS general'.[12]

During early October, German forces in the Betuwe found themselves also fighting Americans. They were from the US 101st Airborne, deployed to replace the bulk of the British 43rd Division, which was pulled out of the line for a much-needed rest. German troops manning the north–south railway embankment detected American paratroopers moving towards Driel on 4 October. They opened up with machine guns and mortars. The following day they attacked, employing two assault guns belonging to the 116th Panzer Division. When these ventured through an underpass beneath the railway embankment, one of them was knocked out by a British anti-tank gun. The other beat a hasty retreat.

Rundstedt's headquarters were warned, '1700 hours, enemy with tanks advanced to railroad embankment from vicinity east of Driel in bitter and close combat'.[13] In the confused fighting,

GERMAN COUNTER-ATTACKS IN THE BETUWE, 1–5 OCTOBER 1944

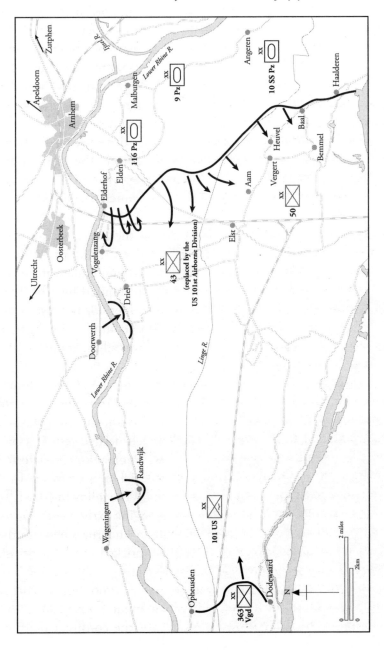

two companies of Panzergrenadiers were surrounded and captured. Only Lieutenant Ernst-Werner Weiss and one other man escaped. This loss forced other units of the 116th Panzer Division to fall back on the railway embankment.

To the west, where the Rhine and Waal were only three miles apart, presented Model with a good chokepoint. The key village in this area was Opheusden, just south of the Rhine, but it was held by the enemy. The 363rd Volksgrenadier Division was directed to attack the Americans at Opheusden, with the benefit of considerable artillery support from north of the river. The division had taken some time to get into position because it had to get over the Rhine using rubber boats and the few ferries.

The Volksgrenadiers opened their attack eastward, at 0600 hours on 5 October, under the cover of fog. When this lifted, Allied shelling forced them to retire. The Germans also put reinforcements across the river to help Oelker, who was still holding the brick factory. The Volksgrenadiers then renewed their attack and by late afternoon had secured most of Opheusden. The fighting continued for another two days, but the Germans were outclassed by the Americans and did not gain much further ground.

The conditions for Oelker's men in his Rhine bridgehead were extremely miserable. They were cold, thirsty, hungry and had little ammunition. Many of his officers were dead, including Major Stuks and Lieutenant Martin. On at least one occasion they were accidentally hit by their own artillery. The survivors cowered in their foxholes, fearful of enemy sniper fire. Oelker asked Tettau twice for permission to evacuate; on each occasion Tettau refused.

Then on 7 October, Model got a call from the Arnhem commandant to say that American bombers had destroyed the bridge. This severely curtailed his offensive operations in the Betuwe. Nonetheless, he saw the irony in the situation; having failed to capture the bridge, the Allies had dropped it into the Rhine. 'Getting supplies across the Rhine is becoming more and more difficult', noted Major Vogelsang, 'especially now, since 50 bombers entirely destroyed the Rhine bridge.'[14] At this point, the remains of the 9th SS-Panzer Division belatedly headed for

Germany, while the 116th Panzer Division was urgently redeployed back to Aachen to counter the Americans.

General von Waldenburg briefly met with Model in Krefeld. 'A short report of the experiences during the battles near Arnhem and a status report of the Division were compiled hastily', grumbled Waldenburg. He complained to Model that his command had been deployed piecemeal in the Betuwe and was now not being given a rest. The field marshal was sympathetic and 'expressed his special praise for the Division, but referred to the very serious situation at Aachen'.[15]

Under constant attack and shelling, Oelker could see no point in staying in his bridgehead any longer. On 10 October he ordered the remains of his battalion to withdraw, much to the fury of Tettau. In the tradition of good commanding officers, Oelker was the very last to leave. Rundstedt now got permission for Model to abandon the Arnhem bridgehead. The 363rd Volksgrenadiers though would have to stay between the Rhine and Waal, south of Wageningen, in order to safeguard the flank of 15th Army.

One of Model's options to deny the Betuwe to the Allies was to flood it. SS-Major Brandt, in charge of the 10th SS Pioneer Battalion, was sent to see how feasible this was. After Brandt made his report, Model opted instead simply to thin out his forward defences. On the night of 13/14 October, the bridgehead was reduced to smaller outposts held by Harmel's men to the south of Arnhem at Elden, Huissen and Angeren, as well as opposite Pannerden. The following day Roestel's weary tank hunter battalion, which had been supporting Battle Group Walther, finally rejoined the division. Harmel was sent 1,600 much-needed reinforcements, but as a third of them were Luftwaffe personnel they were kept at Doetinchem for training.

Essentially, the battle for the Betuwe just fizzled out. The Germans lacked the resources to persist with their attacks. The British and the Americans were stuck in a cul-de-sac and had no desire to waste further effort trying to get out of a dead end. With the onset of bad weather, both sides hunkered down. 'During the winter the Germans flooded the area between Arnhem and Nijmegen', said

General de Guingand, 'and so for a while removed the potential threat caused by our possession of the bridgehead.'[16]

Northeast of 's-Hertogenbosch, on the western side of the Allies' Eindhoven–Nijmegen corridor, the Germans retreated to the Waal and south of Wageningen to the Rhine. On the eastern side of the corridor they retained a sizeable bridgehead over the Maas, west of Roermond and Venlo. On the Dutch coast, 15th Army continued to block the Scheldt. Eventually, after it was forced from the Breskens bridgehead, South Beveland, Walcheren and North-Beveland, it retreated behind the Maas.

Breskens was lost on 22 October, along with almost 13,000 prisoners. Major-General Daser and his 70th Infantry Division surrendered at Middelburg on 6 November. The 60-year old Daser had no real desire to carry on fighting and his actions saved the ancient market town from destruction. Clambering into a British assault boat, he looked a tired and forlorn figure. Although clad in a leather trench coat and field cap, he had the appearance of someone's grandfather, rather than a battle-hardened garrison commander. His naval colleague was even less heroic. Captain Frank Aschmann, in charge of the coastal batteries, simply fled. His deputy Captain Otto Würdemann was captured at Vlissingen, along with Colonel Eugen Reinhardt.

The last organized resistance on Walcheren ended two days after Daser's capitulation. Around 10,000 German troops laid down their weapons, many of whom found themselves under the watchful eye of the Dutch Resistance. Initially some of the surrendering Germans feared they might be massacred, but the Dutch liberation celebrations proceeded without mishap. The port of Antwerp was not open to the Allies until the end of the month.

Student, who had worked so hard to transform 1st Parachute Army into an effective fighting force, relinquished command to General Alfred Schlemm. He found himself placed in charge of a new army group comprising 1st Parachute Army and the newly created 25th Army. The former included the 6th, 7th and 8th Parachute Divisions. Hitler had been formulating plans for his Ardennes offensive since 25 September and wanted to withdraw the 5th Panzer Army from the Aachen area. To do this, 15th Army was redeployed from the Netherlands and replaced by 25th Army under General Christiansen.

Student's long-suffering airborne troops were forced to conduct a final counter-attack in the Betuwe as the year came to a close. This was launched by three companies of the 16th Parachute Regiment against the British at Haalderen in the early hours of 4 December 1944. Under the cover of mortars and machine guns, the lead assault company got into the enemy forward positions, resulting in close-quarter combat. Once it was light, British artillery soon thwarted the attack. The two supporting parachute companies suffered heavy casualties, while the assault company, consisting of 161 men, lost 50 dead, including their commander, and 110 captured. Many of those killed had drowned in the floodwaters.

It was the turn of the 3rd Battalion, 7th Parachute Regiment on 18 January 1945, who attacked the British western flank in the Betuwe. They attempted to clear the British from Zetten in a two-day battle. The German paratroopers failed and suffered 150 killed wounded and captured in the process. Undeterred, a dozen parachute companies then tried to fight their way southeast towards Nijmegen bridge. They were counter-attacked by British infantry supported by Canadian tanks. The Germans were driven from Zetten and Hemmen to the northwest. The fighting in and around Zetten cost the Germans 300 killed or wounded and 400 captured. These last battles achieved nothing but the wasteful loss of yet more lives.

20

Little Consequence

The battle for Arnhem was of little consequence to Hitler, and he chose to ignore it. The very day before the airborne attack, he was warned of the danger, but simply waved such concerns aside. His preoccupations were Aachen and Antwerp, not Arnhem. Rundstedt's assessment on taking command was that the Allies' main line of attack was likely to be towards Aachen on the Belgian border, then the Ruhr and on to Berlin. While Seyss-Inquart had been fretting about the security of the Netherlands, Hitler had lumped ever more responsibility on him at the end of the first week of September. He found himself charged with the construction of the Siegfried Line defences as far as and including Aachen.

Initially Gauleiter Josef Grohé, the Reichskommissar in Belgium and Northern France, had been in control of the Scheldt–Albert canal defences and those to the west of Aachen. Seyss-Inquart was tasked only with the area from the Ijsselmeer to Nijmegen. Once the British were in Brussels, Grohé was relegated to the Aachen–Cologne area. Seyss-Inquart then had to come up with Dutch manpower to renovate a great swathe of Germany's neglected frontier defences. These were to be manned by the Volkssturm, Germany's home guard comprising reluctant old men and young boys and protected by Volksgrenadiers.

By the late summer, Hitler's deluded brain had begun to indulge in strategic fantasies of epic proportions. These were in part backed by the SS, who had been instructed to create a reserve made up of newly formed Volksgrenadier divisions. His senior generals Wilhelm Keitel and Alfred Jodl from the German armed forces high command, Chief of the General Staff Heinz Guderian and Werner Kreipe representing the Luftwaffe found themselves on 16 September alarmed by their Führer's latest grandiose schemes. Gathered at the Wolf's Lair near Rastenburg deep in the forests of East Prussia, they were also alarmed by his deteriorating appearance. He looked much older than 54, his skin was jaundiced and his hands trembled. His heart and stomach were giving him unending problems, which contributed to his volatile temper.

Jodl cautiously opened the briefing by explaining that in the last three months the German armed forces had suffered over a million casualties. Half of these had been in the West. Their surviving forces were establishing new defensive lines in the Netherlands, but they lacked troops with which to hold the forested region of eastern Belgium and Luxembourg – the Ardennes. Suddenly the Führer became animated. 'I have just come to a momentous decision', he exclaimed. 'I shall go over to the offensive', he added, leaning over the map. 'Here, out of the Ardennes, with the objective – Antwerp!'[1]

His generals were flabbergasted. As long as Zangen held the Scheldt, the Allies could not use Antwerp, so there was little point in trying to retake it. Besides, where would the necessary forces come from? Jodl highlighted that the Allies had twice as many divisions in the West. In addition, after landing in the Riviera in August the Allied armies were now thrusting north past Switzerland towards the German frontier. He cautioned that intelligence suggested that the Allies might conduct an airborne attack in the Netherlands.

Hitler would not listen. He was convinced that it was only a matter of time before the British and Americans fell out with the Russians. He could not believe that the capitalist–Marxist alliance would survive much longer. Jodl pointed out the Allies had air superiority. Not a problem, responded Hitler, the Luftwaffe would support his proposed operation with 1,500 aircraft. This was news to Kreipe, who said this would not be possible. For his honesty, he was later sacked. In any case, said Hitler, the attack in the Ardennes would take place during the winter, when low cloud and mist would keep Allied aircraft grounded.

Kreipe noted the offensive would involve '30 new Volksgrenadier divisions and new panzer divisions in addition to panzer divisions from the east'.[2] Guderian was aghast, as inevitably come the winter the Red Army would strike westward from the Vistula. While Hitler seemed oblivious to this threat, he was very afraid that a Russian airborne division might be dropped on the Wolf's Lair. This now bristled with anti-aircraft defences.

Meanwhile, Hitler had more pressing concerns, with the security of the frontier near Aachen. Four days earlier on 12 September, Seyss-Inquart and Grohé confirmed the Americans had pierced the border to the south of the city. This threat was a matter of national prestige and far more important than the defence of the Low Countries. 'There can no longer be any large-scale operations on our part', Hitler warned his generals. He then instructed that 'fanaticism' must be used 'against the trespassers of German soil'.[3] His watery eyes glinting, he went on, 'All we can do is to hold our position or die'.[4]

There seemed to be very little 'fanaticism' being displayed in Aachen. Its military commandant, Colonel Helmuth von Osterroht, was highly dismayed to discover that all the city's cowardly Nazi party officials, along with the police, had fled. They were supposed to have overseen the evacuation of the civilian population. This understandably left people in a state of panic. General von Schwerin, now commanding the 116th Panzer Division, wanted to abandon Aachen, but such a traitorous move could have cost him his life. Instead, when his plans were discovered he was dismissed. Hitler was determined that Aachen would not become the first German city to fall into Allied hands. Should this happen, the Americans could push east to Cologne on the Rhine and then swing north into the Ruhr.

To make matters worse, to the south American troops had reached the river Our, the border between Luxembourg and Germany. Michel Weber, the Burgermeister of the German hamlet of Sevenig, witnessed them arrive in the woods on the far bank on

11 September. They were preceded by three dishevelled German soldiers who fled across the river, one of whom warned Weber, saying, 'Save yourself. We're the last. After us it's the enemy.'⁵ At 1805 hours, an American patrol had crossed into Germany near the village of Stolzembourg. That night they went over between the Luxembourg village of Weiswampach and Sevenig.

Rundstedt was almost captured by American tanks when he visited the Trier area near the German-Luxembourg frontier. Not long after, the Americans had begun to probe Wallendorf to the north of Trier, which was poorly defended. Farther south in France, the Americans had got over the river Moselle between the cities of Metz and Nancy. In response, Rundstedt instructed that 'Every pill-box, every village must be defended until the Allies bleed to death'.⁶ Allied pressure eased up only because they were diverting resources north to the Netherlands.

By mid-September, Rundstedt was able to report to Hitler that he had, temporarily at least, held the Americans at Aachen and on the Moselle. The Allies generously attributed this to the Volksgrenadiers. 'Within the fortifications of the Siegfried Line these divisions have effectively stopped the American advance', reported Canadian intelligence. 'That this success will continue against a full-scale offensive, and when out of the protection of their concrete bunkers, is most unlikely.'⁷

Certainly morale soon proved to be an issue for these units. For example, the 256th Volksgrenadier Division deployed to the Netherlands suffered from disciplinary problems. It had been created from a former infantry unit decimated on the Eastern Front. 'During the last eight days no less than 11 desertions have been reported', noted the divisional commander General Gerhard Franz, 'seven of whom went over to enemy lines.'⁸

Rundstedt knew that whatever the fate of Aachen, the Americans would pay a heavy price trying to secure the enormous neighbouring Hürtgen Forest. This offered a formidable defensive position. It was at this stage the Allies had agreed to try to outflank the Siegfried Line by seizing a bridgehead over the Lower Rhine at Arnhem. The day after the Allied airborne assault, Hitler was focused on his counter-attack against the Americans at Lunéville to the southeast of Nancy. This ended in failure after 11 days of fighting, but ensured stalemate in Lorraine. It also soaked up the majority of Hitler's available Panzer forces. By the end of the month, he had lost 440 tanks and assault guns in the region.

Despite his headlong retreat from France, Hitler was confident the Allies would run out of momentum by the winter. Unusually for him, he largely left his generals in the West to their own devices. Hitler's only real stipulation was that the Channel ports and the Scheldt be held. He was highly pleased when he was informed that Zangen's army had been evacuated over the Scheldt in just two weeks. Afterwards, there was some concern about the Allies' offensive into the Netherlands. Intelligence showed that it involved three ground corps and an entire airborne corps. It soon became apparent that progress of the enemy was painfully slow, especially on the flanks, thanks to the swift actions of Model and Student.

Hitler's fevered mind was still formulating his plan to forestall the British and American push towards the Rhine by recapturing Antwerp. Once he had done that, he would then direct his attentions to the Russians. However, losses on the Eastern Front were causing him acute manpower shortages. While he was able to successfully salvage the remains of army groups B and G from France, Army Group Centre in Russia was a write-off. This meant that Hitler needed to re-equip his tatty divisions in the West as well as create new ones for both fronts. In the meantime, his generals had to make do with what was to hand; any reinforcements were strictly limited. This was why Model, Student and the others had to fight using such a wide range of ill-trained units from the SS, army, navy and Luftwaffe. Hitler's plans left Rundstedt and Model in a very difficult position.

Hitler's Army Group Centre lost almost 30 divisions on the Eastern Front, making it a greater catastrophe than even Stalingrad or Tunis. Army Group North Ukraine, also caught up in the Red Army's maelstrom, lost a similar number. Such losses were irreplaceable. By comparison, Hitler lost 10 divisions at Falaise in Normandy. Staggeringly, during the year a total of 75 infantry divisions had been destroyed on all fronts. These were to be replaced by 66 much weaker divisions.

Most of the depleted Panzer units that escaped from France were withdrawn to Germany to be re-formed ready for the winter offensive. The newly raised Volksgrenadier divisions were also largely held back, the first of which were formed in August 1944. Those that could be spared, along with the newly formed Panzer brigades, were sent to Lorraine to help resist Patton's US 3rd Army on the Moselle. A few others were sent to Aachen.

This explains why, when Model asked for 30 divisions to bolster the Western Front, he did not get anything like this number. German manpower in the West plummeted from early September to mid-October 1944. In that six-week period they suffered 150,000 casualties. Although replacements numbered 152,000, Rundstedt was also forced to give up 86,000 men who were redeployed elsewhere. Little of Hitler's gathering strategic reserve was touched, and Model got only a single Volksgrenadier division to fight in the Betuwe. When Model moved his headquarters to Oosterbeek on 11 September, he warned Hitler that he could not guarantee to hold the Siegfried Line. Rundstedt wanted to withdraw behind the river Waal, on the grounds that this shortening of the front would save five divisions. Hitler refused to sanction such a move.

Even while the fighting was still ongoing in the Betuwe, Hitler would not be distracted from his master plan for Belgium and Luxembourg. Albert Speer recalled, 'On October 12 1944, when the military situation in the West had settled down again… Hitler took me aside… and then revealed that he was going to carry out a great offensive in the West by concentrating all available forces'.[9] This included over a dozen Volksgrenadier divisions, most of which comprised airmen and sailors. On the German southern frontier, Hitler was content that his Colmar bridgehead would keep the Allies distracted, while he also launched an attack into Alsace.

Four days later, Hitler was informed that Aachen had been encircled, along with Colonel Gerhard Wilck's 246th Volksgrenadier Division. In the space of just over a week the Germans had lost

600 dead and 4,500 wounded. Beforehand, Wilck had pleaded in vain with Model to give up Aachen. The trapped defenders, down to 1,200 men, were relentlessly bombed and shelled. 'When the Americans start using 155s as sniper weapons', said Wilck, 'it is time to give in.'[10] On 18 October, he warned, 'Situation in Aachen such that last resistance probably coming to an end'.[11] Three days later, he surrendered the city. The Allies had not gone round the Siegfried Line; instead they had punched a hole through it at Aachen.

Both Rundstedt and Model were against the Ardennes offensive from the start. 'This plan hasn't got a damned leg to stand on',[12] cursed Model. They argued it would be better to use the massing reserve to destroy the American salient at Aachen. The latter might be achievable; Antwerp was far too ambitious for the forces available. Hitler would not be swayed, and in the event they were to be proved right. Ironically, having held the Allies in the Netherlands, neighbouring Belgium was to be his undoing.

Hitler appreciated that the Netherlands remained a cornerstone in his western defences, because it shielded the northern Ruhr and hosted his V-weapon sites. Ultimately he was happy to leave things to Seyss-Inquart and the regional Gauleiters, Friedrich Florian and Fritz Schlessmann. This consigned the country to yet more suffering through the long winter of 1944.

Mary of Arnhem

By the autumn of 1944, any delusions that Anton Mussert may have harboured about the Netherlands being ruled as an autonomous part of a Greater Germany were completely dashed. He had naively lobbied for a confederation of states, with the Waffen-SS acting as its shield. Hitler, though, had never planned to concede any authority to the hapless Mussert. The 2nd SS-Panzer Corps acted as a shield to protect Germany, not the Netherlands. Hitler had once believed in the 'essential soundness' of the Dutch, but no more.[1]

At this stage in the war, although the Germans still controlled three-quarters of the Netherlands, they now had little interest in their Dutch allies. The Dutch people were left to the mercy of a vengeful Seyss-Inquart and Rauter. 'The higher SS leadership considers the Dutch people German', noted Mussert. 'It is terrible. What will come of it?'[2] Early in the occupation, he foolishly thought he could maintain Dutch sovereignty and even grab Belgian Flanders. Now Belgium had been liberated and the Allies were inside the Netherlands. Mussert knew that his days were numbered and he hid away in his office at Korte Vijverberg in The Hague. He did nothing to stop what happened next.

Towards the end of September 1944, the Germans evacuated all civilians from the Arnhem–Oosterbeek area. Around 100,000 people were put on the road towards Apeldoorn. Rumour spread that the Germans were expecting the British to bomb Arnhem; most residents suspected that it was payback time. Any males caught between the ages of 16 and 25 were press-ganged to work on German defences. Slave labour was also shipped in from Rotterdam, while 40,000 others were sent to Germany. The bitter fighting in the Arnhem area that month resulted in some 500 civilian deaths. The dogged German defence of Nijmegen left the population caught in the crossfire, resulting in 2,200 dead and 10,000 wounded. Nijmegen, like Arnhem and Oosterbeek, was left in ruins.

Once back in Arnhem and Oosterbeek, German troops went on a looting spree, ostensibly for goods that could be sent home to bombed German cities. Radios and sewing machines were carted off. They pillaged buildings for any wood they could lay their hands on, to be used in their defensive positions. As a result, houses were stripped of their floorboards, doors and roof joists. In Oosterbeek alone, 8,000 doors were ripped from their hinges to provide covering for German trenches. This left properties open to thieves and the weather. What the Germans could not remove they simply smashed. This vindictive vandalism showed a lack of discipline, or simply a calculated callousness to cow the local population.

In Berlin, Nazi propaganda minister Dr Joseph Goebbels decided to capitalize on the victory at Arnhem. He could not help himself, as success was hard to come by these days. Goebbels sent German citizens Helen Sensburg[3] and Gerda Warke[4] to Hilversum to front Radio Arnhem in October 1944. Sensburg spent a decade in Britain before the war and spoke perfect English, as did Warke, who had lived in America. Helen was pleased to get the call. Her husband was fighting the Russians, so she was keen to do her bit for the war effort. One of Goebbels' propaganda units had taken over the Hilversum radio station the very day after the Dutch Army, under General Henri Winkelman, surrendered in 1940. The fact that Hilversum is between Amsterdam and Amersfoort and nowhere near Arnhem did not matter to German propagandists.

The 31-year-old brunette Sensburg and 24-year-old blonde Warke managed to avoid the predatory attentions of Goebbels. He had a reputation, largely self-propagated, of being an insatiable womanizer. Fortunately for them the 'poison dwarf', as he was known behind his back, had more pressing matters to attend to, such as propping up national morale. Model's defeat of the British at Arnhem provided just such an opportunity.

Sensburg, in her programme titled 'Arnhem Calling', played music, made veiled threats to American, British and Canadian soldiers and reported on the great success of the V-1 and V-2 attacks. 'You can listen to our music, but you can't walk our streets',[5] she taunted. She always closed with 'Goodnight boys. Take care of yourselves'.[6] The British soon dubbed her 'Mary of Arnhem'. Although she broadcast fake news, sometimes her intelligence was worryingly accurate, which demoralized the troops stuck in the mud and snow of the Betuwe.

The Americans soon tired of her antics. 'You are as far as you are going, Yanks', cooed Sensberg over the airwaves. 'Just bring your toothbrush, overcoat, and blanket and the war will be over for you.' She would then read out lists of those captured who were enjoying Hitler's hospitality. In response, the Americans took to calling her 'Arnhem Annie', or those in a more humorous mood resorted to the sobriquet of 'Dirty Gertie'.[7]

Most of the captured British 1st Airborne wounded, including those at the Schoonoord Hotel and St Elizabeth Hospital, were moved to a Dutch army barracks at Apeldoorn and placed in the care of Colonel Warrack. In all, 1,700 casualties and 250 medical staff were gathered there. The Germans even provided ambulances to transport them, as well as what food and medical supplies they could spare. There was a tense moment when a group of senior SS officers arrived at St Elizabeth Hospital to be greeted by a loud raspberry. For a split second they were stunned by this final act of defiance before sweeping on their way.

Major Eckbrecht Freiherr von Olderhausen, the Apeldoorn town commandant, agreed to treat the barracks as a hospital and not a prisoner of war camp, as long as there were no escapes. His gentleman's agreement included leaving the facility under British control. Subsequently, Rauter had Olderhausen arrested on suspicion of colluding with the enemy. The Dutch Resistance had been smuggling British prisoners out under the Germans' noses with ease. Warrack did not trust Olderhausen, but his men seemed to have no trouble getting transit passes. Warrack was even amongst the escapees. Rauter was unaware that Lieutenant-Colonel Schroeder, the German commandant in Amsterdam, was also co-operating with the Resistance. He and Olderhausen were both considered 'good' Germans by the Dutch.

The continued presence of Model's forces meant that the Dutch went hungry. Seyss-Inquart decided to punish the population and ordered a freeze on the movement of food within the German-occupied area. This was in part due to an ugly stand-off over transport in the Netherlands. The Dutch railwaymen, who had gone on strike on 17 September, steadfastly refused to go back to work, leaving the rail network paralysed. In response, the Germans blocked all inland shipping. The Dutch, denied barges and trains, were unable to move food to their cities in the west. Once winter set in and the canals froze, it was impossible to use them anyway. Amsterdam, Rotterdam and The Hague suffered the most as a consequence.

To safeguard against further Allied attempts on the Netherlands, Model flooded one-eighth of the country. This further hampered the movement of provisions and supplies throughout the Dutch provinces. The Allies played a role in this inundation when they bombed Walcheren's dykes. The Germans also rigged more dykes for demolition should the Allies attack again.

The German Army made sure that it did not go hungry. German infantry divisions 'purchased' any food available within 50 miles of the front. Each had its own bakery and butchery companies, responsible for the provision of bread, meat and vegetables. There were three ration scales; front-line troops, lines of communication and home service. German field kitchens were responsible for providing the troops with one hot meal a day; conditions permitting, this was normally at midday. They also supplied the men with hot drinks at lunch and dinner times. In the evening, every man was issued with rations to cover supper and breakfast. This consisted of bread, butter and cheese or sausage.

The butchery companies ordered local farmers to deliver livestock and vegetables to them once a week. Likewise, the bakery companies took all the flour. German infantry still relied on horse-drawn transport, so when meat was scarce they slaughtered their own draught animals. Even after the Allies overran many of their depots, the Germans were able largely to maintain their normal rationing.[8]

The result of all this was that the Dutch starved. During September they existed on 1,500 calories per day, but by the end of the winter they were down to 500 calories, or in some cases even half that. The daily ration was two pieces of bread, two potatoes and half a sugar beet. The latter tasted foul, but it was better than nothing. People resorted to eating cats, dogs, horses and tulip bulbs. 'Porridge cooked in rye and water was a mucky replacement of any minimal meals as offered in the soup kitchens,' recalled Dutchman Harry Kuiper. 'The grey and somewhat brown porridge without a grain of salt or sugar... was just disgusting.'[9] He later discovered that this concoction was normally used as pig feed.

Collaboration became a way to survive. Sergeant Charles Whiting wrote 'consumptive "good" girls sold themselves to German soldiers in the backstreets of Amsterdam for a loaf of hard Army bread or a tin of "Old Man", the standard Wehrmacht meat ration'.[10] The Dutch Resistance struggled to feed 70,000 people who were in hiding, as well as 10,000 fighters. It became known as the 'Hunger Winter' during which some 18,000 people starved to death. The vindictive Seyss-Inquart refused to allow the Allies to conduct food airdrops until late April.[11] This, though, was just the tip of the iceberg when it came to the horrors of the German occupation. The war cost the Dutch 237,000 fatalities.

The continued presence of Hitler's V-weapons at The Hague meant that civilians continued to suffer. On 3 March 1945 the RAF inadvertently dropped bombs on local housing while trying to hit the launch sites, killing 520 and wounding 344. The resulting fires destroyed 3,250 homes and damaged many others, leaving about 20,000 people homeless. Total fatalities in the Netherlands caused by bombing raids by both sides amounted to 6,150 people. Thanks to the activities of the Germans and the Allies, the Netherlands lost 86,000 homes and apartments. Some 7,662 were in The Hague, while Amsterdam and Arnhem were placed second and third for damage.

Mussert's Dutch SS, in the shape of the Landstorm Nederland division, continued to operate against the Dutch Resistance, notably in the Nord-Brabant province and Gelderland. This unit consisted of little more than a couple of weak regiments. Time ran out for SS-Colonel Feldmeijer, one of the senior Landstorm commanders. His car was caught by Allied fighters on the open road on 22 February 1945 and he was killed. Hanns Rauter, the hated SS police chief, found himself targeted by the Dutch. His staff car was ambushed by the Dutch Resistance on 7 March 1945. Luckily for Rauter, who was wounded, a German patrol arrived just in time.

The German hold on the Netherlands was tenuous by 1945. They had about 10,000 men in the Arnhem–Apeldoorn area, with just 1,000 holding Arnhem itself. When the Allies renewed the battle for the Rhineland, it was way to the south of Nijmegen. It was not until early April 1945 that the Germans were completely cleared from the Betuwe. Then on 13 April the British crossed the Rhine and Arnhem was finally liberated. Two German battalions tried to hold out in a factory building, but they were rapidly killed or captured. Four days later the German garrison at Apeldoorn surrendered.

The official German capitulation in the Netherlands took place at Wageningen on 5 May 1945. There were 126,500 Germans in the western Netherlands and another 30,000 in the north. General Johannes Blaskowitz had Major Olderhausen released just in time to act as an interpreter during the surrender negotiations with the Canadians. Along with Blaskowitz's chief of staff, Lieutenant-General Paul Reichelt, they presented themselves at the Hotel de Wereweld to ratify the surrender and face a press conference. The building was shell damaged and it was an extremely sombre affair. Blaskowitz knew the Allies could not dismantle the German administration overnight or there would be chaos.

Seated in the restaurant, Blaskowitz and Reichelt stared ahead impassively as they listened to what was going to happen. Memories of the German victory at Arnhem were long forgotten. One Canadian officer noted the German generals appeared as if they were 'in a dream, dazed, stupefied'.[12] The Germans were initially permitted to retain their weapons; in return, Blaskowitz had to disarm the Dutch SS, remove the demolition charges from the dykes and start clearing minefields. On the way back to his headquarters, he prevented the execution of 30 civilians in reprisal for attacks on German troops. In Dordrecht, Rotterdam and Utrecht panicked Dutch SS and some Germans shot at celebrating crowds. They were swiftly disarmed and jailed on the orders of Blaskowitz. To his credit, he maintained discipline and handed over most of those who were on the Allies' automatic arrest list.

The Dutch SS, with nothing to lose, attempted to resist to the last against the British at Ede, to the northwest of Arnhem and at Renswoude. The pitiful survivors, numbering 1,492 men, finally laid down their arms at Doorn on 10 May 1945.[13] Two days later, a further 53 Dutch SS and German deserters were rounded up. Other Dutchmen, under the command of SS-Brigadier Jürgen Wagner, remained on the Eastern Front until the end of the war. Most of the latter were killed or captured by the Russians; just a few managed to surrender to the Americans at Magdeburg.[14] Léon Degrelle's Belgian SS surrendered to the Russians, though he escaped to Spain.[15] After the war, some 50,000 Dutch were tried as collaborators. Mussert always claimed that his party was supported by such numbers.

The last of Student's stubborn paratroopers surrendered their weapons to the British outside Utrecht, along with the staff of the 88th Corps. The survivors of the 6th Parachute Division capitulated near Zutphen and it took two days to process them. The British were surprised that they were still so well equipped, though their transport was only horse-drawn. The division's very smart-looking officers arrived on Dutch bicycles to finalize formalities. Harry Kuiper saw some of them on the road: 'one day, there was an endless looking column of German POWs marching towards Utrecht city'.[16]

Forlornly the men filed through a house, handing over their binoculars, side arms, watches and other possessions. Their 9mm Lugers were particularly sought after by British souvenir hunters. Then they were marched out into the fields, where they neatly stacked their para helmets and heavier weapons. Such was the fate of what had once been one of Student's crack divisions. They had to wait a week in nearby woods before they marched home. On the way some were pelted with rocks by angry locals. The 7th and 8th Parachute Divisions had already withdrawn and surrendered on German soil.

The 346th Infantry Division was disarmed at Amersfoort, once the home of Helle's Dutch SS, which had performed so badly at Arnhem. In The Hague Canadian troops had to prevent the Dutch from throwing grenades into a compound holding Gestapo and SS prisoners. The Dutch were furious that the SS officers had been left with their Lugers. To the north, German troops were marched onto the airfield at Julianadorp, where they were also dealt with by the lenient Canadians.

Rauter was arrested by the British while still in hospital, and handed over to the Dutch authorities, who executed him. The equally hated Seyss-Inquart was put on trial at Nuremburg and subsequently hanged as a war criminal. General Christiansen, the German military commander in the Netherlands, was sentenced to 12 years in prison by the Dutch for war crimes. He was held responsible for the winter famine and reprisals against the village of Putten. In the event he served only three years before being sent home. Mussert made little attempt to flee to Germany and was arrested by the Dutch Resistance in The Hague. Photographed outside his office in an oversized double-breasted coat and a small trilby hat, he looked a rather pathetic figure. Found guilty of treason, he was shot.

Mary of Arnhem did not escape the liberation either. The Dutch Resistance caught her and she was taken to The Hague. Her interrogators found she was devoted to Hitler and the Nazi cause. As one British officer put it, Sensburg 'had a nice cultured voice with a friendly approach'.[17] A British journalist who interviewed Sensburg described her as a 'wide-eyed, witty, intrusive, understanding type'.[18] To her countrymen she was a patriot, to others she was simply a deluded stooge. Sensburg's greatest wish was to be reunited with her husband, who was a prisoner of war.[19]

For the long-suffering Dutch it seemed as if the occupation would never end. By mid-May 1945 there were still 98,000 German troops in the Netherlands, of whom around 1,000 were armed. The majority of these had not gone until mid-June. General Winkelman, who had signed the Dutch surrender on 15 May 1940, was finally released from German captivity on 12 May 1945. He had fallen foul of German pettiness. Winkelman's crime had been to wear a white carnation, a symbol of protest against the occupation and an act that had incensed Goebbels. The Dutch were now free to wear what they wanted.

Epilogue

Poignant Tragedy

In London, the BBC initially reported Arnhem as 'one of the outstanding operations of the war'; then changed it to 'a valuable stand' by 'a depleted, gallant and undaunted force'.[1] British war correspondent Alan Moorehead belittled German achievements by saying the battle was 'magnified far beyond its strategic importance by the peculiar circumstances and the poignant tragedy of the stranded paratroops'.[2] This is very true. 'It should be remembered that the Arnhem bridgehead was only a part of the whole',[3] cautioned General de Guingand after the war.

For the Allies, it represented an inconvenient and very brief glitch in their war effort. They quickly moved on to other costly operations at Walcheren, the Hürtgen and Aachen. The failure to clear the Scheldt was a far greater disaster, requiring a costly campaign at the end of the year. For the Germans, the battle was simply part of the desperate effort to shore up their front after the collapse in Normandy.

Ultimately, *Market Garden* was thwarted as a result of British mistakes as much as by the German response. Model, Student and Bittrich only just held on. Despite the delays, the British and Americans successfully cut a 60-mile corridor through German lines and took nearly all their airborne objectives. On the whole the quality of German troops involved in the battle was very poor, although who knows what would have happened had Hitler released some of the forces he was assembling for the Ardennes offensive. In consequence, apart from securing Arnhem, all of Model's counter-attacks were beaten off, and he failed to retake Nijmegen, permanently cut the corridor or clear the Allies from the Betuwe. He even failed to destroy both the Nijmegen bridges.

Model could have achieved a much greater victory had he cut the Nijmegen bridges before the British tanks got over them. If that had happened, it would have been impossible to evacuate the survivors of 1st Airborne. Montgomery would then have lost an entire division. He was spared this humiliation by Hitler. Nor would Model have had to fight the battle for the Betuwe. 'Model said, don't blow the bridge because I need it for a counterstroke', recalled Harmel. 'Bittrich and I believed it should have been blown straightaway. We realized we could never mobilize sufficient forces'.[4] Crucially, Model was left in possession of Arnhem and that is all that mattered. It was to be his last victory.

Appendices

Although many of the senior German commanders involved in the battle for Arnhem were good administrators, they were not necessarily experienced combat commanders. Nor were these two skills mutually inclusive. General Kussin seems to have been promoted above his abilities. Certainly he exhibited a complete lack of judgement in absenting himself from his Arnhem headquarters at a crucial moment in the battle. General Zangen had little opportunity to show any real tactical flair, although his oversight of the evacuation across the Scheldt was exemplary. Christiansen, Feldt and Tettau showed little aptitude.

FIELD MARSHAL GERD VON RUNDSTEDT

Rundstedt's military career exhibited remarkable durability throughout World War II. He was born in Ascherleben, near Halle, in 1875, and joined the cadets at the age of 12. He became an infantry officer, followed by general staff training. He fought at the battle of the Marne in 1914 and was then sent to the Eastern Front. Post-war he remained in the army and by 1932 had reached the rank of general. After falling out with Hitler, he was retired in 1938, the first of four such retirements. He returned the following year to oversee the invasion of Poland, commanding Army Group South. He then took a key role in the conquest of France. Afterwards he took charge of Army Group South once again for the invasion of

Russia, only to be sacked in December 1941. Recalled in 1942, he was appointed CinC West. At the height of the Normandy campaign, he was once again sacked and replaced by Model. On 4 September 1944 he was reinstated just in time for the battle for Arnhem. He opposed Hitler's plans for the Battle of the Bulge, and after it failed Rundstedt fell back behind the Rhine. He was replaced on 9 March 1945 and was captured by the Americans on 2 May 1945. He died in Hanover in 1953.

FIELD MARSHAL WALTHER MODEL

Model has been described as the most effective of the Nazi generals. Certainly during the second half of World War II he became Hitler's number one trouble-shooter. He was born in Genthin, near Magdeburg, in 1891. Joining the Imperial Army in 1909, he served as an infantry officer during World War I. Afterwards, Model stayed in the army and by 1934 had reached the rank of colonel. In late 1940 he was promoted to lieutenant-general and commanded the 3rd Panzer Division during the invasion of Russia the following year. In 1942 he took command of 9th Army, which he led with great distinction. After the German defeat at Kursk, Model became CinC Army Group North and then Army Group South. When Army Group Centre collapsed in the summer of 1944, Model was sent to take charge. In mid-August 1944, after stabilizing the crumbling Eastern Front, he was ordered to take command of Army Group B and briefly became CinC West. Following Arnhem and the Battle of the Bulge, rather than be captured, Model shot himself on 21 April 1945.

GENERAL HANS KREBS

Krebs, who was born in 1898, was a career staff officer. He joined the army in 1914. During the late 1930s he served as the German military attaché in Moscow, where he became an expert on the Red Army. During World War II he was the chief of staff for 9th Army, Army Group Centre and then Army Group B. In early 1945 he was promoted to deputy chief of the Army General Staff. In the closing stages of the war, Krebs was given the fruitless task of trying to co-ordinate the relief of Berlin. He committed suicide on 2 May 1945.

GENERAL KURT STUDENT

Kurt Student was born in Neumark, Brandenburg, in 1890. He joined the army but with the outbreak of World War I he was sent for pilot training and transferred to the air force. Subsequently, although Germany was banned from having an air force, Student joined the Air Ministry. Under Hermann Göring he was tasked with creating the Luftwaffe. Then in 1938 he was selected to form Germany's very first airborne division. Student led this with élan during Hitler's early Blitzkrieg campaigns in 1940, but after the botched Crete operation the following year he fell from grace. He was summoned from his desk job in early September 1944 to take charge of the newly forming 1st Parachute Army. Afterwards he was promoted to be an army group commander. Student was captured by the British in 1945 and charged with committing war crimes in Crete. He was found not guilty and died in 1978.

GENERAL GUSTAV-ADOLF VON ZANGEN

Zangen was born in 1892 and served with the army in World War I. During World War II he was a divisional commander on the Eastern Front. He then served in France and Italy before taking over 15th Army in northern France. After his highly successful withdrawal across the Scheldt Estuary, his command played a limited role in the Battle of the Bulge. He surrendered in the Ruhr Pocket and died in Hanau in 1964.

GENERAL FRIEDRICH CHRISTIANSEN

Christiansen, like Student, was a Luftwaffe general. Born in 1879 in Wyk auf Föhr, he started his career as a naval officer. In 1914 he became a naval aviator flying seaplanes on bombing missions over England. When Hitler came to power he joined the Air Ministry and reached the rank of general by 1939. The following year he was placed in command of the Netherlands, a post he held until the very end of the war. From late 1944 he also commanded 25th Army. He died in 1972.

GENERAL WILHELM BITTRICH

Born in Wernigerode in 1894, Bittrich started his military career as a fighter pilot in World War I. He joined the SS in 1932 and climbed through the ranks. He served with the Waffen-SS throughout the early Blitzkrieg campaigns. After commanding an SS-cavalry brigade, he took charge of the 9th SS-Panzer Division in 1943. He then commanded the 2nd SS-Panzer Corps, a post he held until the end of the war. He died in Wolfratshausen in 1979.

GENERAL KURT FELDT

General Feldt was born in Schmentau, West Prussia, in 1897 and joined the army in 1908. He served as a cavalry officer and by the outbreak of World War II he commanded the 1st Cavalry Division. This became the 24th Panzer Division in late 1941 and fought on the Eastern Front. Feldt was assigned to headquarters staff in southwest France in the summer of 1942. By the summer of 1944, he was the Marne sector commander and on 12 September formed Corps Feldt. This unit doggedly counter-attacked the Americans at Nijmegen. After a brief stint on the reserve list, in 1945 he was sent to join German headquarters staff in Denmark, where he ended the war. He died in 1970 in Berlin, at the age of 72.

GENERAL EUGEN MEINDL

Meindl was born in 1892 and he joined the army in 1912, seeing combat during World War I. He led a parachute jump in Norway in 1940 and transferred to the Luftwaffe. During the Crete campaign he was severely wounded. He recovered and commanded Luftwaffe ground units on the Eastern Front with great skill. He then took command of the 2nd Parachute Corps, seeing action in Normandy and the Netherlands. Afterwards he oversaw the evacuation of the Wesel bridgehead. He died in 1951.

MAJOR-GENERAL FRIEDRICH KUSSIN

Kussin's career was wholly uninspired. Born in Aurich in 1895, he joined the army in 1913. He fought in World War I and by 1940 was commanding a pioneer battalion. Placed on the reserve list in 1943, he became the field commander for the Arnhem area only on 3 September 1944. Fourteen days later, he was killed on the day that Operation *Market Garden* commenced.

GENERAL HANS VON TETTAU

Tettau was born in 1888 and joined the army in 1909. Between mid-1940 and early 1943 he commanded the 24th Infantry Division. He then joined the staff of General Christiansen in the Netherlands. His main claim to fame was the battle for Arnhem, where he put pressure on the British western flank. His colleagues disparaged his efforts as plodding and ineffectual. He was captured in May 1945 and not released until 1947. He died in 1956.

Appendix B: Orders of Battle

GERMAN ORDER OF BATTLE

CINC WEST	**FIELD MARSHAL GERD VON RUNDSTEDT**
The Netherlands Reichskommissar (The Hague)	**Dr Arthur Seyss-Inquart**
Commander Armed Forces Netherlands (The Hague)	**Luftwaffe General Friedrich Christiansen**
Chief of Staff	Major-General Hans von Tettau
Head Counter-Intelligence	Lieutenant-Colonel Hermann Giskes
Deputy Head	Major Friedrich Kieswetter
V-1 and V-2 Command	Lieutenant-General Walther von Axthelm
	Colonel Max Wachtel (Max Wolf)
	Major Sommerfeld
SS Police Chief	SS-General Hanns Rauter
2nd SS-Panzer Corps	SS-General Wilhelm Bittrich
9th SS-Panzer Division Hohenstaufen	SS-Colonel Walther Harzer
Chief of Staff	SS-Captain Wilfried Schwarz
10th SS-Panzer Division Frundsberg	SS-Brigadier Heinz Harmel
Chief of Staff	SS-Colonel Otto Paetsch
Reinforcements from early October 1944: 9th Panzer Division 116th Panzer Division	
Division von Tettau	Lieutenant-General Hans Von Tettau
5th SS Artillery Training and Replacement Regiment	SS-Captain Schwappacher

16th SS-Panzergrenadier Training and Reserve Battalion	SS-Major Sepp Krafft
SS NCO School Arnheim	SS-Colonel Hans Michael Lippert
SS Depot Battalion	SS-Major Eberwein
SS Concentration Camp Administration	
Amersfoort	SS-Commandant Karl Peter Berg
Vught	SS-Commandant Hans Hüttig
Security	SS-Captain Paul Helle
Hermann Göring Training Regiment	

ARMY GROUP B	**FIELD MARSHAL WALTHER MODEL**
1st Parachute Army	**General Kurt Student**
12th SS-Corps (from 29 September)	SS-Lieuteant General Kurt von Gottberg
180th Infantry Division	
190th Infantry Division	
363rd Volksgrenadier Division (from 5 October)	
86th Corps	General Hans von Obstfelder
176th Infantry Division	
Battle Group Walther	
6th Parachute Regiment	
107th Panzer Brigade	
Division Erdmann	
15th Army	**General Gustav-Adolf von Zangen (replaced Hans von Salmuth 27 August 1944)**
	General Otto Sponheimer
67th Corps	
64th Infantry Division (Breskens)	

70th Inafantry Division
(Walcheren)
346th Infantry Division
711th Coastal Division
719th Coastal Division
(reassigned to 1st Parachute
Army)
88th Corps   General Hans Reinhard (reassigned
                                         to 1st Parachute Army)

Battle Group Chill
Battle Group Huber
Battle Group Jungwirth
Battle Group Rink
59th Infantry Division
245th Infantry Division
347th Infantry Division
712th Coastal Division
Plus remnants of the 331st, 344th,
345th, and 348th infantry divisions
and the 17th Luftwaffe Field Division
Corps Feldt (from 18 September)   **General Kurt Feldt**
406th Infantry Division
Battle Group Fuerstenberg
Battle Group Goebel
Battle Group Greschick
Battle Group Stargaard
Reinforcements from 20 September:
Battle Group Budde
Battle Group Lewin
Battle Group Molzer
2nd Parachute Corps (from
20 September)   General Eugen Meindl
Battle Group Becker
(3rd Parachute Division)
Battle Group Hermann (5th
Parachute Division, plus elements
of 6th Parachute Division)

ALLIED ORDER OF BATTLE

21ST ARMY GROUP

FIELD MARSHAL BERNARD MONTGOMERY

British 2nd Army

Lieutenant-General Miles Dempsey

30th Corps

Lieuteant-General Brian Horrocks

Guards Armoured Division

Major-General Allan Adair

43rd Wessex Division

Major-General G. I. Thomas

50th Northumbrian Division

Major-General D. A. H Graham

8th Armoured Brigade

Brigadier O. L. Prior Palmer

Royal Netherlands Brigade Princess Irene

Lieutenant-Colonel A. C. de Ruyter van Steveninck

Left Flank Support

8th Corps

Lieuteant-General R. N. O'Connor

3rd Division

Major-General L. G. Whistler

Right Flank Support

12th Corps

Lieuteant-General N. M. Ritchie

53rd Welsh Division

Major-General R. K. Ross

1ST ALLIED AIRBORNE ARMY

LIEUTENANT-GENERAL LEWIS BRERETON

US 18th Airborne Corps

Major-General Matthew B. Ridgway

US 82nd Airborne Division

Brigadier General James Gavin

US 101st Airborne Division

Major-General Maxwell Taylor

British 1st Airborne Corps

Lieuteant-General Frederick Browning

1st Airborne Division

Major-General Robert Urquart

52nd Lowland Division (Airlanding)

Major-General E. Hakewell-Smith

Polish 1st Independent Parachute Brigade

Major-General Stanislaw Sosabowski

Appendix C: German Armour Strength

GERMAN ARMOUR IN THE ARNHEM AREA

2nd SS-Panzer Corps

9th SS-Panzer Division Hohenstaufen
(Areas of Operation: Arnhem–Oosterbeek–Nijmegen–Elst)
42 armoured cars (mostly half-tracks)
2 Jagdpanzer IV tank destroyers
3 Möbelwagen Flakpanzers
1 Flak half-track

10th SS-Panzer Division Frundsberg
(Arnhem–Elst)
7 armoured cars, half-tracks
1 armoured scout car
8 Panzer V Panther tanks
12 Panzer IV tanks
4 StuG III assault guns
1 Flak half-track

Other Armoured Units Involved
6th Panzer Replacement Regiment Bielefeld (battle groups Brinkmann, Knaust and Mielke)
(Arnhem–Elst)
2 Panzer IV
6 Panzer III

Heavy Panzer Company Hummel
(Arnhem–Elst)
12 Panzer VI Tiger Is

506th Heavy Panzer Battalion (Battle Group Knaust)
(Oosterbeek–Elst)
28 Panzer VI Tiger IIs

280th Assault Gun Battalion (Battle Group Knaust)
(Arnhem–Elst)
7 StuG III
3 StuH 42 assault howitzers

244th Panzer Company
(Oosterbeek)
1 Panzer 35S
2 Panzer B2
14 Flammpanzers

Total
51 armoured vehicles
104 tanks and assault guns1

Unaccounted-for reinforcements
Battle Group Knaust
(Elst)
Knaust was also supported by around seven Panther tanks. Most if not all of them had come straight from the factory, judging by the inexperience of their crews and the speed with which they were lost.

GERMAN ARMOUR BETWEEN VALKENSWAARD AND EINDHOVEN

10th SS Tank Destroyer Company
15 Jagdpanzer IV tank destroyers

Unit unknown
1 Panther
2 self-propelled guns

Total
2 armoured vehicles
16 tanks and tank destroyers

GERMAN ARMOUR FACING HIGHWAY 69
(HELL'S HIGHWAY)

107th Panzer Brigade (only regimental strength)

119 half-tracks
4 Flakpanzers
11 Jagdpanzer IVs
36 Panthers

Total

123 armoured vehicles
47 tanks and tank destroyers

Plus miscellaneous assault gun and self-propelled gun units.

GERMAN ARMOUR IN THE BETUWE

2nd SS-Panzer Corps

9th Panzer
Strength unknown

9th SS-Panzer
4 Panthers2

10th SS-Panzer
Strength unknown

116th Panzer
11 Panzer IVs3
5 Panthers4

506th Heavy Panzer Battalion (attached to 9th Panzer)
5 Tigers5

Total

25 tanks

Notes and References

Prologue

1 Cornelius Ryan, *A Bridge Too Far* (London: Hamish Hamilton, 1974), p.153.

2 James Lucas, *Hitler's Enforcers: Leaders of the German War Machine 1933–1945* (London: Arms and Armour Press, 1996), p.99.

3 Ryan, *A Bridge Too Far*, p.71.

4 Ibid.

5 Stephen H. Newton, *Hitler's Commander: Field Marshal Walther Model – Hitler's Favourite General* (Cambridge, MA: Da Capo Press, 2006), p.317.

6 Lt Gen Sir Brian Horrocks, *A Full Life* (London: Collins, 1960), p.213.

7 Ryan, *A Bridge Too Far*, p.160.

8 Ibid.

9 Antony Beevor, *Arnhem: The Battle for the Bridges, 1944* (London: Viking, 2018), p.92.

10 Ryan, *A Bridge Too Far*, p.160.

11 Beevor, *Arnhem*, p.92.

12 Newton, *Hitler's Commander*, p.317. He was wrong because it was only one, the British 1st Airborne Division.

13 Ibid. Sources differ regarding the German reaction at the Tafelberg Hotel. As Antony Beevor points out, 'Some say it was panic-stricken', for example Geoffrey Powell, *The Devil's Birthday: The Bridges to Arnhem, 1944* (London: Buchan and Enright, 1984), p.89. In light of Model's considerable experience in tricky situations this seems unlikely.

14 Ryan, *A Bridge Too Far*, p.160.

15 Chester Wilmot, *The Struggle for Europe* (London: Collins, 1952), p.502.

16 Beevor, *Arnhem*, p.47.

17 Peter Beale, *The Great Mistake: The Battle for Antwerp and the Beveland Peninsula, September 1944* (Stroud: Sutton, 2004), p.14.

18 Wilmot, *The Struggle for Europe*, p.503.

19 Ryan, *A Bridge Too Far*, pp.103–4.

20 Behr very narrowly escaped being captured with the rest of 6th Army at Stalingrad. Serving as an operations officer at General Paulus' headquarters staff, he had been sent to brief Hitler in January 1943. Behr feared his graphic description of the conditions would get him sacked, but instead he ended up on Krebs' staff.

21 Ryan, *A Bridge Too Far*, p.160.

22 Anne Sebba, *Les Parisiennes: How the Women of Paris Lived, Loved, and Died in the 1940s* (London: Weidenfeld and Nicolson, 2017), pp.115–16.

23 Ryan, *A Bridge Too Far*, p.170.

24 Charles MacDonald, *By Air to Battle* (London: Macdonald, 1970), p.13.

25 Ibid., p.14.

26 Ibid., p.15.

27 Wilmot, *The Struggle for Europe*, p.505. Powell, *Devil's Birthday*, gives a slightly higher figure of 435, comprising 13 officers, 73 NCOs and 349 men, p.96.

28 Ryan, *A Bridge Too Far*, p.160.

29 Marcel Stein, *A Flawed Genius: Field Marshal Walter Model, A Critical Biography* (Solihull: Helion, 2010), p.170.

30 Samuel W. Mitcham, *Hitler's Field Marshals and Their Battles* (London: William Heinemann, 1988), p.325.

CHAPTER 1 RACE AGAINST TIME

1 Martin Bormann, *Hitler's Table Talk* (Oxford: Oxford University Press, 1988), p.537.

2 Ibid.

3 These were the 1st Belgian Infantry Brigade and the Royal Netherlands Brigade (Princess Irene's).

4 Wilmot, *The Struggle for Europe*, p.476.

5 Beale, *The Great Mistake*, p.75.

6 Ibid., p.14.

7 Ibid.

8 Hugh R. Trevor-Roper, *Hitler's War Directives 1939–45* (London: Sidgwick and Jackson, 1964), p.272.

9 Ibid.

10 Beale, *The Great Mistake*, p.14.

11 Stein, *A Flawed Genius*, p.163.

12 Ibid.

13 Beale, *The Great Mistake*, p.16.

14 Ibid., p.17.

CHAPTER 2 ZANGEN'S GREAT ESCAPE

1 Beale, *The Great Mistake*, p.18.
2 Newton, *Hitler's Commander*, p.312, and 1st Canadian Army Intelligence Summary 77, 8 September 1944, cited in Donald E. Graves, *Blood and Steel 2. The Wehrmacht Archive: Retreat to the Reich, September to December 1944* (Barnsley: Frontline, 2015), p.4. The latter offers a slightly different translation.
3 Beale, *The Great Mistake*, pp.120–1.
4 1st Canadian Army Intelligence Summaries, Nos 68–86, 5–24 September 1944, cited in Major-General J. L. Moulton, *Battle for Antwerp: The Liberation of the City and the Opening of the Scheldt 1944* (Hersham: Ian Allan, 1978), p.49.
5 Patrick Delaforce, *Churchill's Desert Rats: From Normandy to Berlin with the 7th Armoured Division* (Stroud: Alan Sutton, 1994), p.96.
6 Robin Neillands, *The Desert Rats: 7th Armoured Division 1940–45* (London: Weidenfeld and Nicolson, 1991), pp.250–1.
7 Delaforce, *Churchill's Desert Rats*, p.98.
8 Ibid., p.101.
9 Beale, *The Great Mistake*, p.118.
10 Delaforce, *Churchill's Desert Rats*, p.101.
11 Moulton, *Battle for Antwerp*, p.49.
12 Trevor-Roper, *Hitler's War Directives*, p.276.
13 1st Canadian Army Intelligence Summary 77, 13 September 1944, cited in Graves, *Wehrmacht Archive*, p.25. This source says Urach came from the 50th Infantry Division.
14 1st Canadian Army Intelligence Summary 122, 30 October 1944, cited in Graves, *Wehrmacht Archive*, p.8.
15 RAF Bomber Command dropped 9,750 tons of bombs on Le Havre.
16 Beale, *The Great Mistake*, p.121.
17 Ibid., p.118.
18 Moulton, *Battle for Antwerp*, p.50.
19 Niklas Zetterling, *Normandy 1944: German Military Organization, Combat Power and Organizational Effectiveness* (Winnipeg: J. J. Fedorowicz, 2000), p.267–8.
20 Ryan, *A Bridge Too Far*, p.69.
21 They were subsequently formed into the 167th Volksgrenadier Division under Hocker.
22 Patrick Delaforce, *The Polar Bears: Monty's Left Flank, From Normandy to the Relief of Holland with 49th Division* (Stroud: Sutton, 1995), p.169.
23 Ibid, p.120.
24 Max Hastings, *Bomber Command* (London: Pan, 1999), p.303 and Anthony Verrier, *The Bomber Offensive* (London: Batsford, 1968), p.301.

25 According to Major-General Moulton, the 64th Division was newly arrived from Germany (*Battle for Antwerp*, p.46). However, in Peter Beale's more recent book *The Great Mistake*, he says that it was in the Pas-de-Calais as a 'rest division' and that it withdrew from positions northwest of Lille on 2 September 1944 (p.122).

26 CinC 15th Army Orders, cited in Graves, *Wehrmacht Archive*, pp.8–9.

27 Ryan, *A Bridge Too Far*, p.333, citing Army Group B's War Diary. Ryan felt these figures to be excessive. Albert Seaton in *The Fall of Fortress Europe 1943–1945* (London: Batsford, 1981) (p.158) also uses the figures of 82,000 men and 580 guns. Beale (*The Great Mistake*) and Moulton (*Battle for Antwerp*) both quote higher numbers: 86,000 men, 6,200 horses, 6,200 vehicles and 616 guns (p.120 and p.48 respectively). It is odd that their numbers for horses and vehicles are identical and again seem exceptionally high.

28 Milton Shulman, *The German Defeat in the West* (London: Secker and Warburg, 1947), p.180. Horrocks, *A Full Life*, p.204 repeats this lower figure of 65,000.

29 Wilmot, *The Struggle for Europe*, p.532.

30 Ibid.

31 Seaton, *Fall of Fortress Europe*, p.159.

CHAPTER 3 SIX AND A QUARTER

1   The Nationaal Socialistische Beweging, or NSB, was overtly fascist in outlook.

2   Bormann, *Hitler's Table Talk*, p.344.

3   These were the 83rd and 84th SS Volunteer Grenadier Regiments, commanded by SS-Colonels Viktor Knapp and Martin Kohlroser.

4   Bormann, *Hitler's Table Talk*, p.402.

5   Ibid.

6   Ibid, p.537.

7   R. V. Jones, *Most Secret War* (London: Hamish Hamilton, 1978), p.374.

8   David Bennett, *A Magnificent Disaster: The Failure of Market Garden, the Arnhem Operation, September 1944* (Philadelphia: Casemate, 2008), p.205.

9   Ryan, *A Bridge Too Far*, p.105.

10 Although Laude was arrested by the Gestapo, they failed to catch the other ringleaders, Eugène Colson, Edouard Pilaet, Lieutenant Urbain Reniers and Colonel Scharf. Reniers, codename Réaumur, was a member of the Secret Army. See Beale, *The Great Mistake*, p.139–40 and Moulton, *Battle for Antwerp*, p.18.

11 This was the Princess Irene's Royal Netherlands Brigade, which first came ashore on 6 August 1944.

12 Beevor, *Arnhem*, p.12.

13 Ibid., p.70.

14 Ryan, *A Bridge Too Far*, pp.351–2, and Bennett, *A Magnificent Disaster*, pp.125–6.

15 Ryan, *A Bridge Too Far*, p.105.

16 Max Hastings, *The Secret War: Spies, Codes and Guerrillas 1939–45* (London: William Collins, 2017), p.271. According to Ryan this message was sent on 23 November 1943 (*A Bridge Too Far*, p.328).

Chapter 4 Student's Paras

1 Christa Schroeder, *He was My Chief: The Memoirs of Adolf Hitler's Secretary* (Barnsley: Frontline Books, 2012), p.123.

2 Ibid., p.124.

3 Heinz Wilhelm Guderian, *Panzer Leader* (London: Futura, 1974), p.359.

4 Wilmot, *The Struggle for Europe*, p.478. Seaton (*The Fall of Fortress Europe*, p.158) offers slightly different wording: 'otherwise the doorway to North Germany would be wide open.'

5 British intelligence initially estimated German losses 'were at least 6,000 killed or drowned and 11,000 wounded' (Ministry of Information, *The Campaign in Greece and Crete*, p.62). The invasion of Crete in 1941 involved 22,000 men; 14,000 were paratroops and the rest were from an airlanded mountain division. German casualties numbered 6,698, including 3,352 dead – of which 1,653 were paratroops. Almost 200 transport aircraft were written off. See Callum MacDonald, *The Lost Battle: Crete 1941* (London: Macmillan, 1993), p.301.

6 Ministry of Information, *Campaign in Greece and Crete*, p.51.

7 Wilmot, *The Struggle for Europe*, p.479.

8 B. H. Liddell Hart, *The Other Side of the Hill* (London: Pan, 1983), p.242.

9 George Harokopos, *The Fortress Crete: The Secret War 1941–1944* (Athens: B. Giannikos and B. Caldis, 2001), p.17. Another reason Hitler was annoyed with Student was that the invasion of Crete delayed Operation *Barbarossa*, his attack on the Soviet Union.

10 Liddell Hart, *The Other Side of the Hill*, p.242.

11 Antony Beevor, *Crete: The Battle and the Resistance* (London: Penguin, 1992), p.73.

12 Ryan, *A Bridge Too Far*, p.24.

13 Liddell Hart, *The Other Side of the Hill*, p.429.

14 Ibid., p.243.

15 MacDonald, *The Lost Battle*, p.301.

16 Ibid.

17 Alan Moorehead, *Mediterranean Front* (London: Hamish Hamilton, 1941), p.266.

18 According to reporter Alan Moorehead's sources, this was the result of taking some sort of drug (ibid.). This was probably benzedrine, intended to keep the paras alert and awake.

19 Liddell Hart, *The Other Side of the Hill*, p.429.

20 Ryan, *A Bridge Too Far*, p.23.

21 MacDonald, *The Lost Battle*, p.4.

22 James Lucas, *Battle Group! German Kampfgruppe Action of World War Two* (London: Arms and Armour Press, 1993), p.156.

23 Liddell Hart, *The Other Side of the Hill*, p.429.

24 Beale, *The Great Mistake*, p.117.

25 1st Canadian Army Intelligence Summary 167, 15 December 1944, from 1st US Army G-2 Periodic Report 186, 13 November 1944, cited in Graves, *Wehrmacht Archive*, pp.96–9.

26 *Report on Status of Parachute Divisions Encountered in France*, Canadian 1st Army Intelligence Summary, 11 October 1944, in ibid., pp.88–9.

27 Zetterling, *Normandy 1944*, pp.214–24.

28 All available Luftwaffe reinforcements ended up being sent to the 3rd and 5th parachute divisions so they could take part in Hitler's Ardennes offensive. By December, 5th Parachute Division was almost 16,000 strong, but that was of no help to Student during September. In contrast by early 1945 both the 7th and 8th parachute divisions had a fighting strength of only about 200 men each.

29 Wilmot, *The Struggle for Europe*, p.479.

30 Liddell Hart, *The Other Side of the Hill*, p.429, and Lucas, *Hitler's Enforcers*, p.184.

31 Lucas, *Battle Group!*, p.156.

32 Ibid.

33 Neillands, *The Desert Rats*, p.253.

CHAPTER 5   CHILL ON THE ALBERT

1   First Canadian Army Intelligence Summary 77, 8 September 1944, cited in Graves, *Wehrmacht Archive*, p.6.

2   William Shirer, *The Rise and Fall of the Third Reich* (London: Secker and Warburg, 1960), p.1088.

3   Beale, *The Great Mistake*, p.127.

4   Lucas, *Battle Group!*, p.157.

5   Beale, *The Great Mistake*, p.127.

6   Sir Brian Horrocks, Eversley Belfield and Major-General H. Essame, *Corps Commander* (London: Sidgwick and Jackson, 1977), p.76.

7   Lucas, *Battle Group!*, p.157.

8   Ibid., p.158.

9   Horrocks, Belfield and Essame, *Corps Commander*, p.80.

10 According to Lieutenant-General Brian Horrocks, commanding the British 30th Corps, this was a Panzer Mk IV (ibid., p. 84).

Chapter 6 The Devil Lies in Wait

1 Harry Kuiper, *Arnhem and the Aftermath: Civilian Experiences in the Netherlands 1940–1945* (Barnsley: Pen and Sword Military, 2019), p.113.

2 Martin Middlebrook, *Arnhem 1944: The Airborne Battle* (London: Viking, 1994), pp.93–4.

3 Their full titles were the 9th SS-Panzer Division Hohenstaufen and the 10th SS-Panzer Division Frundsberg. For ease they are simply referred to as 9th and 10th SS throughout, unless a quote mentions them by name.

4 For more on the 9th SS and 10th SS-Panzer divisions' experiences in Normandy, see Anthony Tucker-Jones, *Falaise: The Flawed Victory – The Destruction of Panzergruppe West, August 1944* (Barnsley: Pen and Sword, 2008), pp.113–28.

5 Wilmot, *The Struggle for Europe*, p.501.

6 Also spelt Roestler: see Bennett, *A Magnificent Disaster*, p.65, and Tim Saunders, *Hell's Highway: US 101st Airborne and Guards Armoured Division* (Barnsley: Leo Cooper, 2001), p.56.

7 Ryan, *A Bridge Too Far*, p.100.

8 Ibid., p.101.

9 Ibid., p.102.

10 Wilmot, *The Struggle for Europe*, p.504.

11 Ryan, *A Bridge Too Far*, p.170.

12 Ibid.

13 Ibid., p.171.

14 Maj Gen John Frost, *A Drop Too Many* (London: Cassell, 1980), p.211.

15 Ryan, *A Bridge Too Far*, p.200.

Chapter 7 Bittrich's Quick Reaction

1 Charles Whiting, *A Bridge at Arnhem* (London: Futura, 1974), p.57. Whiting's book was published the same year as Cornelius Ryan's *A Bridge Too Far*.

2 Whiting, *A Bridge at Arnhem*, p.56.

3 Patrick Hook, *Hohenstaufen 9th SS Panzer Division* (Hersham: Ian Allan, 2005), p.91.

4 Ibid., p.86. The traditional German Army lunch was pea soup with chunks of pork in it.

5 Ibid.

6 Ryan, *A Bridge Too Far*, p.172.

7 Ibid., p.203.

8 Max Hastings, *Armageddon: The Battle for Germany 1944–45* (London: Macmillan, 2004), p.50.

9 Ibid.

10 Frost, *A Drop Too Many*, p.217.

11 Robert Kershaw, *It Never Snows in September: The German View of Market-Garden and the Battle of Arnhem, September 1944* (Marlborough: Crowood Press, 1994), p.109.

12 Ibid., p.111.

13 Ibid., p.110.

14 Ibid., p.111.

15 Ryan, *A Bridge Too Far*, p.220.

16 Ibid.

17 Ibid., p.221.

18 Ibid.

19 Kershaw, *It Never Snows in September*, p.118.

Chapter 8 Panzers at Valkenswaard

1 Wilmot, *The Struggle for Europe*, p.502.

2 Ibid., p.503.

3 Ryan, *A Bridge Too Far*, p.107.

4 Wilmot, *The Struggle for Europe*, p.502.

5 Ryan, *A Bridge Too Far*, p.159.

6 Ibid.

7 Whiting, *A Bridge at Arnhem*, pp.62–3.

8 Wilmot, *The Struggle for Europe*, p.503.

9 Ryan, *A Bridge Too Far*, pp.190.

10 Horrocks, *A Full Life*, p. 215. Student credited this German security breach as the main reason for heavy parachute losses in Crete in 1941, because it highlighted German airborne tactics.

11 Ibid., p.215.

12 Wilmot, *The Struggle for Europe*, p.507.

13 'Manpower in Germany', 1st Canadian Army Intelligence Summary, 100, 8 October 1944, cited in Graves, *Wehrmacht Archive*, p.134.

14 Saunders, *Hell's Highway*, p.52.

15 Ibid., p.51.

16 Hook, *Hohenstaufen*, p.34.

17 Powell, *The Devil's Birthday*, p.91.

18 'History of the 279 Magen (Stomach Battalion)', 1st Canadian Army Intelligence Summary, 115, 23 October 1944, cited in Graves, *Wehrmacht Archive*, pp.95–6.

19 Saunders, *Hell's Highway*, p.48.

20 Horrocks, *A Full Life*, p. 211.

21 Saunders, *Hell's Highway*, p.48.

22 Ibid., p.51.

23 Horrocks, *A Full Life*, p.212, and Horrocks, Belfield and Essame, *Corps Commander*, p.90. Wilmot says eight tanks were 'brewed up' (*The Struggle for Europe*, p.507). Ken Ford opts for Horrocks' figure (*Operation Market-Garden 1944 (3): The British XXX Corps Missions* (Oxford: Osprey, 2018), p.39).

24 Kershaw, *It Never Snows in September*, p.98.

25 Saunders, *Hell's Highway*, p.62.

26 Hastings, *Armageddon*, p.57.

CHAPTER 9 AIRBORNE STEPPING STONES

1 Kershaw, *It Never Snows in September*, p.98.

2 Saunders, *Hell's Highway*, p.70.

3 Kershaw, *It Never Snows in September*, p.99, and Saunders, *Hell's Highway*, pp.78–80.

4 Ibid.

5 Beevor, *Arnhem*, p.121.

6 Ibid., p.120.

7 'Manpower in the German Army', 1st Canadian Army Intelligence Summary, 8 October 1944, cited in Graves, *Wehrmacht Archive*, pp.135–6.

8 Robin Neillands, *The Battle for the Rhine 1944* (London: Weidenfeld and Nicolson, 2005), p.109.

CHAPTER 10 FIERCE COUNTER-ATTACKS

1 Saunders, *Hell's Highway*, p.140.

2 Ibid., p.110.

3 Ibid., p.110.

4 Ibid., pp.117–8.

5 See Steven Zaloga, *Lorraine 1944: Patton vs Manteuffel* (Oxford: Osprey, 2000), pp.22–3.

6 Its commander, General Paul Schürmann, escaped from the Minsk pocket in the summer of 1944 with just 30 men. There were so few survivors that his division had to be disbanded. See Anthony Tucker-Jones, *Stalin's Revenge: Operation Bagration and the Annihilation of Army Group Centre* (Barnsley: Pen and Sword, 2009), pp.78–9 and 122.

CHAPTER 11 REICHSWALD ASSAULT

1 Kershaw, *It Never Snows in September*, p.113.

2 Tim Saunders, *The Island: Nijmegen to Arnhem* (Barnsley: Leo Cooper, 2002), p.98.

3 Kershaw, *It Never Snows in September*, p.113.

4 Ibid., p.140.
5 Ryan, *A Bridge Too Far*, p.258.
6 Bennett, *A Magnificent Disaster*, p.72.
7 Kershaw, *It Never Snows in September*, p.142.
8 Tim Saunders, *Nijmegen: US 82nd Airborne and Guards Armoured Division* (Barnsley: Leo Cooper, 2001), p.99.
9 Ibid., p.100.
10 Ibid., p.116.

CHAPTER 12 RESISTANCE AT THE VALKHOF

1 Saunders, *Nijmegen*, p.134.
2 Ibid., p.134.
3 Kershaw, *It Never Snows in September*, p.237.
4 Beevor, *Arnhem*, p.215.
5 Kershaw, *It Never Snows in September*, p.238.
6 Ryan, *A Bridge Too Far*, p.343.
7 Ibid., p.344.
8 Beevor, *Arnhem*, p.218.
9 Ryan, *A Bridge Too Far*, p.351. Beevor questions Harmel's version of events based on the interview he gave to Ryan. Beevor speculates that Harmel claimed he tried to blow the bridge to avoid Hitler's wrath. It seems odd, though, that he would keep up the pretence so long after the war (*Arnhem*, p.220). Dutch Resistance later reported that Jan van Hoof had cut the cable. Unfortunately, he was killed on 19 September so was unable to verify this. The general consensus is that van Hoof did not sabotage the demolition charges: see Kuiper, *Arnhem and the Aftermath*, pp.127–31.
10 Ryan, *A Bridge Too Far*, p.351.

CHAPTER 13 CREATING HELL'S HIGHWAY

1 Beevor, *Arnhem*, p.225.
2 Ibid.
3 Saunders, *Hell's Highway*, p.148.
4 Ibid., pp.167–8.
5 Ibid., p.172.

CHAPTER 14 ARNHEM RETAKEN

1 Hook, *Hohenstaufen*, p.44.
2 Kershaw, *It Never Snows in September*, p.189.

3 Ryan, *A Bridge Too Far*, p.335.
4 Lieutenant-Colonel John Frost's 2nd Battalion, 1st Parachute Brigade.
5 Ryan, *A Bridge Too Far*, p.231.
6 Kershaw, *It Never Snows in September*, p.155.
7 Ibid.
8 Ryan, *A Bridge Too Far*, p.228.
9 Hook, *Hohenstaufen*, p.45.
10 Ryan, *A Bridge Too Far*, p.229.
11 Kershaw, *It Never Snows in September*, p.157.
12 Beevor, *Arnhem*, p.147.
13 Ryan, *A Bridge Too Far*, p.273.
14 Ibid., p.319.
15 Kershaw, *It Never Snows in September*, p.205.
16 Ibid., p.245.
17 Erwin Kirchhof, *Der Westkurier*, 8 October 1944, cited in Graves, *Wehrmacht Archive*, p.57.
18 Louis Hagen, *Arnhem Lift* (London: Leo Cooper, 1993), p.102.

CHAPTER 15 SS IN THE BETUWE

1 Kershaw, *It Never Snows in September*, p.275.
2 Ryan, *A Bridge Too Far*, p.412.
3 Beevor, *Arnhem*, p.302.
4 Ibid.
5 Kershaw, *It Never Snows in September*, p.306.
6 Ibid.

CHAPTER 16 MODEL TRIUMPHS

1 Ryan, *A Bridge Too Far*, p.382.
2 Kershaw, *It Never Snows in September*, p.328.
3 Ibid., p.329.
4 Powell, *The Devil's Birthday*, p.208.
5 Whiting, *A Bridge at Arnhem*, p.219.
6 Major-General R. R. Urquhart, *Arnhem* (London: Cassell, 1958), p.163.
7 Ryan, *A Bridge Too Far*, p.421.
8 Bennett, *A Magnificent Disaster*, p.178.
9 Ryan, *A Bridge Too Far*, p.424.
10 Beevor, *Arnhem*, p.312.
11 Saunders, *The Island*, pp.96–7.
12 Kirchhof, *Der Westkurier*, 8 October 1944, cited in Graves, *Wehrmacht Archive*, p.58.

13 Dirk Bogarde, *Snakes and Ladders* (London: Penguin, 1988), pp.62–3. He
    was born Derek van den Bogaerde and served as such in the British Army, but
    is better known by his Anglicized screen name – Dirk Bogarde.
14 Ibid, p.63.
15 Kershaw, *It Never Snows in September*, p.371.
16 Ibid., p.372.
17 Dirk Bogarde, *For the Time Being* (London: Penguin, 1999), p.22.
18 Ibid, p.23.
19 Dirk Bogarde, *Cleared for Take-Off* (London: Penguin, 1996), p.12.
20 Saunders, *The Island*, p.106.
21 Ryan, *A Bridge Too Far*, p.450. Estimates for German casualties vary
    considerably. Major-General Urquhart cites 7,000 German casualties lost in
    the battle for Arnhem (*Arnhem*, p.187). Kershaw's detailed but incomplete
    survey identified 2,565 for the Arnhem–Oosterbeek fighting plus a further
    1,725 for the surrounding area. This gives 5,175 for Arnhem. He estimates
    some 3,750 for the *Market Garden* corridor, making a grand total of 8,925 (*It
    Never Snows in September*, pp.421–2).

CHAPTER 17 UNREPENTANT ADVOCATE

 1 David Niven, *The Moon's a Balloon* (London: Coronet, 1973), p.241.
 2 Kirchhof, *Der Westkurier*, 8 October 1944, cited in Graves, *Wehrmacht
    Archive*, p.55.
 3 Ibid., p.56.
 4 Bernard Montgomery, *The Memoirs of Field Marshal the Viscount
    Montgomery of Alamein* (London: Collins, 1958), p.297.
 5 Horrocks, *A Full Life*, p.232.
 6 B. H. Liddell Hart, *History of the Second World War* (London: Cassell,
    1970), p.566.
 7 Ibid., p.567.
 8 Alun Chalfont, *Montgomery of Alamein* (London: Weidenfeld and
    Nicolson, 1976), p.271.
 9 Horrocks, *A Full Life*, p.232.
10 Wilmot, *The Struggle for Europe*, pp. 531–2.
11 Montgomery, *The Memoirs*, p.297.
12 Horrocks, Belfield and Essame, *Corps Commander*, p.110.
13 Hastings, *Armageddon*, p.57.
14 Urquhart, *Arnhem*, p.190.
15 Powell, *The Devil's Birthday*, p.96.
16 Ryan, *A Bridge Too Far*, p.215. Interestingly, General Horrocks refutes
    this, saying, 'The capture of this vital document was a great boon to the
    Germans, who thus had a complete picture of what we intended to do' (*Corps*

Commander, p.94). Max Hastings supports this: 'In the absence of high-level decrypts, captured documents became the most prized German sources, of which the September *Market Garden* plan, taken from a dead US officer on a Dutch landing zone in the first hours of the operation, was most notable, and exercised an important influence in making possible that German victory' (*The Secret War*, pp.501–2).

17 Whiting, *A Bridge at Arnhem*, p.139.

18 Dirk Bogarde, *Backcloth* (London: Penguin, 1987), p.113.

19 Montgomery, *The Memoirs*, p.298.

20 Brian Montgomery, *A Field Marshal in the Family* (London: Constable, 1973), p.317.

21 Major-General Sir Francis de Guingand, *Operation Victory* (London: Hodder and Stoughton, 1947), p.382.

22 Ibid., p.383.

23 Captain Harry C. Butcher, *Three Years with Eisenhower* (London: William Heinemann, 1946), p.583.

24 Dwight D. Eisenhower, *Crusade in Europe* (London: William Heinemann, 1948), p.342. Eisenhower hardly references *Market Garden*, choosing to avoid the fact that overall responsibility rested with him. In his subsequent book *At Ease* he avoided it altogether, preferring to focus on D-Day and the Battle of the Bulge.

25 Eisenhower, *Crusade in Europe*, p.340.

26 Carlo D'Este, *Eisenhower* (London: Weidenfeld and Nicolson, 2003), p.618.

27 Arthur Bryant, *Triumph in the West 1943–46* (London: William Collins, 1959), p.227. Field Marshal Brooke was chief of the Imperial General Staff, the most senior post in the British Army.

28 Ibid., p.232.

29 Graham Stewart, *His Finest Hours: The War Speeches of Winston Churchill* (London: Quercus, 2007), p.174.

30 Bogarde, *Cleared for Take-Off*, p.12.

31 Bogarde, *Snakes and Ladders*, p.63. Montgomery made this claim, which was complete nonsense. Montgomery's chief of staff, Major-General Freddie de Guingand, told the press it was about 70 per cent successful. Even Eisenhower called it a 'partial success' (*Crusade in Europe*, p.340).

32 Bogarde, *Backcloth*, p.113.

33 Bogarde, *Cleared for Take-Off*, p.12.

34 de Guingand, *Operation Victory*, p.419.

35 Horrocks, *A Full Life*, p.231.

36 Nigel Hamilton, *Monty: The Field Marshal 1944–1976*. (London: Hamish Hamilton, 1986), p.98.

37 Ibid.

38 Liddell Hart, *The Other Side of the Hill*, p.428.

39 Ibid.

40 Hastings, *Armageddon*, p.68.

41 Kershaw, *It Never Snows in September*, p.376.

42 Godfrey Freeman, *Escape from Arnhem: A Glider Pilot's Story* (Barnsley: Pen and Sword Aviation, 2010), p.134.

CHAPTER 18 PANZER CORPS CONTROVERSY

1 1st Canadian Army Intelligence Summary 241, 25 February 1945, cited in Graves, *Wehrmacht Archive*, p.174.

2 Frost, *A Drop Too Many*, p.224.

3 Wilmot, *The Struggle for Europe*, p.481.

4 The Jagdpanther had gone into production in early 1944, but this was hampered by the Allied bomber campaign. Only about 15 saw action in Normandy. By the end of the year two battalions had been issued with the Jagdpanther, but they were not fully equipped.

5 Powell, *The Devil's Birthday*, p.40.

6 Richard Mead, *General 'Boy': The Life of Lieutenant General Sir Frederick Browning* (Barnsley: Pen and Sword, 2017), p.120.

7 Hagen, *Arnhem Lift*, pp.94–5.

8 Ibid., p.112.

9 Ryan, *A Bridge Too Far*, p.70.

10 Ibid., p.30.

11 Hagen, *Arnhem Lift*, p.94.

12 Urquhart, *Arnhem*, p.35.

13 Michael Smith, *Station X: The Codebreakers of Bletchley Park* (London: Pan Books, 2004), p.184.

14 This work was the responsibility of the RAF's No 35 Reconnaissance Wing and the Royal Canadian Air Force's 39 Reconnaissance Wing, which formed part of the 2nd Tactical Air Force. Their coverage was described as 'patchy'. See Chris Staerck (ed.), *Allied Photo Reconnaissance of World War II* (London: Parkgate, 1998), p.111.

15 See Mead, *General 'Boy'*, pp.155–6 for more on this issue. In the intervening years these photos have become part of the Arnhem folklore, but they have never come to light.

16 'Brian Urquhart's Recollections of Intelligence at Arnhem', interview 15 May 2003, cited in Bennett, *A Magnificent Disaster*, p.242.

17 Beevor, *Arnhem*, p.51, citing Sebastian Ritchie, 'Arnhem: The Air Reconnaissance Story', Air Historical Branch, 2015.

18 At the time of *Market Garden* the Hermann Göring Reserve and Training Regiment's 2nd Battalion had two companies of tank crew, one of assault gun crew and one of armoured car crew. The two tank companies did not

have any Panthers or Tigers and were mainly equipped with the Panzer IV. See 1st Canadian Army Intelligence Summary 124, 1 November 1944, cited in Graves, *Wehrmacht Archive*, p.91.

19 Smith, *Station X*, p.184.
20 Hastings, *The Secret War*, p.409.
21 Powell, *The Devil's Birthday*, p.45.
22 Urquhart, *Arnhem*, p.21.
23 Zetterling, *Normandy 1944*, p.339.
24 Hook, *Hohenstaufen*, p.34.
25 Frost, *A Drop Too Many*, p.224 and Ryan, *A Bridge Too Far*, p.287.
26 Kershaw, *It Never Snows in September*, p.43.
27 Ibid.
28 The Allies were swamped with decrypts. Bletchley Park issued 25,000 to the American and British Special Liaison Units during January 1944 to May 1945 (Hastings, *The Secret War*, p.502).
29 Hagen, *Arnhem Lift*, p.111.
30 Ryan, *A Bridge Too Far*, p.98.
31 Urquhart, *Arnhem*, p.21.
32 Bennett, *A Magnificent Disaster*, p.199.
33 Horrocks, *A Full Life*, p.214.
34 Horrocks, Belfield and Essame, *Corps Commander*, p.83 and 89. Horrocks reiterates this point twice.
35 Horrocks, *A Full Life*, p.214.
36 Horrocks, Belfield and Essame, *Corps Commander*, p.89.
37 Wilmot, *The Struggle for Europe*, p.513.
38 Ryan, *A Bridge Too Far*, p.111.
39 Middlebrook, *Arnhem 1944*, p.67.
40 Alexander Morrison, *Silent Invader: A Glider Pilot's Story of the Invasion of Europe in World War II* (Shrewsbury: Airlife, 1999/2002), p.51.
41 Frost, *A Drop Too Many*, p.200.
42 Ibid., p.224.
43 Ibid.
44 John Nichol and Tony Rennell, *Arnhem: The Battle for Survival* (London: Viking, 2011), p.50.
45 Ibid., p.51.
46 Frost, *A Drop Too Many*, pp.209–10.
47 Ryan, *A Bridge Too Far*, p.280.
48 Hagen, *Arnhem Lift*, p.42.
49 Ibid., p.42–3.
50 Powell, *The Devil's Birthday*, p.238.
51 Ibid., p.48.
52 Frost, *A Drop Too Many*, p.258.

CHAPTER 19 LAST BATTLES

1 Beevor, *Arnhem*, p.359.
2 Albert Speer, *Inside the Third Reich* (London: Phoenix, 1995), p.536.
3 Ibid., p.564.
4 Michael Reynolds, *Sons of the Reich: II SS Panzer Corps Normandy, Arnhem, the Ardennes and on the Eastern Front* (Barnsley: Pen and Sword Military, 2017), p.179.
5 Saunders, *The Island*, pp.141–2.
6 Ibid., p.142.
7 Kershaw, *It Never Snows in September*, p.399.
8 Ibid., pp.395–6.
9 Heinz Günther Guderian, *From Normandy to the Ruhr: With the 116th Panzer Division in World War II,* (Bedford, Pennsylvania: Aberjona, 2001), p.197.
10 Ibid., p.204.
11 David Irving, *The Rise and Fall of the Luftwaffe: The Life of Luftwaffe Marshal Erhard Milch* (London: Weidenfeld and Nicolson, 1973), p.290, citing Milch's diary.
12 Speer, *Inside the Third Reich*, p.536.
13 Guderian, *From Normandy to the Ruhr*, p.200.
14 Ibid., p.204.
15 Ibid., p.205.
16 de Guingand, *Operation Victory*, p.419.

CHAPTER 20 LITTLE CONSEQUENCE

1 Charles MacDonald, *The Battle of the Bulge* (London: Weidenfeld and Nicolson, 1984), p.11.
2 Antony Beevor, *Ardennes 1944: Hitler's Last Gamble* (London: Viking, 2015), p.25.
3 Trevor-Roper, *Hitler's War Directives 1939–1945*, p.281.
4 John Toland, *Adolf Hitler* (Ware: Wordsworth Editions, 1997), p.823.
5 Charles Whiting, *West Wall: The Battle for Hitler's Siegfried Line September 1944 – March 1945* (London: Pan, 2002), p.21.
6 Charles Messenger, *The Last Prussian: A Biography of Field Marshal Gerd von Rundstedt* (Barnsley: Pen and Sword, 2018), p.206.
7 1st Canadian Army Intelligence Summary, 100, 8 October 1944, cited in Graves, *Wehrmacht Archive*, p.131.
8 Charles Whiting, *'44: In Combat from Normandy to the Ardennes* (London: Century, 1984), p.151.
9 Speer, *Inside the Third Reich*, p.555.
10 Guderian, *From Normandy to the Ruhr*, p.225.

11 Steven Smith, *2nd Armored Division: 'Hell on Wheels'* (Hersham: Ian Allan, 2003), p.47.

12 Newton, *Hitler's Commander*, p.329.

CHAPTER 21   MARY OF ARNHEM

1 Bormann, *Hitler's Table Talk*, p.591.

2 Mark Mazower, *Hitler's Empire: Nazi Rule in Occupied Europe* (London: Penguin, 2009), p.203.

3 Also spelt Sandsberg.

4 Also known as Markov.

5 Stephen E. Ambrose, *Band of Brothers* (London: Simon and Schuster, 2017), p.164.

6 Paul Holt, '"Mary of Arnhem" is in custody in Holland', *Daily Express*, interview, 13 May 1945.

7 Major Dick Winters, *Beyond Band of Brothers* (London: Ebury Press, 2011), pp.157–8.

8 By the time the British liberated Amsterdam, the German garrison was down to 1,000 calories a day.

9 Kuiper, *Arnhem and the Aftermath*, p.2.

10 Whiting, *A Bridge at Arnhem*, p.262.

11 By 7 May 1945, the Allies had managed to drop 10,680 tons of food: see Michael Jones, *After Hitler: The Last Days of the Second World War in Europe* (London: John Murray, 2015), p.200.

12 The Surrender of Colonel-General Blaskowitz 5 May 1945, War Diary GSHQ, 1st Canadian Corps, Appendix 43, cited in Richard Giziowski, *The Enigma of General Blaskowitz* (Barnsley: Leo Cooper, 1997), p.402.

13 They consisted of 77 officers and 1,415 men from the 84th SS Volunteer Grenadier Regiment: see Delaforce, *The Polar Bears*, p.240.

14 Some 20 Dutch volunteers serving in the Waffen-SS received the Knights Cross of the Iron Cross for gallantry.

15 Controversially, Degrelle remained the most decorated foreign member of the Waffen-SS.

16 Kuiper, *Arnhem and the Aftermath*, p.196.

17 Delaforce, *The Polar Bears*, p.226.

18 Holt, '"Mary of Arnhem"'.

19 As of 30 May 1945, Captain Sensburg was reportedly held by the Red Army.

EPILOGUE: POIGNANT TRAGEDY

1 Richard Collier, *The Warcos: The War Correspondents of World War II* (London: Weidenfeld and Nicolson, 1989), p.180.

2 Chalfont, *Montgomery of Alamein*, p.253.
3 de Guingand, *Operation Victory*, p.419.
4 Newton, *Hitler's Commander*, p.320.

APPENDICES

1 Hook, *Hohenstaufen*, P.34.
2 Guderian, *From Normandy to the Ruhr*, p.193.
3 The 116th listed these tanks on 24 September before it redeployed from Aachen, so not all of them may have been available (ibid., p.184).
4 Ibid.
5 Ibid., p.193.

Bibliography

Publications

Ambrose, Stephen E. *Band of Brothers*. London: Simon and Schuster, 2017

Badsey, Stephen. *Arnhem 1944: Operation Market Garden*. Oxford: Osprey, 1993

Beale, Peter. *The Great Mistake: The Battle for Antwerp and the Beveland Peninsula, September 1944*. Stroud: Sutton, 2004

Beevor, Antony. *Ardennes 1944: Hitler's Last Gamble*. London: Viking, 2015

Beevor, Antony. *Arnhem: The Battle for the Bridges, 1944*. London: Viking, 2018

Beevor, Antony. *Crete: The Battle and the Resistance*. London: Penguin, 1992

Bennett, David. *A Magnificent Disaster: The Failure of Market Garden, the Arnhem Operation, September 1944*. Philadelphia: Casemate, 2008

Bogarde, Dirk. *Backcloth*. London: Penguin, 1987

Bogarde, Dirk. *Cleared for Take-Off*. London: Penguin, 1996

Bogarde, Dirk. *For the Time Being*. London: Penguin, 1999

Bogarde, Dirk. *Snakes and Ladders*. London: Penguin, 1988

Bormann, Martin. *Hitler's Table Talk*. Oxford: Oxford University Press, 1988

Brooks, Richard. *Walcheren 1944: Storming Hitler's Island Fortress*. Oxford: Osprey, 2011

Brown, Chris. *Arnhem: Nine Days of Battle*. Stroud: Spellmount, 2014

Bryant, Arthur. *Triumph in the West 1943–46*. London: William Collins, 1959

Buckingham, William F. *Arnhem 1944: A Reappraisal*. Stroud: Tempus, 2002

Butcher, Captain Harry C. *Three Years with Eisenhower*. London: William Heinemann, 1946

Chalfont, Alun. *Montgomery of Alamein*. London: Weidenfeld and Nicolson, 1976

Cimino, Al. *The Story of the SS: Hitler's Infamous Legions of Death*. London: Arcturus, 2019

Clark, Alan. *The Fall of Crete*. London: Anthony Blond, 1962/London: Cassell, 2004

Clark, Lloyd. *Operation Market Garden: Netherlands 17–25 September 1944*. London: Ministry of Defence, 2004

Collier, Richard. *The Warcos: The War Correspondents of World War II*. London: Weidenfeld and Nicolson, 1989

de Guingand, Major-General Sir Francis. *Operation Victory*. London: Hodder and Stoughton, 1947

Delaforce, Patrick. *Churchill's Desert Rats: From Normandy to Berlin with the 7th Armoured Division*. Stroud: Alan Sutton, 1994/London: Chancellor Press, 2001

Delaforce, Patrick. *Monty's Iron Sides: From the Normandy Beaches to Bremen with 3rd Division*. Stroud: Alan Sutton, 1995/London: Chancellor Press, 1999

Delaforce, Patrick. *The Polar Bears: Monty's Left Flank, From Normandy to the Relief of Holland with 49th Division*. Stroud: Sutton,1995/2003

D'Este, Carlo. *Eisenhower*. London: Weidenfeld and Nicolson, 2003

Eisenhower, Dwight D. *Crusade in Europe*. London: William Heinemann, 1948

Fitzgerald, Michael. *Hitler's Secret Weapons of Mass Destruction: The Nazi Plan for Final Victory*. London: Arcturus, 2018

Ford, Ken. *Operation Market-Garden 1944 (2): The British Airborne Missions*. Oxford: Osprey, 2016

Ford, Ken. *Operation Market-Garden 1944 (3): The British XXX Corps Missions*. Oxford: Osprey, 2018

Forty, George. *7th Armoured Division: The 'Desert Rats.'* Hersham: Ian Allan, 2003

Freeman, Godfrey. *Escape from Arnhem: A Glider Pilot's Story*. Barnsley: Pen and Sword Aviation, 2010

Frost, Major-General John. *A Drop Too Many*. London: Cassell, 1980/Barnsley: Pen and Sword, 2009

Giziowski, Richard. *The Enigma of General Blaskowitz*. Barnsley: Leo Cooper, 1997

Graves, Donald E. *Blood and Steel 2. The Wehrmacht Archive: Retreat to the Reich, September to December 1944*. Barnsley: Frontline, 2015

Guderian, Heinz Wilhelm. *From Normandy to the Ruhr: With the 116th Panzer Division in World War II*. Bedford, Pennsylvania: Aberjona, 2001

Guderian, Heinz Günther, *Panzer Leader*. London: Michael Joseph, 1952/ London: Futura, 1974

Hagen, Louis. *Arnhem Lift*. London: Leo Cooper, 1993

Hamilton, Nigel. *Monty: The Field Marshal 1944–1976*. London: Hamish Hamilton, 1986

Harokopos, George. *The Fortress Crete: The Secret War 1941–1944*. Athens: B. Giannikos and B. Caldis, 2001

Hastings, Max. *Armageddon: The Battle for Germany 1944–45*. London: Macmillan, 2004

Hastings, Max. *Bomber Command*. London: Pan, 1999

Hastings, Max. *The Secret War: Spies, Codes and Guerrillas 1939–45*. London: William Collins, 2017

Hook, Patrick. *Hohenstaufen 9th SS Panzer Division*. Hersham: Ian Allan, 2005

Horne, Alistair and Montgomery, David. *The Lonely Leader: Monty 1944–1945*. London: Macmillan, 1994

Horrocks, Lieutenant-General Sir Brian. *A Full Life*. London: Collins, 1960

Horrocks, Sir Brian, Belfield, Eversley and Essame, Major-General H. *Corps Commander*. London: Sidgwick and Jackson, 1977/London: Magnum, 1979

Irving, David. *The Rise and Fall of the Luftwaffe: The Life of Luftwaffe Marshal Erhard Milch*. London: Weidenfeld and Nicolson, 1973

Jones, Michael. *After Hitler: The Last Days of the Second World War in Europe*. London: John Murray, 2015

Jones, R. V. *Most Secret War*. London: Hamish Hamilton, 1978

Kent, Ron. *First In: The Airborne Pathfinders*. Barnsley: Frontline Books, 2015

Kershaw, Robert. *It Never Snows in September: The German View of Market-Garden and the Battle of Arnhem, September 1944*. Marlborough: Crowood Press, 1994/Hersham: Ian Alan, 2011

Kuiper, Harry. *Arnhem and the Aftermath: Civilian Experiences in the Netherlands 1940–1945*. Barnsley: Pen and Sword Military, 2019

Liddell Hart, B. H. *History of the Second World War*. London: Cassell, 1970

Liddell Hart, B. H. *The Other Side of the Hill*. London: Pan, 1983

Lucas, James. *Battle Group! German Kampfgruppe Action of World War Two*. London: Arms and Armour Press, 1993

Lucas, James. *Hitler's Enforcers: Leaders of the German War Machine 1933–1945*. London: Arms and Armour Press, 1996/London: Brockhampton, 1999

MacDonald, Callum. *The Lost Battle: Crete 1941*. London: Macmillan, 1993

MacDonald, Charles. *By Air to Battle*. London: Macdonald, 1970

MacDonald, Charles. *The Battle of the Bulge*. London: Weidenfeld and Nicolson, 1984.

Mazower, Mark. *Hitler's Empire: Nazi Rule in Occupied Europe*. London: Penguin, 2009

McNab, Chris. *Hitler's Armies: A History of the German War Machine 1939–45*. Oxford: Osprey, 2011

McNab, Chris (ed). *Hitler's Elite: The SS 1939–45*. Oxford: Osprey, 2013

Mead, Richard. *General 'Boy': The Life of Lieutenant General Sir Frederick Browning*. Barnsley: Pen and Sword, 2017

Messenger, Charles. *The Last Prussian: A Biography of Field Marshal Gerd von Rundstedt*. Barnsley: Pen and Sword, 2018

Middlebrook, Martin. *Arnhem 1944: The Airborne Battle*. London: Viking, 1994/Barnsley: Pen and Sword, 2017

Mitcham, Samuel W. *Hitler's Field Marshals and their Battles*. London: William Heinemann, 1988

Montgomery, Brian. *A Field Marshal in the Family*. London: Constable, 1973

Montgomery, Field Marshal. *The Memoirs of Field Marshal the Viscount Montgomery of Alamein*. London: Collins, 1958

Moorehead, Alan. *Mediterranean Front*. London: Hamish Hamilton, 1941

Morrison, Alexander. *Silent Invader: A Glider Pilot's Story of the Invasion of Europe in World War II*. Shrewsbury: Airlife, 1999/2002

Moulton, Major-General J. L. *Battle for Antwerp: The Liberation of the City and the Opening of the Scheldt 1944*. Hersham: Ian Allan, 1978

Neillands, Robin. *The Battle for the Rhine 1944*. London: Weidenfeld and Nicholson, 2005

Neillands, Robin. *The Desert Rats: 7th Armoured Division 1940–45*. London: Weidenfeld and Nicolson, 1991/London: Aurum Press, 2005

Newton, Steven H. *Hitler's Commander: Field Marshal Walther Model – Hitler's Favourite General*. Cambridge, MA: Da Capo Press, 2006

Nichol, John and Rennell, Tony. *Arnhem: The Battle for Survival*. London: Viking, 2011/London: Penguin, 2012

Niven, David. *The Moon's a Balloon*. London: Coronet, 1973

Paterson, Michael. *Voices of the Code Breakers: Personal Accounts of the Secret Heroes of World War II*. Newton Abbot: David and Charles, 2007/Barnsley: Greenhill, 2018

Powell, Geoffrey. *The Devil's Birthday: The Bridges to Arnhem, 1944*. London: Buchan and Enright, 1984

Quarrie, Bruce. *Fallschirmjäger: German Paratooper 1935–45*. Oxford: Osprey, 2001

Quarrie, Bruce. *German Airborne Troops 1939–45*. Oxford: Osprey, 1983

Quarrie, Bruce. *Hitler's Samurai: The Waffen-SS in Action*. London: Patrick Stephens, 1985

Quarrie, Bruce. *Hitler's Teutonic Knights: SS Panzers in Action*. London: Patrick Stephens, 1986

Reynolds, Michael. *Sons of the Reich: II SS Panzer Corps Normandy, Arnhem, the Ardennes and on the Eastern Front*. Barnsley: Pen and Sword Military, 2017

Ripley, Tim. *Elite Units of the Third Reich: German Special Forces in World War II*. Miami: Lewis International, 2002

Ruffner, Kevin Conley. *Luftwaffe Field Divisions 1941–45*. Oxford: Osprey, 1990

Ryan, Cornelius. *A Bridge Too Far*. London: Hamish Hamilton, 1974

Sarkar, Dilip. *Arnhem 1944: The Human Tragedy of the Bridge Too Far*. Barnsley: Frontline, 2018

Saunders, Tim. *Hell's Highway: US 101st Airborne and Guards Armoured Division*. Barnsley: Leo Cooper, 2001

Saunders, Tim. *Nijmegen: US 82nd Airborne and Guards Armoured Division*. Barnsley: Leo Cooper, 2001

Saunders, Tim. *The Island: Nijmegen to Arnhem*. Barnsley: Leo Cooper, 2002

Schroeder, Christa. *He was My Chief: The Memoirs of Adolf Hitler's Secretary*. Barnsley: Frontline Books, 2012

Seaton, Albert. *The Fall of Fortress Europe 1943–1945*. London: Batsford, 1981

Seaton, Albert. *The German Army 1933–45*. London: Weidenfeld and Nicolson, 1982

Sebba, Anne, *Les Parisiennes: How the Women of Paris Lived, Loved, and Died in the 1940s*. London: Weidenfeld and Nicolson, 2017

Shirer, William. *The Rise and Fall of the Third Reich*. London: Secker and Warburg, 1960

Shulman, Milton. *The German Defeat in the West*. London: Secker and Warburg, 1947

Simpson, Tony. *Operation Mercury: The Battle for Crete, 1941*. London: Hodder and Stoughton, 1981

Sixsmith, E. K. G. *Eisenhower as Military Commander*. London: Batsford, 1973

Smith, Michael. *Station X: The Codebreakers of Bletchley Park*. London: Pan Books, 2004

Smith, Steven. *2nd Armored Division: 'Hell on Wheels'*. Hersham: Ian Allan, 2003

Speer, Albert. *Inside the Third Reich*. London: Phoenix, 1995

Staerck, Chris (ed). *Allied Photo Reconnaissance of World War II*. London: Parkgate, 1998

Stein, Marcel. *A Flawed Genius: Field Marshal Walter Model, A Critical Biography*. Solihull: Helion, 2010

Stewart, Graham. *His Finest Hours: The War Speeches of Winston Churchill*. London: Quercus, 2007

Telp, Dr Claus. *The Advance from the Seine to Antwerp 25 August – 30 September 1944*. London: Ministry of Defence, 2005

Thomas, Nigel. *The German Army 1939–45 (5): Western Front 1943–45*. Oxford: Osprey, 2000

Toland, John, *Adolf Hitler*. Ware: Wordsworth Editions, 1997

Tout, Ken. *In the Shadow of Arnhem: The Battle for the Lower Maas, September–November 1944*. Stroud: The History Press, 2009

Trevor-Roper, Hugh R. *Hitler's War Directives 1939–45*. London: Sidgwick and Jackson, 1964

Tucker-Jones, Anthony. *D-Day 1944: The Making of Victory*. Stroud: The History Press, 2019

Tucker-Jones, Anthony. *Falaise: The Flawed Victory – The Destruction of Panzergruppe West, August 1944*. Barnsley: Pen and Sword, 2008

Tucker-Jones, Anthony. *Stalin's Revenge: Operation Bagration and the Annihilation of Army Group Centre*. Barnsley: Pen and Sword, 2009

Urquhart, Major-General R. R. CB, DSO. *Arnhem*. London: Cassell, 1958/ London: Pan, 1972

Verrier, Anthony. *The Bomber Offensive*. London: Batsford, 1968

Weighly, Russell F. *Eisenhower's Lieutenants: The Campaigns of France and Germany 1944–1945*. London: Sidgwick and Jackson, 1981

Whiting, Charles. *'44: In Combat from Normandy to the Ardennes*. London: Century, 1984

Whiting, Charles. *A Bridge at Arnhem*. London: Futura, 1974

Whiting, Charles. *Siegfried: The Nazis' Last Stand*. London: Pan, 2003

Whiting, Charles. *West Wall: The Battle for Hitler's Siegfried Line September 1944 – March 1945*. London: Pan, 2002

Williamson, Gordon. *The SS: Hitler's Instrument of Terror*. London: Amber, 2002

Williamson, Gordon. *Waffen-SS Handbook 1933–1945*. Stroud: Sutton, 2003

Wilmot, Chester. *The Struggle for Europe*. London: Collins, 1952

Winters, Major Dick. *Beyond Band of Brothers*. London: Ebury Press, 2011

Zaloga, Steven. *Lorraine 1944: Patton vs Manteuffel*. Oxford: Osprey, 2000

Zaloga, Steven. *Operation Market Garden 1944 (1): The American Airborne Missions*. Oxford: Osprey, 2014

Zetterling, Niklas. *Normandy 1944: German Military Organization, Combat Power and Organizational Effectiveness*. Winnipeg: J. J. Fedorowicz, 2000

DOCUMENTARIES

Carruthers, Bob. *Arnhem with Tom Hicks*. Visions of War, 2014

Garofalo, Robert. *Remembering the Battle of Arnhem*. Rock on Digital, 2018

Gormlie, Chris. *Arnhem 1944*. Archive Media, 2009

Grinberg, Sherman. *Battlezone: WWII Arnhem and over the Rhine*, Episode 1 *Arnhem*. Timeless Television, 2018

Vigar, Bruce. *Arnhem: A Bridge Too Far*. Leading Edge Productions, 2001

Index

References to maps are indicated in **bold**; references to notes are indicated by n.